MW00621015

Speakeasy

By

R. G. Bluemer

Publisher
Grand Village Press
Granville, Illinois 61326

M&D Printing
Henry, Illinois 61537

Front Cover – Machelle's Backstreet
959 Ninth St., LaSalle, Illinois.
Back cover – Club LaSalle
1026 First St., LaSalle, Illinois

1

Acknowledgments

The author is especially grateful to the staff of the Peru Library, especially Shirley Sharpe, for their help in locating the numerous local photographs and other material used in this work. The Putnam County Historical Society volunteers at Pulsifer House in Hennepin and Cathy Oliveri at the Hennepin Court House were also most helpful.

A number of individuals were very cooperative in sharing their memories, experiences, expertise and/or materials with regard to this historic period. Special mention must be made of Ray Marliere (Metamora), Mark Scheidecker (Ottawa), Lyle Kennedy (Streator), Larry Wilkins (Sparland), Patricia Breen (Streator Historical Society), John Shimkus (Granville), Jeno and Margaret Bonucchi (Granville), Edwin and Corinne Eckerd (Mark), Art Piccioli (Mark), Fritz Ballerine (Granville), Joe Englehaupt (Granville), John Redshaw (Hennepin), William Dresbach (Peru), Ted Flesburg (Peru), James Hebel (Peru), Machelle Urban (LaSalle), Dennis Kaszynski (LaSalle), Steve Shutt (LaSalle), and Matt VanWyk (Morris).

In addition, the author is grateful for the scholarly advice of his father, Glenn Bluemer, his wife, Peggy Bluemer, and Debbie Korn, who spent countless hours in proofreading the manuscript.

Table of Contents

Introduction

Introduction

The Prohibition Era was unique in the history of the nation, which was recovering from experiences of WWI. Many citizens wanted a return to the normalcy of the pre-war years, but others were ready to adopt a new lifestyle.

The 1920's was a decade of technological innovations and social change. Another wave of immigrants flooded the country. Moral values were challenged. Into this mix was injected a new national law that affected almost every citizen and alien resident alike. Old ethnic habits were hard to change as the government imposed new and, to some, unenforceable regulations.

The story detailed in this work is a microcosm of how the social and economic life in rural areas, small towns and cities in America was affected by the 18th Amendment and the Volstead Act. The stereotypical view of America in the 1920's has been perpetuated as a decade of gangland violence used to control the production and distribution of illegal beer and whiskey. In reality, it was much less dramatic for the average individual. In the Illinois Valley, the "criminals," for the most part were ordinary businessmen, shopkeepers and farmers, who were trying to make a living, albeit sometimes in defiance of the prohibition laws. While a few individuals profited from the widespread graft, most of those who were caught were simply fined or received short jail sentences.

The term "speakeasy," used in reference to the secret drinking establishments of the prohibition era, was not widely used in the Illinois Valley until the 1930's. In most cases, there were no secret passwords. However, the windows of the taverns were often covered with heavy drapes or other materials to avoid detection by the authorities. These neighborhood "soft drink parlors," as they were called, relied on a constant supply of home-brewed beer, wine, and moonshine, which was often produced in local neighborhoods. Often overlooked by local authorities, the illegal stills, as well as the local "speakeasies," were frequently the targets of county and federal authorities.

The material found in this work is based entirely on front-page stories published in local newspapers, court records, and personal interviews. The author in no way intends to defame neither any individuals nor their families who may have been associated with any illegal activities. As far as can be determined, all of the facts are correct. Documentation of all relevant material has been provided at the end of this work.

It should be noted that the spelling of individual's names might be appear to be incorrect. The local newspaper reporters in the 1920's tended to spell names, especially the Italian and Polish names, the way they sounded. Newspapers, at times, even changed spellings for the same individuals from issue to issue. Even court records indicate different spellings for those coming before the bench on different occasions. The author tried to be as precise as possible in using the correct spellings and apologizes if the reader takes exception.

Chapter One
The Breweries of the Illinois Valley

Commercial development in the Illinois Valley included the building of several breweries. On the east side of LaSalle along Little Vermillion Creek, Louis and Jeremiah Eliel established the LaSalle Brewery Co. in 1855. By 1865, the brothers had constructed a large stone building in which their crew of up to 20 men produced up to 30,000 barrels of beer every year. Oscar Eliel, a son of one of the brothers, apprenticed as a brewmaster and eventually took on the full responsibility for the production of the malt and Pilsner beer. The business grew in size until four stone buildings were needed. To keep the beer cool, the kegs were stored in four tunnels dug into the hillsides along the Little Vermillion. The local saloons purchased both barrels and ponies. Sometimes customers drove up in wagons and buggies to purchase their beer. A pony (1/8 barrel) cost about 90 cents. (Housby, J.and G., *An Antiquarial Look At LaSalle and the Illinois Valley*, 1984, pp 47-48.)

Eliel Brewery workers. Date unknown. James Hebel collection.

Another little known operation along the Little Vermillion was built in Troy Grove. The Doffner Brewery was actually southeast of the village, but Mr. Doffner also operated a tavern on the current site of the Wild Bill Hickock State Park. Constructed around 1860, the three-story brewery made use of the natural surroundings. A cave was cut out of the sandstone cliffs along the river to store the beer and keep it cool.

In Peru, two major breweries were built. In 1847, William Rausch founded the Peru Beer Co. near the waterfront on the corner of Rock and Putnam Streets. The extension of the Rock Island Railroad placed the tracks right over the underground vaults where the beer was stored. A newer plant was built in 1851 at the corner of Farm and Center Streets. Rausch took on P.K. Behrends as a partner until 1857 when he sold his interest to Mr. Behrends and Mr. Kitzinger. Rock Island freight trains stopped with supplies and carried away the company's products. Eventually Behrends became the sole owner by buying out Kitzinger's interest.

Wagons were waiting to pick up supplies from a Rock Island train in front of the Behrends Brewery in Peru. Peru Library collection.

In 1868, Behrends sold his interest in the brewery to a group of businessmen who formed the Peru Beer Company. Andreas Hebel and Herman Brunner acquired controlling interest in the company in 1872 and renamed it, Hebel and Brunner. Hebel held the position of plant foreman, and Brunner took charge of the bookkeeping. When Andreas Hebel died in 1886, his son, Andrew Hebel, took over the joint management of the company with Brunner. Charles Herbold, the foreman at the plant, purchased Brunner's interest in the brewery in 1888, and Hebel and Herbold became partners of the renamed Peru Beer Co.

Steamboats from the LaSalle and Peoria Packet Line were also used to transport beer in the early days. Peru Library collection.

While tied up on the north bank of the Illinois River near Water Street, workers loaded beer barrels on the deck of the *Fred Swain.* Peru Library collection.

Hebel and Brunner brewery workers. Date unknown. James Hebel collection.

The brewmaster conducted a number of tests to insure the high quality of the various beers. William Hebel collection.

A charter was drawn up, and the company was incorporated in 1889. Charles Herbold held the position of superintendent, and Andrew Hebel was the secretary-treasurer.

In order to cool the brew, ice was harvested from the backwaters of the Illinois River. At the turn of the century, a refrigeration unit was installed. In 1901, the plant was producing 20,000 barrels of beer annually. The best known of its products was called "Favorite Stock." But there were many others including Hebel's Special and Muenchener Style Special.

Andrew Hebel joined the Peru brewery business when his father died in 1886. This lithograph illustrates the main buildings with the company office on the bluff overlooking the plant. James Hebel collection.

Andrew Hebel at work in the company office on Bluff Court in Peru. Besides his duties as president and general manager of Peru Beer, Andrew was a member of Peru's Liberty Fire Co. No. 1 and became mayor of the city in 1894 when H. Rausch resigned. He was elected mayor in 1895 and served until 1897 during which time the city acquired Washington Park. He was also president of the Hygienic Institute and the 1st National Bank of Peru. He died in October 1937 at the age of 72. William Hebel collection.

The old Peru Beer Co. office, which was located on the north bluff of the Illinois River was the scene of all the financial transactions. William Hebel collection.

Accountants and secretaries were kept busy recording the weekly receipts and taking orders for beer shipments. Records and payments were kept in a Mosler safe (at left). The interior of the office is being restored by James Hebel, the great, great grandson of the founder. William Hebel collection.

Huge copper cookers held thousands of gallons of beer.

The raw beer was cooled by wort chillers before yeast was added to the brew.

Beechwood tanks held the beer while it was fermenting. Photos from William Hebel collection.

The finished beer was stored in kegs in the "government room." Tax stamps were applied to each keg as they were placed in cold storage. William Hebel collection.

In the early days, Peru Beer was only shipped in kegs to local taverns. Thirty teams of horses were used before the advent of beer trucks. William Hebel collection.

Another bottling plant was built after this picture was taken. William Hebel collection.

Racking the kegs in the keg and bottling department. William Hebel collection.

Another load of Peru beer headed to local taverns. Dennis Kaszynski collection.

It wasn't long before horses were replaced at the Peru Beer Co. with modern trucks. Circa 1911.

A case of empties from the James Hebel collection.

For many decades, hundreds of men found employment at the Peru Beer company. James Hebel collection.

The company took an active role in community events. At left - Exhibit of Peru Beer Company products at a carnival held Nov. 21-26, 1910.
Original photo by Schwindeman. Peru Library collection.

Parade float photos from James Hebel collection.

The other major brewery in Peru was the Star Union Brewery. In 1845, Fred Kaiser constructed his buildings along Water Street on the west side of town. It was later sold to Benjamin Ream. In 1880, the name "Star Union" was changed to the "Union Brewery." Henry Hoerner took over as plant manager, and the fame of the plant spread across the Midwest. At that time, the "Cellars" building, which was constructed from Joliet limestone, was added to the facilities. Here the beer was fermented, aged, and stored in the refrigerated warehouse.

Star Union employees. Unknown date. Dennis Kaszynski collection.

Left: A rare "Star Select" poster from pre-prohibition days. Circa 1914. Dennis Kaszynski collection.

****

Following page - The lithograph shows the layout of the brewery buildings, Circa late 1800's. Source- Star Union booklet.

17

In 1880, the Cellars building was constructed. An overhead bridge connected the structure to the brew house. Peru Library collection.

Around 1890, a huge horse barn was added to the complex. An automatic feeding system, designed by a Westclox employee was used to dispense oats and hay every morning to the 60 horses. It took a full time crew to care for the horses and arrange the horse collars and nickel and brass harnesses. Gaily-painted horse-drawn wagons hauled beer to local taverns and ice to homes and hospitals. It took two teams of horses to pull the wagons loaded with beer kegs up "Brewery Hill." Horses were used until 1910 when trucks began to replace them. Being a good businessman, Hoerner sold the used mash to local farmers, who used it for fertilizer. The barn was still used for storage but was finally torn down in 1964.

In addition to the brewery, Star Union owned a number of bars and other buildings throughout the Illinois Valley. In 1913, a distribution building was constructed in DePue on the north side of 4th Street across from the phone company. Since the Rock Island tracks ran though the village, it was more convenient to ship beer from Peru by rail. The DePue building had a cooling room to store the beer. Ice was cut each winter from Lake DePue and packed in layers of sawdust so that it would last most of the season. The building was equipped with a set of tracks so that cases and pony barrels could be moved with little effort. A team and wagon were used to bring orders to taverns. When business was slow the same wagon was used to haul barrels of fish into town from the lake. During rare emergencies, the wagon was pressed into service to haul fire equipment. Frank Fowler operated the Star Union tavern at 222 W. 4th St.. Others who ran the place over the years were Chris Gieler and John Lindquist. In the 1930's the building was remodeled as a grocery store.

Henry Hoerner was born in Baden, Germany in 1850. He immigrated to America at the age of four with his parents. The family first lived on a farm in West Brooklyn. Later he moved to Mendota and worked for the Illinois Central Railroad. He rose to the position of IC yardmaster in LaSalle after only one year. His relationship with the brewery began in 1880 when he purchased the stock of William Meyer, Fred Schulte and Fred Seepe. Eventually, Hoerner accumulated 2/3's of the company stock. The other principal partner was Philip Link who held the remaining stock. Hoerner retired in 1930. (Photo reprinted from LaSalle *Daily Post* Oct. 25, 1940)

Hoerner was not only the past president of Star Union Brewery but also served the community in a number of high profile positions. He was first elected mayor of Peru in 1888 and served a total of 14 years. He died at the age of 90 on Oct. 24, 1940. He was one of the oldest citizens of Peru.

Henry Hoerner was president and manager of the Star Union brewery until 1930. Management was then taken over by his son, Martin. Following Martin's death in October 1937, his sister, Kathryn Hoerner Ellis, took charge. Peru Library collection.

One of the original stock certificates in the Star Union Brewery dating from the 1890's is signed by company Secretary Jacob L. Link and counter-signed by President Henry Hoerner. The watermark on the certificate indicates a par value of $100 for each of the 950 shares. LaSalle Historical Society, Utica.

The breweries also took an interest in the social life of their employees. Pictured is a picnic being enjoyed by employees of both the Star Union Brewery and the Peru Beer Co. at Holly Grove south of Peru. Date circa 1911. Peru Library collection.

Several buildings made up the Star Union complex. The bridge walkway at right connected the Cellars refrigeration building with the rest of the plant. During the early history of the plant, a deep well was drilled so that there would always be a plentiful supply of fresh water. With the addition of mechanical refrigeration, it was no longer necessary to cut blocks of ice from the Illinois River and store them in caves during the rest of the year to keep the beer cool. Peru Library collection.

Few of the original Star Union wooden kegs still exist. This example is located in the LaSalle Historical Society's museum on the Illinois-Michigan Canal in Utica.

Rock Island trains stopped at the loading docks to pick up beer or to bring in supplies and the hops and barley used in fermentation. The hops were imported from Oregon, Washington and California in 200-pound bales and then refrigerated to preserve the flavor and aroma. Barley malt was ground to make mash. Peru Library collection.

During the prohibition years, the brewery continued to produce Star Model near beer, soft drinks such as ginger ale and root beer, and artificial ice. The company was renamed Star Union Products Company during the 1920's.

A major fire in 1925 gutted the interior of much of the plant, but Henry Hoerner decided to rebuild instead of abandoning the brewery. When the 18th Amendment was repealed in 1933, it went back into the beer business under the name of Star Union Products. Oscar Wablin had the job of brewmaster when beer was legalized. He had gained much experience in his previous employment in breweries in Europe and America. Star Union Brewery could turn out up to 180,000 barrels annually. It was the oldest brewery in Illinois and the oldest industry in the Illinois Valley.

A rare bottle of Star Union's Gota Lejon Pilsner keg beer. John Shimkus collection.

23

A Star Union Brewery parade float represented the old fashioned method of distributing the beer. Wagons were replaced and trucks hauled the beer faster and to more distant markets. Peru Library collection.

Star Union Brewery was always active in community events. Here is another example of a float they built for a local parade.
Peru Library collection.

The company produced a variety of beers. Gota Lejon Pilsner beer was bottled in half-gallon containers, as was the standard Star Model beer. Every spring there was a batch of Star Model heavy Bock beer. Star Union's Sepp'l Brau was the premium brew.

Star Union products from John Shimkus collection

In 1928, the company changed its name to the Star Union Products Co. Upon retirement in 1930, Henry Hoerner's son, Martin H. Hoerner, became president and treasurer. Leslie M. Link served as secretary of the firm. His sister, Kathryn, took the position of vice president and succeeded her brother upon his death. Irene Hoerner moved to the position of vice president.

The Link family continued their interests in the operation. Lester M. Link was the secretary, and Howard L. Link took on the responsibilities of treasurer. Link took charge of beer production from 1935 to 1955 when he retired and moved to Texas. Looking back on his career with the company, Link said that the best years were immediately after WWII. In those days, a half-barrel was selling for about $6. The marketing area extended from Galena in northwestern Illinois down to Peoria.

Competition from the larger breweries in Wisconsin and St. Louis was narrowing the profit margin so on September 10, 1963, the company was sold to the Ace Brewing Company of Canada.

Jacket emblem worn by Star Union employees. John Shimkus collection.

Finally, the president of the Chicago branch of the Canadian company, Allen Schultz, announced on Jan. 6, 1966, that they were shutting down the Peru plant after a 120-year history. Three days later, the final bottle of Star Union beer was filled. The plant was obsolete and too expensive to maintain according to the Ace spokesman, but Canadian Ace agreed to continue to manufacture beer in the Chicago brewery using the Star Model label.

William Dresbach, who had worked at the Peru brewery since 1957 as its sales manager, bought the property from Ace on May 1, 1968. He sold all of the buildings except the one at the corner of Pike and Brewster. Ron Yanke and Victor Andres purchased the remaining buildings. Dresbach used the lone facility to distribute Grainbelt Beer, Star Model Beer, and Pabst Blue Ribbon. The holdings of Yanke and

Andres were sold again in 1973 to Charles Schopf of Justice, Illinois. Richard Fell became a co-partner the following year. They hoped to make a profit by tearing down the buildings and selling the scrap. A large portion of the plant was demolished in 1975. Only two buildings remained from the original complex. Finally, city engineers determined that the remaining "Cellars" and the masonry building on the northwest corner of Pike and Brewster were dangerous and ready to collapse. So the wrecking ball was taken to the "Cellars." The old bottling building owned by Dresbach was still standing in 2003.

Advertising for taverns and restaurants in the Illinois Valley was not nearly as prevalent in the late 1800's and early 1900's as it is today. Peru Beer did advertise to popularize "Favorite Stock." Star Union did not run ads in the World War I newspapers. However, the Peru Beer Co. ad (far right) was run in almost every issue of the LaSalle *Daily Post Tribune* in 1917. Once prohibition began, virtually all advertising of alcoholic products - even near beer - disappeared.

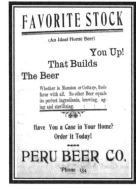

Anheuser-Busch placed many ads for a non-alcoholic soft drink called Bevo in 1917. They opened a brand new factory in St. Louis, Mo. for the production and described the hundreds of new jobs they created. The copy at left says that Bevo can be ordered from Baker Brothers, a wholesale distributor in LaSalle and Streator. The ingredients were never described, but the product was said to be wholesome and refreshing. It could be ordered at hotels, restaurants, grocery stores drug stores, soda fountains – almost anywhere that soft drinks were sold.

Ads like these, which appeared in the 1922 LaSalle-Peru city business directory, tell much about the impact of the Volstead Act. Note the emphasis on root beer and malt "tonic" and the manufacture of ice.

Another major brewery in the Illinois Valley was the Ottawa Brewing Association. The company manufactured a number of products, but one of the most popular was Shabbona Beer. This real beer (2.75%) was forced out of production when prohibition started, but the business struggled on by producing soda and near beer for a time.

One of the products produced by the Ottawa Brewing Association was Ottawa "Hop," a non-alcoholic drink.
This original label was printed in red and black lettering with a yellow background.

Another of the Ottawa brewery products was Shabbona Tonic. It used the same coloring scheme as the Hop label. The individual pictured is a rendition of Chief Shabbona

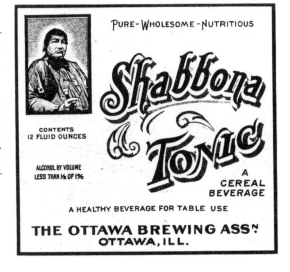

Ottawa Brewery from *Ottawa Old and New*

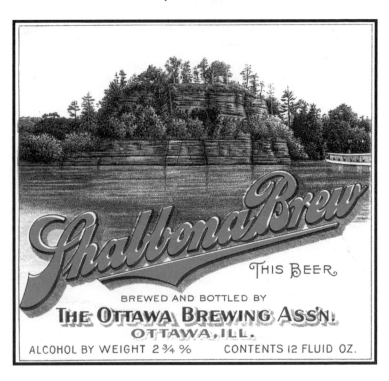

Grundy County also had a famous brewery located in Morris. Its founder, Louis Gebhard, came from Germany in 1866 and constructed

his brewery along the Illinois-Michigan Canal. Steamboats brought cargoes of barley, Bavarian hops and other ingredients to the brewery dock. Large quantities of corn grown locally in Grundy County were also used in the plant. The main buildings were located only a short distance from the canal. The complex was located on the east bank of Nettle Creek.

View of Gebhard Brewery looking north across the Illinois-Michigan Canal.

Malt was raised to the seventh floor of the brew house and descended by gravity as it went through various processing stages until it reached the first floor. The plant was capable of turning out 125 barrels daily. One major accident occurred on Dec. 13, 1873 when the second floor of the brew house collapsed due to the excessive weight of 400 bushels of barley.

Louis Gebhard died in 1886. His son, William, continued managing the plant for over 30 years.

The brewing house was seven stories high and measured 50' x 120'. The brew house, which was built on a limestone foundation with red brick walls and interior steel supports, was finally completed in 1896.

To the south of the brewing building was the malt and bottling house. Although smaller, it followed the same basic construction of a limestone foundation topped with red brick (pictured below).

View of the Gebhard complex from Nettle Creek.

The brick bottling house was constructed in 1888. Gebhard Brewery turned out up to 250 barrels of beer a day while WWI raged in Europe. Local taverns in Morris bought up much of the production although some beer was shipped to surrounding communities. Pony barrels sold for only $1. In the taverns, a glass of beer cost a nickel. As with other breweries, the Gebhards established a number of distribution points in Morris.

In 1905, two new cooling units were added to the stock house- a 35-ton and a 50-ton machine. They were driven by Corliss engines and could bring the temperature down to freezing. The building was well insulated and could maintain freezing temperatures for several days if the power failed.

The Gebhard brewery stock house was three stories in height and covered 6000 square feet. It was constructed from steel and brick and had asphalt floors. William added it in 1904. View in 2003.

The Gebhards were firm believers in the "stewardship of wealth" philosophy and paid their workers some of the highest wages in Morris. Beer production ended in 1919 at the plant when prohibition began. The buildings were sold and converted to flour milling.

William passed away in 1922 at the age of 65. From the age of eight, he had spent his entire life as a resident of Morris. He was active in the political life of the community serving as an alderman for several terms. He also was a Mason and a director of the Farmers and Merchants National Bank until the year before he died. He was highly respected in the community and on the day of his funeral the chamber of Commerce requested that all businesses remained closed during the funeral out of respect for the distinguished citizen.

The abandoned Gebhard brewery still stands near the I-M Canal on Washington Street. Birds fly through the broken windows of buildings that served as an economic focal point for Morris, Illinois.

Chapter 2
Making it the Old Fashioned Way

With the inability of the breweries and distilleries to legally continue the production of real beer and whiskey, local residents devised different schemes and methods to continue the production of various concoctions of alcoholic beverages. The methods of making wine and beer were ageless, but because of the Volstead Act, it was necessary to go underground and out of sight to continue production. In some cases, the operations were so deceptive that the authorities never did find out where the brew was being made. Even in the 21st Century, Illinois Valley residents reminisce about how stills were successfully hidden from federal agents. Following are a few examples of how homemade alcoholic beverages were produced locally during prohibition.

In DePue, Illinois, the Marliere family had maintained a tavern long before prohibition went into effect. Naturally, it became one of the many so-called "soft drink" parlors during the 1920's. But when the law was working against a once thriving operation, there were only two choices available to maintain the family business. A few soft drink parlors stayed within the law and purchased soda or near beer from Star Union or Peru Products. The alternative solution for many establishments, however, was to find an illegal source of home brew, wine, or moonshine to satisfy thirsty patrons and hope that their tavern wasn't raided.

According to Ray Marliere, his grandfather, Ernest Marliere, was a fisherman as were many of the DePue residents. Ernest's brother and partner, Hector, was a fisherman and farmer – another helpful occupation when corn became a very useful local commodity.

Set in the backwaters of the Illinois River, Lake DePue, stretched back almost to the now-abandoned coal-mining town of Marquette. It was large and deep enough to offer good fishing. Protecting the calm waters of the lake were a series of strips of land interspersed with sloughs. DePue fishermen used large flat-bottomed boats with platforms for the storage of hoop nets 8'-10' in diameter. These nets, which were 20'-30' in length, were let out behind the boats by a 2-3 man crew. Families had their own favorite spot that was recognized as exclusive by fellow fishermen. The boats would be out for hours waiting for the nets to fill. The many fields of corn and reed-filled marshes surrounding the lake and fingerlets of land extending into the lake easily concealed another activity – fermenting corn mash. The men realized that by putting half-barrels of mash in their boats, the gentle, undulating swells filtering into the lake from the traffic on the Illinois

River would aid the fermentation process as the boats bobbed with each passing wave. By leaving the mash barrels on the boats for some time, the activity was virtually immune from detection by federal agents. This relatively safe and secure method of producing moonshine was maintained throughout prohibition.

Frank Marliere (1852-1937) owned one of the taverns in DePue during the prohibition years. Although there is no record of Frank's inventory, no records were found indicating that the tavern was ever raided. However, with his sons bringing into town something more than that day's catch from Lake DePue, Ray speculated that the Marliere tavern continued to have an adequate supply of illegal liquor through the 13 years of prohibition. The tavern continued to operate after the 21st Amendment was ratified, but a different owner took over before 1939.

The Marliere tavern located on 2nd St. in DePue. (Ray Marliere collection).

Although most attention by law enforcement authorities was paid to the large breweries and illegal distilleries that used huge vats for fermentation and large copper kettles to produce alcohol, thousands of individuals made small quantities of alcohol for their personal use during prohibition. Grain was readily available, and the devices needed to manufacture alcohol were easily acquired.

While the mix was heating, steam would evaporate and be piped through the small threaded tube at the top of the slightly domed lid. To this, a coiled copper pipe was attached. As the vapor cooled and condensed, the pure moonshine alcohol dripped into another container. The process was incredibly simple. Coloring and flavoring could be added if desired. A popular food coloring in the Illinois Valley came from the juice of raisins. This gave the clear moonshine the appearance of whiskey. Some individuals even found old labels from popular pre-prohibition brands to give their product the appearance of the bonded whiskey.

This copper still was typical of the cookers used in producing small batches of alcohol. It could be filled with water and grain and placed on a home stove. (Jeno Bonucchi)

Another example of the copper cookers used in producing small batches of moonshine was owned by James Turchi of Mark.
Art Piccioli collection.

Making beer was a little more involved since more ingredients were needed. Barley, hops, malt, and yeast, all legally available, were slowly fermented for a few days. Timing was very important. If the brew fermented too long, the beer would be "flat," but if the aging was not long enough, it would lack a kick. Another problem in making "home brew" was the tendency of yeast to settle on the bottom of bottles. If the beer was poured out too quickly, the yeast would mix with the liquid and give it an unpleasant taste.

Bootlegging sometimes turned into a family enterprise. Lyle Kennedy of Streator recalled how he and his brothers helped his dad, Willard, make home brew in two 20-gallon crocks from which they would fill seven to eight cases of 12-ounce bottles. It was Lyle's job to add a teaspoon of sugar to each bottle. If too little sugar was added, it wouldn't be strong enough. But if too much was added, according to Lyle, "It would erupt from the bottle like warm champagne when opened." The young boy also had the duty of capping each bottle-another exacting chore. If the cap wasn't flat on the lip of the bottle, the gas would escape, and the beer would go flat. His brothers also helped out. They had the unpleasant job of scrubbing out the old bottles before they were filled. Sometimes the yeast hardened on the bottom of the old beer bottles making it difficult to scrape out. It also smelled bad. Bottling beer was done seven days a week in the basement of their home. Lyle got so fast at capping by the time he was 12 that another bootlegger even paid him to cap his bottles.

One method of "improving" near beer was converting it into needle beer. The Star Union brewery generally obeyed the law and produced only near beer and soda pop. Willard Kennedy and his son would follow the Star Union beer trucks as they made deliveries to neighboring towns to the east and northeast of Streator. However, they stayed out of Joliet because of the danger from Spike O'Donnell, a Chicago gangster, who controlled the beer business in that area. Willard would go to the speakeasies, which were also known as "blind pigs," and insert a large hypodermic needle under the tax stamps sealing the bung holes on the kegs. The glass barrel of the syringe, which was about two inches in diameter and 15 inches long, was slowly filled with the near beer. Then the same quantity of alcohol was injected into the barrel. This increased the alcoholic content by about ten times the original amount.

Beer and moonshine weren't the only illicit drinks being produced. The Italian communities found in the Illinois Valley, especially in the coal-mining towns of Bureau and Putnam Counties, had for years produced large quantities of wine. In rural communities, residents frequently grew their own grapes. Locally, the Concord and Niagara varieties were popular. Every fall, at harvest time, the grapes would be first put through a type of grinder, according to Jeno Bonucchi of Mark, Illinois. This broke the skins and caused the clear juice from the fruit to run into barrels. Later, the skins were put through a wine press to extract the remaining liquid. It was important not to crack the grape seeds since this would release the oil in the seeds and ruin the flavor. The liquid would ferment in the barrels for 2-3 weeks and then be transferred to other barrels. The barrels were usually old whiskey barrels that distillers could not use. A family might have a supply of about five barrels filled with wine to last the year. Generally the authorities, especially local police, did not bother individuals who made wine for home consumption. Some individuals, however, made much more and sold it to local saloons.

Not everyone who wanted to make wine bothered to grow their own grapes. Wholesalers from Ladd and Spring Valley would make the rounds taking orders from local residents. It was all perfectly legal.

Typically, it would not be unusual to place an order for a quarter of a ton of California grapes. The grapes would be shipped to Ladd and Spring Valley in Milwaukee RR boxcars loaded with 20-pound crates. From those stations, trucks would make the final deliveries. In Granville, residents could go down to the town depot when the Milwaukee freight stopped and pick up their orders right out of the boxcars.

Wine presses could be constructed with a little ingenuity. Guiseppi Zagnoni, a resident of Mark, Illinois, constructed one in the early 1900's and produced thousands of gallons of red and white wines over the course of more than 70 years. Guiseppi used both wild grapes from Putnam County and cultivated grapes from California. The grapes were placed in the hopper on top to break the skins. They would then be placed in 55-gallon barrels for several weeks to ferment. Then small batches would be placed in a small

container and covered by two semicircular wooden inserts. The covered container was placed under the press screw to squeeze the remaining juice from grapes. The liquid would pass through the openings in the container and flow off the boards into another container. Then the liquid was bottled. Families sometimes made upwards of 300 gallons a year for personal use.

The current owner of the press, his daughter, Corinne Eckerd, said that her father made his last batch of wine in the 1970's. It was a very good vintage. The last bottle was opened in 2003.

Chapter Three
1919
The National Debate

World War I was the setting that brought forward the national debate over the abolition of alcohol in America. The Women's Christian Temperance Union with headquarters based in Evanston, Illinois had fought for many years to ban drinking. Notorious leaders like Carry Nation took the issue to an extreme with personal attacks on demon rum in the early 1900's. The Anti-Saloon League also joined the fray with their political lobbying. Conservative religious ministers extolled the evil consequences of drinking.

Facing wartime shortages, conservation measures seemed appropriate during WWI. The National Prohibition Act, introduced by Congressman Andrew Volstead of Minnesota, was also referred to as the War Prohibition Act. It was the legal tool to enforce the 18th Amendment, which was ratified on Jan. 29, 1919. The law specified that the sale and manufacture of intoxicating liquors would be illegal until the end of WWI and the termination of demobilization as determined by the President, Woodrow Wilson. Although the military confrontation in France had ended with the armistice on Nov. 11, 1918, Wilson had not declared an end of hostilities due in part to the lack of Senate ratification of the Treaty of Versailles, which he had helped to negotiate. The White House made it known that the President's stance against wartime prohibition would not be reversed until the Senate ratified the Versailles documents. By Oct. 28, 1919, both houses of Congress had overridden Wilson's veto of the Volstead Act. (1) Strict prohibition laws were to be implemented effective Jan. 16, 1920.

The next step was to fund the programs necessary to enforce prohibition. In a conference bill, Congress authorized the expenditure of $2.4 million. The Bureau of Internal Revenue was ordered to turn over evidence of violations of the law to the Department of Justice for prosecution of offenders. The main product being targeted was beer containing 2.75 percent alcohol. The new law only allowed for alcoholic beverages containing less than one-half percent alcohol.

Time was of the essence for liquor producers. Wartime prohibition was to end as soon as Wilson declared an end of hostilities, and constitutional prohibition was to begin in Jan. 1920. In the interim, liquor producers hoped to dispose of available stocks. A legal challenge arose when the Federal District court in Louisville, Kentucky held that wartime prohibition was illegal because it deprived holders of bonded liquor the right to dispose of their supplies. The court further noted that if the bonded liquor could not be sold, the owners would stand to lose $300,000. The main arguments upheld were that the law violated the 5th Amendment right of the brewers to compensation for their property. They asserted that, with the cessation of hostilities and the demobilization of the military, the war was over.

In the federal district court in Chicago, Judge Carpenter faced the contentions of the Hannah and Hogg liquor distributors. Residents in Chicago were preparing for a wild night, and saloons were ready to resume business as soon as a favorable ruling was handed down. Judge Fitzhenry in Peoria was confronted with a similar problem. But they were hesitant to rush to judgment until the United States Supreme Court had rendered a decision.

Some courts moved forward, however. In New York, the Jacob Rupper Breweries and others sought the release of their stocks of alcoholic beverages, but Federal Judge Learned Hand ruled that wartime prohibition remained a valid exercise of the congressional power. A similar decision was handed down in Baltimore restraining the Maryland Distilling Company of Baltimore from obtaining its bonded alcohol. (2)

On Nov. 20, 1919, the Supreme Court received a brief from Attorney Wayne Wheeler on behalf of the Anti-Saloon League. This organization argued that the beer brewers were using 32 tons of sugar annually as well as enough grain to feed seven million people. The brief also pointed out that three million tons of coal and millions of teams and wagons as well as hundreds of thousands of freight cars were being used by the industry back in 1917. The U.S. Assistant Attorney General Fryerson contended that wartime prohibition would not end until the President or Congress made it official. (3)

The issue was of major importance to the liquor industry, since 2.75 beer, which was worth millions of dollars, was being withheld from the market. Attorney Elihu Root, who represented the brewers, argued that the seizure of private property by the government without compensation to the owners was unconstitutional. He went on to state that Congress had intended to give the industry one year to dispose of its inventory before constitutional prohibition went into effect. The beer in question had been manufactured before Congress passed the Volstead Act on Oct. 28. (4)

Finally on Dec. 15, 1919, the Supreme Court ruled. Speaking for the majority, Justice Louis Brandeis stated that wartime prohibition was legal and would continue in force until the President or Congress formally proclaimed an end to the war. However, the legality of the Volstead Act and the question of alcohol content was undecided. The decisions in the Louisville federal district court were reversed. The

Supreme Court also ruled that no compensation to the liquor industry should be exacted from the government because wartime prohibition did not go into effect until July 1, 1919, more than six months after the legislation was passed. There was ample time to dispose of liquor supplies. The court also pointed out that the liquor could be exported from the United States. Regarding the issue of the actual end of hostilities, the court held that even though 91% of the army had been demobilized, the President would have to make a formal declaration of peace. That was the only way to officially end the war according to Brandeis. (5)

For the liquor industry, this was a major setback and a victory for the "drys." In the storehouses around the country there was an estimated $1 billion of intoxicating liquor waiting to be sold. Even the federal government would suffer a loss of $4.4 million from the tax revenue it stood to collect on the whiskey sales. The only hope was that the ban would be lifted before Jan. 16, 1920.

Immediately following the court decision, attorneys for the liquor industry went to work seeking to overturn the 18th Amendment. In Rhode Island, New Jersey, and New York cases were filed. Ohio attempted to withdraw ratification of the prohibition amendment in a referendum. Action in Congress discouraged the liquor interests, however, when the House agricultural committee voted 16-3 against the repeal of the Volstead Act. (6)

Chapter 4
1920
Prohibition Raids Begin

On Jan. 5, 1920, the Supreme Court in a 5-4 decision upheld the provisions of the Volstead Act. The lawyers of the liquor industry maintained that Congress had exceeded its authority in defining intoxicating liquor at anything more than one-half percent alcohol. The only loophole for the average citizen was the court's ruling that this did not apply to homemade beer and wine for private consumption.

Other court cases regarding prohibition and the Volstead Act would continue to challenge the "drys" and law enforcement officials. But beginning with 1920, state's attorneys and local police departments began an earnest effort to control the manufacture, sale, and transportation of liquor in all forms that exceeded the legal alcohol limit set by law. It became one of the most newsworthy activities documented in the local press. Raids became almost a daily occurrence in the Illinois Valley. Surprisingly, the notorious gang violence frequently associated with the 1920's was almost non-existent in the Illinois Valley.

The Prohibition Era is defined in most history books as beginning in January 1920 and continuing until the ratification of the 21st Amendment in 1932. It must be remembered however, that arrests were also made under the authority of wartime prohibition. For instance, in Bureau County, Sheriff Leonard D. Spaulding had been making arrests for the manufacture and sale of alcoholic beverages since July 1, 1919. As might be expected, the number of cases coming before judges and justices of the peace in the Illinois Valley increased noticeably after 1920.

On Jan. 8, 1920, Sheriff Spaulding raided the home of Catherine Peters of Spring Valley. His men burst into the home and lined up everyone against the wall while they conducted the search. A ten-gallon keg of wine and a five-gallon jug of a concoction loaded with raisins and oatmeal were confiscated. Peters and the brew were taken to the Bureau County jail. She was charged with selling and manufacturing liquor as well as conducting a disorderly house and running a gambling den. (1)

The next day, the action moved to the south side of the Illinois River not far from LaSalle. After conducting surveillance operations for a month, federal revenue agents struck with such surprise that the arrest of Nick Tubitch of Oglesby was made without violence. Tubitch, who was considered the ringleader of the moonshine operation, rented a seven-acre plot a mile northeast of Lehigh Cement. Hidden in a cave-like area on the property, the federal agents found a still in full operation. A copper boiler was situated on an old stove. The steaming liquid from the sealed boiler flowed through a "cooling worm" and condensed into a white liquid generally referred to as "moonshine." By adding some prune coloring, the liquid was being passed off as genuine "whiskey." It was reported that there was enough "whiskey" already made to satisfy the needs of an individual for three years. Besides the finished product, the agents confiscated the 1920's-type still (a variety used during wartime prohibition), raisin mash and prune coloring. It was estimated that the still was capable of producing 12 gallons of brew every day. At a retail price of $27 a gallon, operations brought in an average of $324 every day.

Tubitch's partner in crime, Washko Coyetsison, was in charge of sales through his LaSalle residence at 217 First Street. An additional stockpile of the illegal alcohol was confiscated there. Three other men and two women were also arrested at the LaSalle boarding house and admitted to knowing about the alcohol sales. However, they were released after convincing authorities that they had no connection with the operation. LaSalle County Deputy Sheriff Armstrong took custody of Coyetsison and Tubitch on charges of "moonshining." The federal penalty for the manufacturing of whiskey could be as high as 15 years in prison and a $5000 fine, but such penalties were seldom imposed. This was one of the largest operations to be shut down in the area. (2)

Rock Island trains were constantly passing through the Illinois Valley, and the Sunday morning freight that passed through Morris on January 11, would have seemed very ordinary except for the four guards posted on every car. One might have thought it was a cross-country gold shipment as the train headed east to its final destination in Pennsylvania. It wasn't a shipment of gold but rather tankers of port wine from California wineries. Since prohibition outlawed all beverages with more than 1% alcohol, this cargo was also illegal so it was being shipped under special government sanction as a "medicinal" product. After passing through Morris, one of the cars developed a hot box, and the train had to stop in the little town of Elburn, Illinois, about 40 miles west of Chicago. During the stopover, 700 gallons of the wine mysteriously disappeared on Sunday night. Revenue agents were able to recover 500 gallons on Monday, but the rest was gone. (3)

Another incident involving the railroad occurred in Bureau County. Princeton Sheriff Spaulding was working with railroad detectives on a series of boxcar robberies. As a result of the investigation, the authorities discovered three operations in Ladd and another one in Seatonville. Eight people were arrested. They were sharing a single still found on a gas plate and a quart of moonshine had already been made in the cellar of Joe Pasquali, an ex-convict. The other locations only had mash vats. A raid at the home of Bassilo Bruno resulted in the confiscation of two barrels of moonshine. Bruno, a brakeman for the Chicago, Milwaukee and St. Paul RR, had two concoctions fermenting. One was a mix of raisins and corn meal syrup. The other was grape pulp. Bruno tried to con the investigator saying that he was simply making some caustic potash, an acid that he needed in his job as a welder. In a remote section of Seatonville, Pete Cioni was also arrested. He had all the ingredients for "white mule." There were sacks of corn meal and bran and six cans of Kayro syrup. Ernest Cassagrande claimed he was a fruit merchant. He had sold over 30 carloads of grapes to the Italians of Spring Valley and Ladd. In spite of his denial of moonshining, enough incriminating evidence was found in his home to warrant his arrest. The other men were arrested for the theft of clothing from the boxcars. Four quarts of Green River whiskey also was found in one of their rooms. (4)

While local officials were trying to control the moonshiners in the Illinois Valley, politicians in Washington were offering amendments to the Volstead Act. Congressman Sabath of Illinois proposed the legal manufacture of beer with three-percent alcohol and wine with nine per cent alcohol. The Congressman also proposed that physicians be allowed to prescribe either a pint of alcohol every 10 days or a quart every 15 days. The justification for these amendments, according to Sabath, was that whiskey was the only effective remedy for the widespread influenza that was gripping the country. This would also allow for the disposal of the huge quantities of liquor being held in the hundreds of federal and private warehouses. The Illinois representative limited his proposal by outlining a policy of restraint. His measures would not take effect until 60 days after the Supreme Court ruled that such disposition was legal. The "drys" immediately voiced their opposition to Congressman Sabath's proposals. (5)

Meanwhile, LaSalle Sheriff Curt Ayers continued to enforce the federal law. A raid was conducted on Feb. 26, 1920 at the home of Louis Vicini in Naplate (the National Glass settlement southwest of Ottawa). Mrs. Vicini allowed the sheriff and his men to inspect the home. During the search of the house, the sheriff found a keg of raisin mash, which Mrs. Vicini admitted was used to make some homemade wine. In the shed behind the house, Ayers also found a still and two kegs of beer. Continuing the search, the police found another keg of wine and a jug of moonshine. Ayers proceeded to the glass factory, where Louis was employed and arrested the man. Vicini, the father of eight young children, protested that he had made the single batch of moonshine so it could be added to his wife's coffee since she was ill. It made no difference to Ayers, who confiscated all the evidence and took Vicini to the Ottawa jail. (6)

LaSalle County Sheriff Curt S. Ayers served from 1918-1922.

In mid-March, the national debate over the constitutionality of the Volstead Act was in full swing. Several different appeals were before the courts. In New Jersey, a complaint was filed concerning the enforcement policies. The state claimed that the entire amendment was inappropriate since it infringed on state sovereignty. In New York, a complaint was filed charging that the Lincoln Safety Deposit Co. should not be allowed to remove liquor from private vaults as required by the law. The owner of the liquor, William Streete, contended that personal liquor could be kept in private homes. In these and other cases, the "wets" seemed to be facing a losing battle as lower courts ruled that the Volstead Act was constitutional. (7)

The Supreme Court finally ruled on an Ohio referendum nullifying its ratification of the 18th Amendment. The "wets" had hoped to delay the enforcement of the law. Finally, a sweeping decision was handed down in June 1920. Chief Justice White admonished the Congress for not having specifically defined their interpretation of "intoxicating liquor" but agreed with the majority to uphold the validity of the prohibition law. In taking this position, the appeals of six states, New Jersey, Rhode Island, Massachusetts, Wisconsin, Missouri, and New Jersey, were denied. The Court ruled that the amendment was legal; all states would have to abide by its provisions; and only another vote by three-fourths of the states could change it.

All the legal maneuvering did not help local bootleggers such as Dimtrich Grazow of Ottawa. Arrested on March 19, 1920, he finally was brought before Judge Landis on May 20 charged with three counts of violations of the prohibition law. Although the penalty in this case could be up to of 11 years in prison with a fine of $2000, the maximum sentence was seldom imposed. (8)

While many of the prohibition violators were before the Ottawa federal court, many of the arrests were being conducted in other cities in LaSalle County. In September 1920, Sheriff Ayers walked into the tavern at Twin City Park in Peru and inquired if he could get a little schnapps from bartender Ben Magierski. The bartender reached behind the counter and pulled out a bottle containing a clear liquid, which he poured into a whiskey glass. The sheriff immediately recognized the drink as "white mule," a distillate of prunes, raisins and alcohol, which was frequently found in local "soft drink" establishments. Ayers identified himself as the sheriff to the astonished bartender and then called for the owner, Fabian Ciganovich. Attempting to resolve the incident, Ayers was offered $50 as hush money. Ciganovich couldn't believe that the sheriff wouldn't accept the bribe stating, "Why the other man settled this case." Ayers learned that a former federal revenue agent had accepted bribes but had now moved from the LaSalle district and was no longer employed by the federal government. Magierski and Ciganovich were both eager to swear that the agent had accepted money in the past. The two men were then taken to the Ottawa jail to face charges. (9)

Ciganovich went before Judge C.S. Stough on Oct. 18 and received a relatively light sentence of $75 and costs since this was his first offense. The Peru man was only one of ten brought before Judge Stough that day on charges of liquor law violations. Three other men, T.F. Willett, Joseph Metzger, and Charles McLain had been arrested for selling liquor at the Willett and Metzger saloon in Oglesby and were freed on $500 bail pending a formal court hearing. (10)

Sheriff Ayers was making headlines in the local papers almost every day. Raids were not limited to individual "soft drink" parlors but also included arrests made on the highways as trucks carrying the illegal contraband crossed the county. On Oct. 22, 1920, Ayers was tipped off by a farmer who reported that a truck was stopped with a flat tire along the Chicago Road five miles northeast of Ottawa. He arrived on the scene; examined the cargo; and found 18 barrels of beer bound for LaSalle. The driver contended that it was near beer with less than a half percent alcohol. Indeed, the metal labels on the barrels indicated that the contents were within the legal limits. Nonetheless, Ayers was suspicious and, after one sip of the brew, determined that it was over the limit. The truck, which was owned by the Milton Express and Packing and Shipping Co. of LaSalle was going no further with its load. Ayers called for another truck from Ottawa, and the barrels, each of which contained 32 gallons of the "real stuff," were transferred to the sheriff's custody. The Milton driver was not detained further. As soon as his companion had returned from LaSalle with a new tire, they were allowed to continue their journey without the beer.

Returning to Ottawa, Ayers had to determine where to hold the evidence. He finally decided to have the barrels unloaded in his fenced-in yard until the court ordered disposition of the evidence. In the meantime, a sample of the evidence was taken to Ottawa High school for testing.

Professor Tydemann, the science teacher, determined that the brew was 3.1% alcohol, far above the legal limit of one-half percent. (11)

The case finally moved into the courts where DeMille Milton, owner of the Milton Truck Co. of LaSalle, faced charges of transporting illegal beer. In liquor violations when the defendants were caught red-handed, the accused realized the futility of requesting a jury trial. Circuit Judge Harry Reck fined Milton $100 and costs. The confiscated beer, which was still sitting in the sheriff's back yard, was eventually poured down the sewer. (12)

Liquor laws were flagrantly violated in the Illinois Valley. The situation grew so bad in Oglesby that the city council finally drew up an ordinance to deal with the problem. It was patterned after a similar provision in the Ottawa city codes. Effective Dec. 18, 1920, all "soft drink" parlors in Oglesby would have to pay a $50 license fee and remove all curtains and screens. Any establishments handling intoxicating liquors would be found guilty of violating federal, state, and local laws and face fines $25 to $200. In addition, samples of all drinks would have to "be furnished on demand of any police or commissioner of the city." (13)

Although many of the local soft drink parlors were violating such ordinances, more often than not, the police raided private homes. In one case, Miss Effie Doan, the LaSalle prohibition officer had been tipped off that an Oglesby resident, Henry Day, had a considerable amount of illegal liquor. A raid was soon conducted at Day's house south of the town. Searching the premises, Sheriff Ayers found all the components necessary to manufacture liquor. Parts of a still, coloring, empty jugs and an empty whiskey barrel were seized. Day could not raise the $500 bail immediately so he spent the night in jail. (14)

It seemed to be a hopeless battle for the authorities. Illinois Attorney General Edward Brundage specifically targeted the LaSalle-Peru-Ottawa area for enforcement. Why were these three cities mentioned by name? He explained that these cities "have been continuously selling liquor in violation of the law." He also threatened other downstate saloons. A dozen law suits were filed in the Chicago federal court to address the disregard of the law held by liquor sellers. (15)

The attorney general's message came through loud and clear to LaSalle Mayor Peter Coleman (pictured at right). He ordered Chief of Police Doyle to make the rounds of all the "soft drink" parlors to let the proprietors know that the law was going to be enforced. He closed his letter to the chief with an emphatic, "I mean what I say."

Rumors quickly spread among the anxious tavern owners that a U.S. marshal was in Ottawa with numerous injunctions handed down by Judge K.M. Landis of the Chicago district court. State's Attorney Harry F. Kelly explained that work was in progress to make sweeping arrests. There was no lack of evidence. Four undercover investigators had made visits early in December to eleven saloons in LaSalle County and purchased bottles of liquor, which they kept for evidence. (16)

As expected, the authorities descended on a dozen taverns in LaSalle, Peru and Ottawa the following day. "Bud" Pickens of Ottawa was one of the deputy U.S. marshals serving injunctions and summonses for tavern owners to appear before the court of Judge Landis.

There was no indication of the eventual penalties that might be handed out. They typically varied from temporary or permanent injunctions to prohibit the sale of liquor, fines or imprisonment. Jail time was usually reserved for those accused of multiple offenses. Kelly announced to the press, "This is just the beginning of a general housecleaning in LaSalle, gambling as well as illicit sale of liquor. The sooner those affected realize it, the better." (17)

Some saloonkeepers apparently did not believe that a crack down was imminent and that the mayor meant what he said. So based on a tip from a couple of drunken brawlers, the following afternoon, Dec. 20, 1920, the Gapenski and Jozwiak tavern at 1003 First Street was visited and Gapenski was arrested. City Attorney W.J. Aplington said that Mayor Coleman instructed his police department to arrest any business selling illicit liquor, no matter how big or small. This was just the beginning of the effort to clean up LaSalle. Not only liquor was seized in a series of raids but also gambling equipment including punchboards and slot machines. (18)

Chapter 5
1921
Ayers' Final Effort

The prohibition crusade continued into the new year with the arrest and indictment of T.W. Willett, an Ottawa tavern owner. The case was unusual in that Willett demanded a jury trial. In most cases, the offenders of the Volstead Act simply pleaded guilty and paid a small fine. The witnesses against Willett, William Munshay and Charles Parker, claimed that they had purchased liquor in his saloon. However, Willett had two witnesses who swore that the accusers were themselves drunk before they came into the establishment. When Willett refused to serve them, a fight ensued outside of the tavern, and the prosecution witnesses were arrested. Later at the station, they said that Willett had sold them the liquor. The jury came back with a "not guilty" verdict. (1)

Such verdicts were rare. The district court of Judge K.M. Landis was flooded with prohibition cases. Investigations in February led to the issuing of warrants against Anton Friedrich and John Rottner, owners of the tavern at 601 First St. in LaSalle and Eddie Franken, who was accused of serving liquor in his establishment at 235 First St. in LaSalle. With warrants in hand, Marshal Tom Pickens left Chicago for LaSalle to serve the court papers. (2)

A few days later, Landis handed down two more injunctions. This time the warrants were issued against Burt Bungart of the Bungart and McInerney tavern at 621 First in LaSalle; Alex Galessi, owner of the Favorite Bar in Peru; and John Fitzgerald, who owned another LaSalle saloon. Before Landis issued the warrants, he questioned Arthur Smith about how he carried out the investigation at the Galessi place. The judge wanted to know how Smith determined that the 50-cent glass of moonshine was the real thing. When Landis asked Smith if the drink had any effect on him, the investigator replied, "I spit it out before it had a chance to affect me." Landis was especially disturbed when he heard that half-pints of liquor had been purchased for $5.50 at the Fitzgerald and Zimney saloon. After asking the defense attorney, W.A. Panneck, if he would need the confiscated liquor for an appeal, the attorney said it was not necessary. Thereupon Landis poured the booze into a cuspidor filling the courtroom with the smell of liquor. (3)

The battle continued with a raid by Sheriff Ayers at 1219 First St. LaSalle, the Mike Shapuka saloon. A thorough search resulted in the confiscation of several gallons of moonshine, a small bottle of which was found behind the bar and the rest in an upstairs storeroom. Another search warrant was executed at a bar owned by P. Monterastelli at 359

First Street. The bartender was caught trying to hide a pint of liquor in his pocket while the search was underway. The next day Monterastelli pleaded guilty and was fined $300.

Following the morning raids, Ayers men hit five more soft drink parlors in East Wenona but came up empty-handed in three of the locations. However, at the Malady saloon, they caught the bartender trying to dump moonshine into a sink before it could be confiscated. Seeing the approaching officers, the bartender, who had been sitting outside rushed inside and went behind the bar to wash some glasses. Ayers told the man to step aside as the liquid was running down the drain of the sink. A sample was gained of the "water" being used to clean the glasses. Later chemical analysis revealed that the liquid was 25% alcohol! The Malady saloon was also a gambling establishment. Ayers seized a slot machine, poker table, black jack table, and a craps table along with 400 poker chips.

The sheriff's other big haul was at the Emil Vallero saloon. Vallero's was outfitted for gambling in a similar fashion as the Malady bar. Ayers confiscated 1,500 poker chips and a dozen decks of poker cards at Vallero's. There was so much evidence that Ayers had to send for a truck from Ottawa to collect most of the material. The large tables and slot machines were temporarily stored in the first floor hallways of the Ottawa Court House. (4)

On March 21, Judge H.B. Reck heard the testimony of the state's attorney that was gathered in recent raids. George Malady was fined $300 for violation of the search and seizure law and another $200 for maintaining a gambling establishment. (5) Charles Mazetti of Oglesby was also hit with a gambling fine. Evidence was presented that he kept a small slot machine at his Walnut Street establishment. That was enough to have him arrested for "gaming." Mazetti received the minimum fine of $100 since there were no other prior violations. Nor was there any evidence of alcohol in the soft drink parlor that was operated by his wife while he worked at the cement mill. (6)

On April 1, 1921, it appeared that the liquor industry would be granted some relief from the government's tight grip on the tens of thousands of gallons of liquor that had been impounded in bonded warehouses. National Prohibition Commissioner Kramer partially lifted the ban. Unfortunately for the owners, the sale of liquor in the warehouses would be restricted to retail drug stores only, and this would be tightly regulated. Only pharmacies with government permits would be allowed to buy from the distillers. To make matters worse for the liquor industry, Kramer set a date of May 15, 1921 for all liquor distilleries to go out of business. (7)

Nothing seemed to change in the Illinois Valley. So the number of raids, especially on local taverns, increased. It wasn't just the illicit liquor that agents were seizing. There was also a determined effort to halt widespread gambling. But like the liquor penalties, the fines became nothing more than a routine cost in conducting a business. On April 8, 1921, two owners of Streator bars appeared before the Ottawa court having been on bail since their arrests in February. Joe Liptak (423 Main Street) and Gus Eicheberger (110 Bloomington) pleaded guilty and paid their $200 fines. Two LaSalle men, Jacob Massock and John Savinik, also admitted to running gambling houses on First Street in LaSalle and were fined $200 (8)

While most of the county officers were busy with raids in the major cities of the Illinois Valley, they did not hesitate to carry out investigations in the smaller towns as well. On April 21, the Bureau County sheriff and his deputies arrived at the tavern of Mike Karus in Seatonville. The place was deserted when the police walked in around 9 p.m. At first, all they spotted were two females with a bottle on the table.

Sheriff Spaulding was not deterred after not finding any significant quantity of liquor in the bar itself. Karus had acted suspiciously with his speedy exit to the rear of the building. Outside, the flickering light of a kerosene lantern illuminated the bartender, who was suspiciously currying a horse in the barn. Spaulding made a careful search of the grounds; found two gallon-bottles of liquor buried in some weeds; and arrested Karus, who was taken to the Princeton jail. (9)

The next day, a sting operation trapped a pair of booze peddlers who just arrived from Sandwich, IL. The episode began when A.J. Zeigler and his companion, W. Bolan, checked into a local Ottawa hotel. At 6 p.m. Zeigler suggested that some of the bellboy's friends might be interested in the "mighty fine liquor" he was carrying. Knowing that the hotel manager was insistent that no booze be allowed on the premises, the bellboy went immediately to his friend, Patrolman Tom Reilley. Wearing civilian clothes, the officer accompanied the boy to Zeigler's room. Once inside, Reilley, agreed to pay $31 for a quart of apricot brandy and a quart of gin. Reilley explained that he didn't have quite enough money and asked Zeigler to accompany him to a nearby office in the Moloney Building. They rode the elevator to the second floor and walked into the office of Ottawa Mayor Y.B. Weeks. Brandishing his badge, Reilley informed the astonished Zeigler that he was under arrest. A search of the hotel room where Zeigler was staying produced two additional quart-bottles of brandy and another quart of gin. Although Zeigler was found to be a salesman for the All-In-One Oil Co. and taking orders for automobile oil, he was also making money on the side by selling liquor to hotel guests. The next day, Zeigler and his roommate

Bolan were arraigned on the charge of violation of the Illinois search and seizure law. (10)

Moloney Building Ottawa, Ilinois. *Ottawa Old and New: 1823-1914*

A few days later, Sheriff Ayers and three deputies raided four saloons in Peru and Oglesby. Ayers and Deputy Campbell went into Schneider's Happy Corner bar. Ed Schneider tried to resist but to no avail. Ayers seized a couple of bottles filled with moonshine together with a half-pint of bonded whiskey behind the bar and a two-gallon jug of moonshine found in the basement. Ayers' other deputies, Armstrong and Frazier, searched the Woodshank bar at Fourth and Pike Streets but couldn't find any illegal liquor. Next the searchers drove across the river to Oglesby for a raid on Gregorich's. The owner threatened to take on the entire squad but had second thoughts. Evidence was everywhere- empty raisin boxes, a keg of raisin mash, stocks of raisins. Then the sheriff and his men hit the Masakas bar where they found a three-gallon jug of moonshine. (11)

While neighborhood saloons were a favorite place for county sheriffs to target for a raid, law enforcement officials were also aware that there were many stills hidden away in remote areas of the Illinois Valley. One such location was an old house located a half-mile west of the Hickory Point schoolhouse eight miles southwest of Ottawa. Rumors had been circulating that the abandoned shack in Fall River Township was the site of a moonshine operation. Sheriff Ayers and Deputy Sheriff Tom Armstrong entered the building and found Frank Bala, who said he knew nothing of any still or hidden liquor. He even invited the pair to search the place. Finding nothing upstairs, the investigators descended into the basement of the dilapidated structure brushing way the thick cobwebs as they walked across the muddy floor. They quickly spotted a five-gallon jug holding three gallons of moonshine and a copper boiler.

Confronted with the evidence Bala admitted that his brother-in-law, Joe Aleike, had come to the area from East Chicago and was making the liquor. Before leaving, Ayers destroyed a half-barrel of raisin mash by soaking it in kerosene.

Aleike was tracked to Marseilles and apprehended on the road about a half-mile south of the city. Under questioning, he admitted that he was the one operating the still. His excuse was that he couldn't find a job and was trying to make a little cash. Both Bala and Aleike were taken to the Ottawa jail. On April 26, they faced Justice of the Peace Koenig, who continued their case due to the heavy caseload of the state's attorney. (12) Two weeks later, the two men had their day in court. Judge Reck sentenced Aleike to 150 days. Bala argued that he had nothing to do with the moonshine operation but pleaded guilty anyhow and was sentenced to 80 days in the Ottawa jail. (13)

City officials were also fed up with the flagrant violations of the law. Oglesby Mayor Hugh McCann was adamant about drying up his city. He ordered Chief of Police John McCann to inform all of the soft drink establishments that the search and seizure law and the 18th Amendment were going to be vigorously enforced. In an interview with a LaSalle Tribune reporter he said, "Conditions are such that it has become time to call a halt. There are some soft drink establishments, which have absolutely no respect for the law. In fact they hold it in utter contempt. When a man goes into one of these places perfectly sober and emerges in ten minutes in an intoxicated condition, it stands to reason that there is law violation somewhere." The mayor went on to describe a specific incident of a Saturday night dance where the men were so drunk that a near-riot ensued. "The saloons in the city of Oglesby will have to obey the law. The law says that intoxicating liquor must not be sold-and that's the law we intend to enforce." (14)

The mayor's threat was soon carried out with raids on the saloons owned by Nick Harochivich and Louis Orlandini. Evidence was seized for analysis. Concerning the samples taken, Police Chief McCann stated, "If it shows that the alcoholic content violates the law, there will be prosecution." (15)

John McCann first served as an Oglesby night police officer during the administration of Mayor William Lindsay. In 1919 his brother Hugh McCann was elected mayor, and John was appointed Police Chief. *Oglesby Our Home Town,* Oglesby Historical Society.

The Oglesby cleanup continued with sheriff's raids on five private homes and a soft drink parlor on May 16. The Gregorich saloon located on top of the hill in Crocketsville was again targeted. The officers found illicit liquor, two quarts of moonshine and wine.

The raid on the home of William Anzeleer almost turned deadly. Upon entering the premises, the sheriff and his deputies were threatened with a gun battle when one of the three occupants threatened to shoot the sheriff and his "gang." After handcuffing the occupants, Ayers found a trapdoor in the bedroom leading to a 6' x 6' concrete vault. Inside was a complete still and two gallons of moonshine. Moving on to Anton Chepanski's home, the sheriff found another still and all the ingredients for making moonshine. A barrel containing raisin mash was seized at the home of John Chemish. It looked like no one was home at the home of Anton Pogues, but as the sheriff's men were about to leave, Pogues was spotted crawling out from under his house. Ayers got down on his hands and knees to search under the house. He found a 10' diameter dugout filled with 18" of water. Just under the water he discovered a gallon-jug of moonshine. Finally, the home of Charles Vlavidek was searched, but nothing was found. (16)

Raids continued throughout the Illinois Valley. A few days later, attention shifted to Bureau County and the discovery of the "Russian connection" in Shelby Township. The sheriff had been trying to find the source of widespread moonshine distribution in DePue for some time. It was widely known that a Russian woman was taking orders for moonshine. One day, the sheriff followed her back to the farm owned by Paul Krishtopanovich and his wife. The property was located about three miles north of DePue and isolated from prying eyes. The land consisted mainly of timber and pasture – generally unsuitable for farming. The farmhouse itself was set back a mile from the nearest road.

While searching the farmhouse with two other officers, W.C.Weigle and Louis Sonnenberg, they found an operating still and ten gallons of moonshine. The couple even had an official government gauge to check the alcoholic content. It was a good batch - 100 proof. Under interrogation, his wife confessed to having made the liquor.

As they were leaving, a DePue butcher arrived. He claimed that he was there to slaughter a calf for the family. Spaulding, who was suspicious of the butcher's real intentions, insisted on staying to watch the butcher carry out his work. In short order, the butcher sheepishly admitted that all of the animals were too small to slaughter. Spaulding grinned and said, "I guess we got the calf (moonshine) that you came for."

Authorities had long felt that the Russian's still was part of an operation being funded by a gang of bootleggers in DePue.

Krishtopanovich lamely excused his actions saying, "Everybody's makin' it. Me make it for my own use." He denied selling the moonshine. After further questioning, he admitted to selling "white mule" in order to pay off the $7,000 mortgage on the farm. Later, he was brought before Judge J.R. Prichard in Princeton and offered to settle for $125. Instead, he was bound over for trial and released after posting a $500 bail. Eventually he was fined $200. (17)

Two months later, the sheriff accompanied by the Bureau County state's attorney and Deputies Simpson and Robinson raided the Russian farm again with the same results. This time they found Mrs. Krishtopanovich tending another batch of 100 proof "white mule," which was being brewed in a copper boiler on a stove in the basement. At first, the Russian woman attempted to offer the officers a bribe. Realizing the futility of her pleas, she tried to destroy the damaging evidence. The woman, who was described as an "Amazon" and "strong as an ox," dumped the boiler spilling the contents. Then she smashed a gallon of the "white mule." Flying into a rage, the woman threatened to smash another bottle on the head of State's Attorney Johnson. However, Deputy Robinson blocked her advance so she tried to hit him instead. Then Deputy Simpson grabbed the bottle from her hand and wrestled her to the ground. It took three men to subdue the large woman as she struggled to get loose. The authorities arrested both the husband and wife; confiscated ten gallons of the white mule; and dumped 11 barrels of fermenting corn mash.

Appearing before Judge Prichard for the second time in two months, bail was set at $1000. Typically second offenses resulted in a jail sentence as well as a fine. Since the man was a farmer, the judge agreed to allow him to harvest his meager crops and then enter a guilty plea. (18)

Seldom, if ever, were reports of bootlegging published in the Putnam County newspapers. However, the court records indicate that numerous stills were in operation in several villages. Only a few cases were before the court in 1920, such as those of Hyman Brownstein, Simon Kalens and Henry W. Anderson, who were all accused of transporting moonshine through the county.

One of the embarrassing events in the county's history came in July 1921. It was common knowledge that large quantities of illicit brew were being shipped out of the county. Finally, Putnam County State's Attorney Faletti ordered a raid on the home of his next-door neighbor and good friend, Dick Bracco. Twelve cases of beer, destined for Spring Valley and Seatonville, were seized in Bracco's home. Deputy Sheriff Ed Berta moved the brew to the Standard jail where he felt the evidence would be safe until a court hearing.

The Standard Village Hall built in 1909 as its appears today pictured from the rear where the theft of the evidence took place in 1921. The window bars have been covered and some of the entrances have been bricked in.

However, in the morning, it was found that 11 of the 12 cases were empty! During the night, unknown individuals had used a fireman's pole to reach through the bars of the jail and pull the cases to within arm's reach of the window. Removing the lid of each case, the parties took out the bottles. Although there were suspicions as to the culprits, no arrests were made. (19)

The sale of illegal beer, wine, and moonshine brought a number of Putnam County residents into the court in 1921. Alfonse Mazzini, who was found guilty of selling liquor in 1920 was again brought into court for the same offense a year later. The December 1921 docket listed the names of Joe Panier, William Constantino, Tony Bertone, Mike Benetone, Machioli Ordolfi, Joe Troy, and Mike Orlandini. The accused in almost every case pleaded guilty as charged. Judge Henry Gunn disposed of most of the cases involving selling liquor in Mark, Standard and Granville with simple fines. Only when the judge found that the accused had a previous appearance before the court was the fine increased substantially.

It wasn't just adults who were involved in bootlegging. In the summer of 1921, three boys, Harry Coulter, Nick Wolfe and Harold Hay, were arrested for peddling wine. The boys had set up their operation on the river across from the Bellrose sand quarry. The weeds and brush along the side of the road concealed their stockpile of wine kegs. The young men had acquired a nice selection of wines including grape, pineapple and dandelion. Sheriff Ayers seized four kegs containing about 30-35 gallons. Officer Cisco arrested Hay and Coulter when they stopped

1921 Hudson

their Hudson touring car along the road; went into the bushes; and returned with a gallon of wine. Wolfe escaped temporarily but was picked up by the sheriff the following day. (20)

Another arrest was made on August 9 when Clarence Mischke, the son of a former deputy sheriff, William Mischke, was picked up. He had evaded the police and was wanted for the robbery of the Peru police magistrate, John Mischke, the boy's uncle. The boy had raided the wine cellar of his uncle who was away on vacation at the time. Hay had turned state's evidence and was released. The information led to the eventual apprehension of the Mischke boy. (21)

Seatonville was the scene of another big bust for Sheriff Spaulding in the summer of 1921. The location of an operating still was revealed to the sheriff while interrogating a couple of men picked up for drunkenness. The men said that they bought their booze in an abandoned miner's house near the mine. For some time, there had been an increasing amount of bonded whiskey being sold in Bureau County. Accompanied by Deputies Axel Dahlgren and Fred Dunbar, Spaulding went to Seatonville around midnight and found the two abandoned houses located east of the old coal company store. Inside the buildings, they found a bottling operation complete with 300 quart bottles, corks, counterfeit revenue stamps to give the appearance of bonded whiskey, coloring for the "whiskey," corrugated wrapping paper for the bottles, and eight gallons of "whiskey." All of the material was hauled away to Princeton in the early morning hours.

Acting on a hunch, the sheriff returned a few hours later and spotted a Cadillac in front of the house. The owners of the car, Albert Olson and Ernest Hartig, were found in the house that had just been raided. They were later charged with manufacturing liquor in prohibition territory. The sheriff had received information that the Cadillac was

1921 Cadillac

being used to transport the liquor to area towns.

Spaulding continued his investigation by questioning Hartig's father who lived in the adjacent house. Although the elder Hartig denied knowledge of the moonshine activities next door, the sheriff searched his house and found 100 pounds of raisins in the cellar. The man could give no explanation for the large quantity of dried fruit other than to say that some fellow whose name he couldn't remember just left the raisins in his cellar. (22)

In spite of the continued efforts of LaSalle law enforcement authorities, the liquor business continued to prosper in a number of locations. In early August 1921, a three-man team consisting of Assistant Police Chief Bolad, and Officers Ryan and McQuade raided a house at 1017 Canal Street. There they arrested Dusan Deide and John Urbanch and confiscated numerous jugs and bottles of "white mule," tubs of mash, and parts of a still. At the court hearing the following day, Urbanch paid his bail money, but Deide had to sit it out in the Ottawa jail since he didn't have sufficient money for the bond. (23)

Old LaSalle County jail in Ottawa. Peru Library collection.

In a dramatic series of raids in DePue's White City, eight men were arrested in their homes by the sheriff. A torrential downpour did not slow down the operation as the sheriff's men waded through ankle-deep mud to search the homes of more than a dozen suspects. Over a two-day period, the LaSalle *Daily Tribune* reported that John Mitz, Charles Sternes, Frank Luigi, Ben Karuth, John Gerbeck, Pearl Wasilewski, Victor Semedero, and Joe Soreka were all found in violation of the prohibition laws. State's Attorney Johnson filed legal papers against all of the accused the following day. (24)

One of the most successful raids in the area followed a short time later. Working on a tip on Aug. 4, 1921, Sheriff Ayers and Deputy Charles Campbell visited the house of Dominic Meceni and Frank Pirania on St. Vincent Avenue near the Illinois Central tracks. The men willingly invited the officers into their home and denied any involvement in liquor manufacturing. Searching the basement, in plain sight they found 16 barrels holding 600-800 gallons of moonshine and wine. A continued search turned up a large still. A gasoline-powered air pump together with a well, which was dug near the still, completed the setup.

The still was in operation at the time of the raid, and a glass gallon-jug under the still was almost full. The men were apparently using a Ford truck and a Ford touring car to distribute the liquor to individuals and local saloons in LaSalle. The accused were loaded into two trucks together with all the liquor and equipment and taken to Ottawa.

1921 Ford Touring Car

The sheriff later told reporters that this was the biggest raid he knew of in northern Illinois. The story did not end there. Two days later, Deputy Sheriff Fred Stedman arrested Tony Tonbeani of LaSalle. He admitted to being the distribution agent for the operation selling to towns along the IC tracks. (25)

The cases against bootleggers and saloon owners were crowding the court calendars in Bureau and LaSalle Counties. In the late summer of 1921 during a six-week period, Bureau County had 30 cases pending – all dealing with violations of the liquor laws. In one case, Robert Blum, who owned a saloon in Spring Valley, was arrested on July 19 for illegal sales to two detectives from the attorney general's office. In a rare jury trial, they testified that Blum had purchased a couple of glasses of whiskey; took a taste; and, without swallowing, went outside and spit the brew into a bottle. The jury found Blum guilty, but his lawyer filed for an appeal. Joe Zaletta from Spring Valley also asked for a jury trial. In another hearing, Cyrill Tilly pled not guilty to manufacturing illicit liquor on his farm near Mineral. When the sheriff raided his house, Tilly defended his actions by claiming that the liquid was "hop tonic," which he used instead of coffee because it was a healthier drink. The judge set his bond at $1000. (26)

While dozen of cases for violations of the Volstead Act were being held in the Illinois Valley, there was a legislative move in Washington to allow the manufacture of 2.75 beer. The violations of the law were so prevalent nationwide that legalization was considered as an alternative. Besides, the government needed the tax revenue. Senator Calder of New York introduced a bill that would have taxed beer at $5 a barrel and raised the tax on other liquors from $2.20 to $6 a gallon. The proposal could generate $175 million for the federal government. (27)

Such bills were becoming more common in the Congress, but still lacked the necessary votes for passage.

Legal attacks on public officials and law enforcement officers were sometimes used as a ploy to divert attention from the real bootleggers. One local incident was described in the LaSalle *Daily Tribune* on Sept. 19, 1921. According to the article, an Ottawa police officer, Jesse Holmes, was accused of being a "booze peddler" along with Ed Werner, a marble cutter at the Jobst monument works, and James Kerrigan. Dr. Dana Palmer, City Commissioner of Public Health and Safety, had the complaint against Holmes signed by Sheriff Ayers and Pete Farrell.

The charge against the 13-year police veteran was somewhat suspicious. His accuser, Pete Farrell, was the brother of William Farrell, who was shot during the robbery of the Dennison grocery store on East Superior St. in Ottawa. In fact, when Holmes was brought before Palmer, he denied the allegations, claiming that Pete Farrell was sore about the shooting of his brother, William, and wanted to get even with the police. He went on to say that his brother and the other accomplices, Joseph Farrell and Ed Fox, were all drunk when they tried to rob the store. He claimed that they had purchased their liquor from Holmes. Saying, "I guess I might as well come clean," Fox also claimed that Holmes sold him the booze. The robbers testified that Holmes was operating a still in the basement of his home on Superior Street only a block west of the Dennison store.

In his defense, Holmes recommended that the sheriff could search his place from top to bottom and stated, "If you find any evidence of a still or moonshine, you can lock me up." To which Pete Farrell replied, "What's the use of searching now after you had all the stuff removed this morning?" At that point, Holmes and Farrell went into a shouting match. Then Farrell pointed to Motorcycle Officer Walt Hisler and said, "There's another one of Holmes' booze peddlers" At this point, an altercation was about to break out between Holmes and Farrell, but they were stopped by other people in the room. Farrell continued with his allegations claiming that Holmes was selling moonshine to city officials and that Commissioner Daugherty was one of them.

In an interview with a reporter from the LaSalle *Daily Tribune*, Holmes denied all accusations stating emphatically, "I have never made nor sold any booze. And I defy anyone to prove that I have. I offered to let the Sheriff or Dr. Palmer search my house. They did not accept my offer." The police officer added, "If I had been making and selling booze, do you suppose I would have been crazy enough to sell any to a man like Farrell?" The only admission that Holmes did make was the legal fermentation of some tomato wine, none of which he ever sold. Ed

Werner said that he had not gotten any booze from Holmes but rather from Kerrgian, who refused to make any comment about the source of the moonshine. (28)

On September 26, Holmes stood before Justice Koenig, but Ed Fox, the state's attorney's star witness, never showed up at the hearing. Werner, who was also on trial for bootlegging, admitted that he did not purchase the illicit liquor from Holmes but rather got it from Kerrigan. Pete Farrell also admitted that he got the liquor before the Dennison robbery from Werner. With insufficient evidence against the Ottawa officer, Koenig dismissed the charges. (29)

Apparently the widespread violations of the law and implications of ineffective law enforcement was beginning to shake up Ottawa city officials. While the case against Holmes was in progress, Dr. Palmer decided to ask for the badge of Chief of Police James Crowe. Although Palmer stated that it had nothing to do with the Holmes case, he did comment, "Recent happenings indicate that Crowe has failed to bring the department up to the necessary standard. He (Crowe) must go." (30)

The LaSalle County Court House has changed little since the prohibition era.

In the meantime, Ayers and Deputy Charles Campbell conducted raids in Mendota that resulted in the arrests of Oscar Leifheit and William Carney. Responding to complaints that liquor was being sold out of their houses, the law officers, with search warrants in hand, first went to the Carney home located a block and a half west of the race track. There they found a gallon of "high grade" moonshine. The Leifheit home located in the southwestern part of Mendota was the site of a large cache of liquor-six gallons of moonshine. Only Leifheit was taken to the Ottawa jail. Carney, a local cigar maker and owner of considerable property in Mendota, was allowed to turn himself in the following day.

Both were expected to plead guilty and pay the customary $300 fine for bootlegging. (31)

While modern day civil libertarians would vehemently oppose the use of force in making any arrest especially ones that might insinuate racial prejudice, physical force was an acceptable defense in the need to preserve evidence or to apprehend a suspect. One case that stood out was that against George Jenkins, an African-American. The man was well built standing 6 feet tall and weighing about 300 pounds. Responding to a tip, on Sept. 22, 1921, Ayers and Deputy Campbell visited the man at the Mendota Fair Grounds. Jenkins was thought to be operating a clothes cleaning and pressing business. Sheriff Ayers found Jenkins and another African-American sitting in Jenkin's very expensive, Winton-6 touring car. Entering the tent, Ayers inspected a coffeepot sitting on a stove in the tent. The liquid in the pot was not coffee but moonshine. Continuing the search, the sheriff next found a gallon-jar filled with more liquor under some straw in the corner of the tent.

Winton's with six-cylinder engines first made their appearance in 1907.

Ayers went outside and ordered the men to come out of the car. Suddenly Jenkins rushed out and lunged at Deputy Campbell trying to knock the "coffee" from the deputy's hand. When some of the evidence was spilled, Campbell shouted, "Don't do that again if you know what's good for you." The suspect charged at the deputy again, but Ayers was on the spot and hit Jenkins over the head with his black jack. The stricken man pleaded, "Please don't hit me again." The sheriff needed no further action, and Jenkins came along quietly. Jenkins' companion in the car was allowed to go free since there was no evidence that he had purchased any liquor. (32)

At his arraignment, Jenkins, a prosperous resident of Spring Valley, was accused of possession and sale of liquor. The charge of liquor sale was dropped in return for a guilty plea on the charge of possession. He was fined $200, but since he could not pay the fine, he was sentenced to 60 days in jail. (33)

Ottawa Police Chief Ben Ford was in charge of three more raids in Ottawa on Oct. 6, 1921. Samples of "grape juice" were taken from the soft drink parlors of Joe Bluth at 510 W. Superior and Matt Bayuk's establishment at the corner of Chestnut and Lafayette for analysis.

Another wine sample was obtained at George Tertezns' saloon on the corner of Chestnut and Superior. Since there wasn't concrete evidence that the proprietors were selling anything containing more than one-half percent alcohol, no one was arrested. (34)

What did they do with all the evidence one might ask? It had to be disposed of somehow. Frequently a moonshine "party" was announced in the local paper. Upon a judge's order, the sheriff, in the presence of a number of witnesses, dumped the brew. One such occasion occurred on Oct. 19, 1921 in Ottawa. The "party" was scheduled for 4:30 p.m. for the disposal of the cache collected in the raids of Frank Pirania and Dominic Meceni in August. At the appointed time, Sheriff Ayers with the assistance of Deputy Frank Frazier, Jailer George Stevens, and several trustees took the 15 barrels seized in the LaSalle raid out to the curb on Jackson Street near the jail. Two other barrels were considered to be of such high quality that they were requisitioned for use in county hospitals for medicinal purposes. The bung plugs were pulled out of the barrels marked for disposal, and a sample was taken from each numbered barrel to make sure that some other liquid had not been substituted while the barrels were stored. William Tydeman, chemistry instructor at Ottawa Township High School, determined that the brew registered 11 to 30 percent alcohol. About 50 people watched for an hour as the barrels of mostly "Dago Red" were emptied into the city sewers. (35)

The first jury trial in LaSalle County on a bootlegging case involved Michael Zabkar, the owner of a LaSalle saloon. It was common knowledge that no jury would ever convict a saloonkeeper in LaSalle County. In the view of many residents, there was too much sympathy for the business owners who were providing a desired product.

Defendants usually pleaded guilty when caught in the act, but Zabkar wanted to fight it out in court. In March 1921, Sheriff Ayers had found two barrels of moonshine in the Zabkar saloon. It seemed like an open-and-shut case, but Zabkar decide to rely on the sympathies of the local populace.

The trail dragged on for some time. Finally, Judge Harry Reck instructed the jury to bring back a finding of guilty even if the sheriff didn't have a search warrant and whether or not a sale was actually observed. Rather, Reck observed, the location of the liquor in a saloon should be sufficient to find Zabkar guilty of the sale as well as possession of illicit liquor. Zabkar's defense attorney argued that the sheriff was picking on a "poor foreigner" while hundreds of other saloons in the county "were violating the prohibition law unmolested." Judge Reck instructed the jurors, "What someone else does has no bearing on this case."

It took the jury seven hours to come to a decision because one or two of the jurors continued to vote "not guilty." During their deliberations, the two barrels of "evidence" were moved into the jury room. Each juror had the opportunity to personally test the liquor to decide if it had an alcohol content above the legal limit. Apparently there was quite a bit of testing of the evidence during the lengthy deliberations, but those in the courtroom said that the jurors were sober when they returned their verdict at 12:30 a.m. Zabkar was found guilty of two of the four charges against him. (36)

The dry crusade was running strong in Congress. In mid-November, 1921, the Senate finally banned the use of beer for medicinal purposes 55-22 and sent it to President Wilson for his signature. In addition, physicians were limited to 100 prescriptions for liquor every three months. Doctors could still prescribe one-half pint of wine or whiskey for medicinal purposes over a ten-day period. The Commissioner of the Internal Revenue was given the authority to change the formulations of prescription medicines used as a beverage. However, the law provided that those searching homes in a malicious manner without a warrant and without probable cause could be fined $1,000. (37)

The local crusade continued. On Dec. 1, 1921, the Ottawa *Republican Times* described how the mayor of Leland caught a bootlegger in his town. When the afternoon Burlington passenger train arrived in Leland, the village marshal, William Campion, became curious since one of the passengers was carrying two gallon-jugs of some liquid and no other baggage. The marshal notified Mayor O.M. Danielson, and the two men proceeded to the Anderson carpentry shop. When the mayor and marshal entered the business, they found that the newcomer, George Demmen of Aurora, sitting at a table with Leland residents Ollie and P.F. Setter along with the jugs of moonshine which had just been sold. It was determined that the Aurora man had been coming to the Leland community frequently with moonshine. Now he was headed to the Ottawa jail where he would spend the night before having his day in court. (38)

Back in Ottawa, Chief of Police Harvey LeRette, conducted a raid at the home of Antone "Tony" Carchia. Rumors of moonshine sales led the chief to find one drunk patron and other evidence of liquor sales. The house located on south Main stood next door to another building where the county sheriff had made a similar raid and found a moonshine operation in progress. (39)

In October 1921, federal agents raided a number of local saloons in the county and from their investigations, it was determined that most of their real beer and near beer was coming from the Ottawa Brewery, which was renamed Ottawa Products company. Warrants were issued in

December for Max Stahl, company vice president, John Damgard, secretary-treasurer, and T.L. Grot, president of the company. (40)

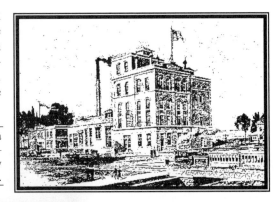

At right-Ottawa Brewing Assn. 1907 – McCoy's Ottawa City Directory.

One of the major events in Ottawa affecting beer production was the closure of the Ottawa Brewing Company. The business was located near Champlain Street and the Rock Island RR. Ottawa Root was one of its non-alcoholic products.

Within days, rumors spread that the company was being fined $25,000. Most of the workers were laid off, and all production was halted. To make sure than none of the contents were removed from the plant, three revenue agents guarded the brewery. A complete inventory of the plant was conducted. An investigation was underway to determine how long the plant had been producing real beer after the prohibition law went into effect. (41)

There was still plenty of liquor for the local taverns, which were constantly threatened by raids. In Ottawa, the sheriff closed down the saloon operated by Harry Moss on Court Street and the Harrison House on Main Street. Two pints of moonshine were found in the basement of the Harrison House. A similar amount was found at the Moss saloon. The Clifton Hotel bar also was inspected but found to have no incriminating evidence – only a quantity of grape juice. (42)

Before the end of the year, additional raids were conducted on homes around the Rock Island depot in Peru. Near the Illinois Zinc Co. along Brunner Street, the sheriff's men targeted Joe Guzier and Joe Washiwicz. Three other locations further north on Center Street were the homes of John Zuchorski, John Rowinski, and Anton Labosenski. Every one of the accused had moonshine on the premises. At the Labosenski house, there were also three barrels of mash. Rowinski was the only one who apparently did not have a still, but there was evidence that he was selling liquor. (43)

In northern LaSalle County, the village of Earlville was the scene of another raid. While walking the tracks west of the village around 9 p.m., Chief of Police H.S. Minor passed a Burlington bunk boxcar He could smell the fumes of fermenting grain coming from a small stack on the car. Upon opening the door of the car, he found two Russians with a still and 30 gallons of mash. The men were section hands for the Burlington, and they had taken over one of several uninhabited bunk cars on the siding. They denied any guilt when the sheriff arrived to take them back to Ottawa. This was the first time that a still had been seized in the village. (44)

New Year's Eve was not a day to celebrate for John Aldrich and his son. They appeared before Judge Koenig on charges of manufacturing moonshine and implicated another man, George Kline, a resident of Marseilles. Clyde Aldrich, who was also on trial as a moonshiner, corroborated their testimony. He said that he knew Kline was using potatoes to make moonshine in a shack on Covel Creek. Based on the testimony, Ayers took Kline into custody later in the day. (45)

Clifton House in Ottawa where the hotel bar was searched for prohibition violations in 1921, but only grape juice was found. *Ottawa Old and New.*

Chapter 6
1922
Small Operations Begin To Grow

The new year had hardly begun before the LaSalle County sheriff was finding more moonshine. A search of the property of John Stockdale of rural Norway turned up a 50-gallon barrel filled with corn mash, some gallon jugs, a small quantity of moonshine and a large copper boiler. Stockdale did not deny that he was using the mash, but he claimed it was for his hogs. There were no cooling coils in the apparatus. Stockdale had draped a cloth over the copper boiler. This collected the vapors, and the liquid could be squeezed out. It was the newest method. Stockdale was taken before Judge Koenig and put up the $500 bond so he would not have to spend a night in the Ottawa jail. Ayers kept up his search and in the little town of Millington found Jesse Lee and his son Arthur with several bottles of moonshine in their possession. (1)

One of the names in the bootlegging business that was in the newspaper headlines on numerous occasions was Joseph Latino of Streator. He was implicated in selling liquor to minors when two Streator High School students said that they had purchased drinks in Latino's soft drink parlor in Streator. One boy claimed it was 110 proof alcohol. Together with a young man, Max Dunn, they said they bought a pint from Latino. Another young man allegedly paid Latino $1 for a pint. He and another boy were arrested at the Streator fair grounds in September 1921. (2) Altogether six people testified against Latino. The state's attorney also produced a pint of moonshine that was seized as evidence in a raid. In his defense, Latino denied selling intoxicating liquor in his soft drink parlor. His bartender, Sidney Robertson, defended his boss. William Price testified that on New Year's Eve, the bartender had thrown out some youngsters demanding a drink. Robertson told them, "Latino's is not that kind of place!" Latino's defense attorney claimed that the boys were not "little angels" and would not hesitate to lie. Unfortunately, the attorney was not persuasive enough. The jury found Latino guilty of selling liquor. (3)

Most of the arrests were routine; those arrested were seldom belligerent. Sometimes, in fact, they were most accommodating. In the spring of 1922, two patrolmen, Walloch and McInerney, found two unsteady individuals near the corner of First and Marquette in LaSalle. Walloch asked one of the individuals what they had in their heavily loaded suitcases. One of the men responded, "moonshine." At that moment, the handle of one of the suitcases snapped, and the luggage fell to the sidewalk with the distinctive sound of breaking glass followed by a stream of liquid seeping from the bag. Officer Walloch addressed the men, "You'd better come with me." They were taken to the LaSalle lockup and booked under the names of Joe Smeg and Anton Kutchavier. The two men were not strangers to the area. Smeg owned a saloon on First Street on the east side of the city, and Kutchavier was his neighbor. While they slept in the jail, their suitcases were inspected and found to be packed with jugs of moonshine apparently destined for Smeg's tavern. (4)

DeMarco's ice cream parlor and candy kitchen in Leland was the scene of another raid by LaSalle Deputies Campbell and Frazier. Armed with a search warrant, the officers were invited in by the proprietor, A. DeMarco, who told them at the outset that they wouldn't find anything. A thorough search resulted in the confiscation of a jug and two bottles containing booze and a number of empties smelling of liquor. DeMarco, who came to Leland from Hinckley, IL three years earlier, admitted his guilt. He explained that this was the first time he had ever purchased any moonshine, but he couldn't remember the name of the man who sold it to him. (5)

The local newspapers did not carry as many stories about the smaller raids being carried out in 1922. The LaSalle *Daily Post* tended to focus on the more significant crimes. For example, on July 12, Ayers was conducting a search of the home of Martin Orechowski at 1415 Prospect in Peru. Neighbors had been complaining about the sales of "hooch." In spite of the denials by the homeowner of any wrongdoing, Ayers made a thorough search of the basement where he found a still that was said to be one of the newest and capable of producing a gallon an hour. The sheriff also found a five-gallon keg that had a key lock on the faucet. Orechowski produced the key for the sheriff. Trying to come up with an explanation for the still, Orechowski explained that he only made it as a rubbing liniment for his leg since he suffered from rheumatism. To that the sheriff replied, "If this would help your rheumatism, you ought to be cured long before this for you've made enough of the stuff." Out in the yard Ayers found a half dozen barrels for making mash. Before leaving, the sheriff destroyed 200 gallons of mash by dousing it with kerosene. The still was added to the sheriff's impressive and growing collection of distilling equipment. (6)

Searches of people's homes and taverns tended to be the main occupation of the police in the 1920's. However, the traffic in illicit liquor was, on occasion, stopped on the highway. Luther McCoy and Ray Johnson had been arrested in Putnam County for transporting booze through Magnolia and were found guilty in January 1922.

In LaSalle County, a farmer had tipped of the sheriff that a suspicious car was stopped on the road six miles northwest of Ottawa. When the sheriff arrived, he found a Ford runabout with its lights on

Ford Runabout

parked along the road. In the back seat were two gallons of moonshine. On the opposite side of the road, he found Pete Johnson of Wedron sleeping in the weeds. Johnson said that he purchased the liquor in LaSalle for his personal use. But he had a memory lapse and couldn't recall the name of the man who sold it to him. He was charged with transporting liquor on a public highway. (7)

Bureau County authorities continued to crack down on the numerous saloons in Spring Valley in the fall of 1922. The tavern owners had become more sophisticated during the course of hundreds of raids. Instead of storing large quantities of liquor in the bars, only a small quantity that could easily be dumped was actually on the premises. The larger supplies were hidden outside.

One of the sadder cases involved a widow, Mrs. Lena Madalozza, who was trying to run a tavern on West Dakota Street by herself after her husband was murdered in a robbery. She also fooled the police when she hid a small bottle of moonshine in her skirt pocket and slipped out the side door while the inspectors were distracted. She tried to conceal the small bottle behind a billboard but was caught in the act. When she finally appeared before the judge at her hearing, she explained the hardship she endured when the couple's previous bar at the corner of Terry and Dakota in Spring Valley burned to the ground. The judge had little pity and fined the woman $784. (8)

The soft drink parlor and tobacco store of Charles Rolando of Seneca was the target of Sheriff Ayers on October 15. On Saturday afternoon, the sheriff and Deputy Campbell found a box lying on its side concealing a removable floorboard. Under it, they found five half-pints of moonshine. The officers then searched all the men in the establishment and found one man with a pint of moonshine in his possession. He admitted that he bought it from Rolando. An arrest warrant was also served on the previous owner, Louis Scarini, who still lived upstairs. (9)

Newly elected Sheriff Ed Welter, who was not well known by the customers, fooled Joe Woodshank of Peru in a raid on Dec. 17, 1922. The sheriff seized bottles containing moonshine, wine and genuine pre-Volsteadian beer. (10)

Chapter 7
1923
Replacing the Breweries

Judges in LaSalle County had little sympathy for booze peddlers. Appearing before the court on Jan 8, 1923, Joe Kutlich pleaded guilty to having moonshine at his soft drink establishment in Oglesby. But he explained to the judge that he had to do it to make enough money to support his wife and 15 children, none of whom was beyond their teen years. Kutlich still had to pay the $100 fine as did Louis Pocius and Mary Somenzi whose bars were also raided by Sheriff Welter. (1)

LaSalle County Sheriff Ed Welter had a long and distinguished career in law enforcement. He served three terms: 1922-1926; 1930-34; 1938-1942.

Welter continued to hit both soft drink parlors and homes in Oglesby. Lucindo Colombi and another man, Joe Archetti, who roomed at the Colombi home were picked up and charged with making moonshine. They argued that they were not making it but merely bought it from some fellow whose name they could not remember. The fine for manufacturing was always stiffer than that for possession. There was also the suspicion that the men had been involved in a recent robbery of merchandise from a Rock Island boxcar. (2)

Sheriff Welter was persistent in his attempts to dry up LaSalle County. Joe Woodshank was arrested again. Other raids were made on the taverns operated by Matt Bayuk and Frank Vallet in Ottawa and the Pete Yanitis saloon at 135 First St. in LaSalle. Little booze was found in any of the bars, but two slot machines were found in the Ottawa establishments. (3)

While the Ottawa brewery had been shut down for manufacturing real beer in 1921, the breweries in Peru continued to operate producing legal beverages. For instance, Peru Products had the local Coca-Cola bottling franchise as well as bottling their near beer. Responding to numerous tips that Peru Products was also making real beer, Mark Potter of the local prohibition office led in the arrests of several officers and workers at the brewery. Those arrested were Andrew Hebel, president, Al Hebel, vice president, George Sippel, brewmaster, and Joe Blitsch and Frank Stachowiak, deliverymen. The prohibition agents seized 125 cases of beer in the plant and another 75 cases being transported by Blitsch and Stachowiak. The beer was taken to the LaSalle post office for storage until the hearing. (4)

After producing tonics for a time, the Ottawa Brewing Association also went back to fermenting real beer as well. In April 1923, federal agents seized a truck as it pulled away from the company loading area. It was loaded with over 19 barrels of real beer. The two men in the truck, Carl Gebhardt and Charles Berta, were arrested. The president of the Ottawa Products company, W.J.Reardon, also ran the Illinois Beverage Co. in Chicago. It too was raided. (6)

Another raid was conducted at the Star Union Brewery a few days later. Four revenue agents descended on the plant early on Monday morning, February 19, when two trucks were stopped as they left the plant. The vehicles were carrying 38 half barrels and two full barrels of beer. The agents went to the brewery and found it in full operation. Employees were filling 14 half barrels and 3 full barrels. To make sure that none of the brew would be removed, the agents drained all the fermentation vats. All of the seized barrels were also moved to the LaSalle post office and stacked along side of the 200 cases found on the Hebel trucks. Later in the afternoon, warrants were served on the plant owner, Henry Hoerner, and his brewmaster. The following day, John Welch, the bacteriologist at the Hygienic Institute, determined that the beer was 4% alcohol. (5)

Soft drinks and near beer were the only products supposed to be found in the bottling department of the Star Union Brewery. Peru Library collection.

71

On May 24, 1923, four of the men associated with the Star Union Brewery, Henry Hoerner, Rudolph Bender, Marshall Koebel, and Charles Link were in the Chicago district court presided over by Judge Adam Cliffe. Three prohibition agents testified that the plant was a major source of alcoholic beverages distributed throughout northern Illinois. (7) A government chemist also testified that the samples taken from the 180 seized barrels indicated an alcohol content that varied from 3.58% to 4.12%.

Since the beer would normally continue to ferment over time, the defense attorney wanted to know how long it had been between the time that the beer was seized and the tests were conducted. The chemist replied that it was a couple of days but that mercury had been added to the beer to stop the fermentation process. (8) Another defense contention was that the employees at the plant had mistakenly filled the barrels from Vat No. 7 which contained beer that had not been de-alcoholized instead of the near-beer in Vat No. 11. (9)

The case went to the jury on May 28. The verdict was guilty. The Star Union's president, Henry Hoerner, and other officials were fined as much as $1000 each. It was also ruled that the plant should be closed for a period of one year. Two days later, Judge Cliffe also closed down all legal near-beer operations as well as the real beer production of Peru's other brewery, the Peru Products Co., for a year and also fined the company $2000. The judge did allow the company to continue its ice-making operation since Peru Products was one of the chief sources of ice for the entire LaSalle-Peru area. (10)

This rare ad appeared in the July 12, 1923 issue of the LaSalle *Daily Post*. During Prohibition, there was very little advertising of liquor of any kind in the Illinois Valley. Even near beer (less than ½ % alcohol) was not promoted in the Illinois Valley even though the Star Union Brewery in Peru was one of the largest distributors in the Mid-West. John A. Littau of LaSalle was a distributor of the Anheuser-Busch products.

While most attention was focused on the outcome of the Peru breweries trial, Sheriff Welter continued his efforts to dry up LaSalle County. Back in February, a raid at the home of A. Regal at 638 LaSalle St. near the Matthiessen Athletic Field netted 20 gallons of moonshine. The lame "rheumatism" defense by Regal did not impress the sheriff who said, "You must have a pretty bad case of rheumantics." as he loaded the gallon-jugs into his car. Other raids were conducted in Oglesby at the soft drink parlors owned by John Kulitch and C. Berardome. (11)

The amount of moonshine, wine, and beer confiscated in the Illinois Valley was only a small fraction of the national totals. In a period of six months in 1922, 6.7 million gallons of liquor and mash along with over 7,000 stills were impounded or destroyed nationwide. Violence associated with the raids locally was either non-existent or minor, compared to the country as a whole, where 12 prohibition agents were killed and another 323 wounded. No doubt the syndicates were angered by the loss of almost $7 million worth of liquor and equipment. (12)

Although the statistics for sheriffs, town marshals, and investigators in the Illinois Valley may not have been as impressive, most officers felt compelled to uphold the law. And so the struggle continued unabated and with more urgency every year. Each raid was viewed as a small battle in the ongoing war with bootleggers. Herb Seibert's bar on Calhoun Street and Pete Massock's place at 1521 Water Street in Peru along with the soft drink parlor of Joe Meglich in Oglesby were all found to have small quantities of moonshine behind the bars. Many of the owners had either gotten wise to the raids by tips or had learned that it wasn't worth the $100 in fines that the courts handed down. (13)

A massive crackdown in Ottawa began at the end of July. All but three of the owners of the 29 soft drink parlors in the city were hauled into court and charged with the sale of liquor. The case against George Zirkle, owner of the tavern at 423 W. Madison was concluded quickly. He paid $56.15 for the fine and court costs. Most of the accused simply paid the fine. But Joe Bluthe and Joe Vidie demanded explanations for the specific charges before committing to a guilty plea. (14)

Not every attempted arrest went as planned. On October 3, Prohibition Commissioner Harry Bellrose left his hotel room at 7:45 p.m. and was joined by Herman Kammer and W.F.Walling who were waiting for him outside of the Ottawa Hotel. In the alley near the hotel, they heard the sounds of barrels being dropped to the pavement. Walking into the alley and armed with his .45 caliber revolver, Bellrose and the deputies discovered two men unloading barrels from a Reo Speed Wagon. One of the men protested that none of the 14 barrels contained any illegal liquor. Suddenly the other man jumped into the truck. Bellrose yelled, "Get the number" as the truck sped down the alley. The accomplice ran into the Zellar Inn and escaped through the front of the hotel. The enforcement officers followed the bootleggers truck, but the Ford roadster they commandeered was no match for the Reo truck that raced out of the city on Ottawa Ave.

Back at the crime scene, Bellrose ordered the 15 half barrels to be moved to a local garage. He anticipated that the bootleggers might return for their cargo to either steal the beer or doctor it to lower the alcohol level so he personally stayed up all night guarding the evidence. Sure enough around 10 p.m. a Reo Speed Wagon and two other trucks carrying additional kegs and guards were seen driving through Ottawa. However, a search of the city failed to find any of the vehicles. (15)

A restored 1922 Reo Speedwagon similar to the one used in the 1923 bootlegging encounter in Ottawa

Another load of illegal moonshine was intercepted in the spring of 1923, but because of various delays, the case did not go to trial until November. The accused bootlegger, Pete Doukezas, was known for operating one of the largest stills in the county in Mark. His operations were said to extend not only into Bureau and LaSalle Counties but also as far south as Peoria and Pekin. Authorities had been aware of the man's activities for two years but previous attempts to arrest him were unsuccessful. While making his rounds in his brand new 1923 Buick, "Moonshine Pete" was stopped in Seatonville.

1923 Buick

In the back seat were 40 gallons of whiskey. Although the hearing was originally slated for the court of Judge Prichard in Princeton, Doukezas' lawyer asked for a change of venue to the court of Judge Taylor at the Hennepin Court House in Putnam County. The defense lawyer was wary of Judge Prichard's penchant for being tough on liquor violators. (16)

The LaSalle sheriff was making steady progress in his campaign to dry out the county. A warehouse on the north bank of the Illinois River near Peru Plow and Wheel was searched in November. The building rented out to a "J. Brennan" was unguarded. Welter and Deputy Rasmus Benson quickly discovered 75 barrels of beer. Welter called for two large trucks to come from Ottawa to pick up the evidence. Since Mr. Brennan left no address or phone, it was impossible to locate him. (17)

It was no wonder that the federal and city authorities in Chicago could not stop the flow of beer and whiskey. It was well known that there were many sources of real beer coming into the city from Elgin, Joliet, Peoria and other cities with their numerous breweries. As in the towns of the Illinois Valley, there were thousands of cellar distilleries within the city limits. One of the more popular drinks because of its potent "kick" was black fig wine, which sold for $6 a gallon in the city. To his credit Chicago's Mayor Dever had shut down over 2,300 saloons. Only 200 known bars were still in operation as Christmas 1923 approached. (18)

Traditional New Year's drinking binges were going to be a thing of the past as far as the city authorities in Marseilles were concerned. It was decided to close down every soft drink parlor as a "public nuisance and threat to the public health." The LaSalle *Daily Tribune* listed the businesses of Fernando Balatto, Wedron Wanner, Joe Marz, Baptista Lansranki, Joe Galbate, and Henry Koine to be served with temporary injunctions. A huge quantity of evidence had been accumulated regarding dates of illegal purchases, the type of drink, and alcohol content. Some samples were 90 to 120 proof. (19)

The closing of the Star Union and Peru Products plants were significant accomplishments for Sheriff Welter in 1923. But he was determined to make even more progress in the new year.

Chapter 8
1924
Cracking Down

It was a sorry sight for beer lovers along the Fox River on March 5, 1924. With the closing of the breweries in Peru and Ottawa, it became more difficult, but not impossible to obtain the amber ale. Revenue agents put another major supplier, the Elgin Ice and Beverage Co. out of business. The court ordered U.S. Marshal Levy to dispose of the seized evidence. The vats and other brewing equipment were destroyed, and 3,000 barrels of beer were dumped into the Fox River. (1)

While the raids on the big distilleries around Chicago were making headlines, federal revenue agents, which the local paper described as the "sponge squad," continued "mopping up" the numerous saloons on First Street in LaSalle in April. The violations were based on investigations conducted on Feb. 26. Operators of saloons from the west end to the business district of LaSalle were served with warrants. Newspaper reports of the day provided details including the names and addresses of the accused. Furthest west at 110 First Street was Anton Pagoni's tavern. At 237 First Street was the Walter Rix bar. John Rottner and Anton Friedrich were arrested at their business at 601 First Street. Three blocks to the east at 945 First Street, the agents arrested Battesta Sampo. One block east at 1059 First Street, a warrant was served on John Novak, and at 1219 First Street, the authorities visited Stanley Koskosky. The total amount of illicit liquor confiscated was only 25 gallons-most of which was wine in the larger establishments. There was also pre-war whiskey and moonshine of recent manufacture. (2)

Another late night raid in April was conducted by Sheriff Welter at the home of Nick Yapich in Oglesby. Nick wasn't at home, but his wife tried to convince the sheriff that there was nothing illegal in the house. After reading his search warrant, the sheriff and Deputy Benson searched the upstairs but found nothing. With her scared children clinging to her skirt, Mrs. Yapich continued to insist that there was nothing in the cellar except some mush. Welter said he would just give it a quick look to give her a "clean bill of health." Finding a barrel in a corner of the cellar, the sheriff pulled off the top and found the "mush." It looked more like fermenting corn mash to the sheriff. He called up to the woman, "If this is mush you must expect a lot of company to help you eat it." Barrel after barrel was discovered until they totaled 15 - all filled with "mash" not "mush." Then a large number of jugs and bottles were found around the cellar. Finally, one of the largest and newest stills the sheriff had ever seen was discovered. There was so much evidence and so little space for storage at the sheriff's office that Welter and Benson simply destroyed the still and poured kerosene over the 800 gallons of mash. They returned to Ottawa with 15 gallons of moonshine that they also found. Welter told Mrs. Yapich to have her husband report to the Ottawa court the following Monday morning. (3)

On April 30, Welter with all his deputies, and six additional officers conducted raids on ten different drinking establishments in Ottawa, Utica, LaSalle and Peru. The Laas and Madic soft drink parlors in Ottawa came up with a clean bill. In Utica only one of three taverns, that of J. Hannum, was not violating the law. The J. Roth business was found with a quart of "moon," and Sherman Cole's place had a pint of liquor hidden. In LaSalle at the Rock Island Inn at 237 First Street they found a gallon of wine. Further west in Peru, they visited the Turn Hall saloon recently purchased by the former bartender, Carl Ulrich. There they found a pint of booze. Of the ten businesses Welter searched, five were doing business within the law, or, if they had any alcohol, it was well hidden from the authorities. (4)

Peru's Turn Hall Opera House – 1908. Peru Library collection.

The court in Bureau County was also making progress enforcing the Volstead Act. A DePue saloon owner, Anton Sorchjich had his place raided on April 14, 1924. The Princeton judge sentenced him to 60 days in jail and fined him $300. He had tried to destroy a small flask of moonshine. Another 60-day sentence and $100 fine was handed out to August Koehler of Spring Valley for possessing illicit liquor. When officers raided the Henry Thomas Buffet in Bureau, Charles Ackerholm of Bureau tried to stop the officers. He got off with a $1 fine and a day in jail because he had been in jail since the raid. In one of the rarer jury trials during the month, Martin Chaido was convicted of having ten barrels of wine in the Spring Valley Prosperity Club. The club's bartender, John Ragio, was fined $250 for selling liquor. Another Spring Valley man, Mike Knezwich, had his hearing for sales of liquor delayed until June. A Tiskilwa resident, Hugh Ryan, was involved in an auto wreck back in February. In the resulting investigation, the officer found that Ryan was transporting alcohol. That cost him over $100. (5)

In June, even more raids were conducted in LaSalle County. The operations, coordinated by Major Hamel Ridgeway of Chicago, resulted in the arrests of ten operators of soft drink parlors. Twenty-seven agents arrived on the Rock Island train in Ottawa at 11:37 a.m. Their searches led to the arrest of William Block, John Gehrig, Cleto Monterestelli, Elbert Monterestelli, Mary Post, Stan Mazurkilvich, Frank Kincheski, Victor Alicki, John Boris, and Joe Vidick. The largest seizure of evidence was at the Monterestelli saloon where 20 gallons of

moonshine was found. Although the actual owners were not present in several cases, the bartenders were all arrested. A total of 18 defendants were taken to LaSalle's city hall (left) to post bail of $1000. It had taken weeks of investigative preparation and tips by an Anti-Saloon agent before search warrants were obtained and the raids were conducted. The tri-city region had been under constant surveillance because of the constant violations of the Volstead Act. (6) A considerable amount of alcohol was removed from the various locations. The largest amount seized included 712 bottles and 12 ½ barrels of beer. The confiscated evidence also included 122 gallons of moonshine, 101 gallons of wine, 27 gallons of whiskey, and 81 gallons of alcohol. Trucks had to be brought in to haul away the evidence to the city hall. Samples were taken of some of the larger quantities of evidence and then the kegs and bottles were destroyed. Five of the Chicago-based agents stayed overnight at city hall while the rest returned to their home office. (7)

In spite of the notoriety associated with the large-scale operations against tavern owners, individuals in the privacy of their homes were also arrested. Frequently, warrants were obtained after complaints by neighbors were filed with the sheriff or state's attorney. One elderly gentleman, J. Sherman, was found to have six bottles of moonshine stashed in his flour bin. The 80-year old man also had a working still in the basement of his Peru home. In spite of Sherman's advanced age, Welter felt that it was necessary to close down the man's operation. (8)

It was a constant battle for the sheriff who did not let up the pressure for a single day. The house at 206 Third in LaSalle was found to have a large quantity of "hooch." A still was found at John Zupancic's saloon at 1016 Third, and Nick Sronovich, who lived at 817 Canal, was also arrested for prohibition violations. (9)

On July 2, 1925, the *Spring Valley Gazette* gave its readers some insights as to how the Bureau County bootleggers were making small-scale sales to customers in nearby Walnut. The local deputies were tipped off that a hollow tree was being used to hide the illegal booze. After staking out the area, the deputies were able to arrest Leo Potts and a young boy who had just procured a small bottle of moonshine from its hiding place. The Deer Grove man implicated Guy Larson as his connection. Larson was later arrested and fined $200.

At the end of July, Welter and Deputy Sheriff Benson found two stills. The first was the Frank Lopatka home at 1234 Fourth. The initial search turned up nothing. But at the last minute, Welter spotted a locked trap door. The opening led to the basement where the sheriff found two gallons of moonshine along with a still. Another still was found at 335 Sterling in LaSalle. The homeowner, Mike Karkas, was arrested, and the ten gallons of moonshine in his basement were seized as evidence. (10)

Meanwhile in the Streator area, Police Chief John Hopkins stopped a truck driven by Frank Koster of Peoria. The chief found six barrels of beer that the Peorian was driving from Joliet to Peoria. The chief kept a small sample but destroyed most of the beer. Koster was later fined $500 for transporting illegal beer. (11)

Following the November elections, a new State's Attorney, Russell O. Hanson, took office and began a crusade against alcohol that was unprecedented in the history of the Illinois Valley. He was the Valley's own version of the more famous federal agent, Elliot Ness. And like the famous Chicago Treasury agent's "Untouchables," "Hanson's Raiders" would descend upon illegal brewing operations like a plague of locusts.

Beginning on Dec. 3, 1924, the raids were designed to completely stamp out all liquor production and sales. First, Hanson went after the alcohol in Utica. One of the individuals they tried to net was none other than the Dan Neary, the son of the Utica village president. Hanson was also preoccupied with closing down "second offenders." As early as Nov. 13, Hanson's undercover agents began to collect evidence in Utica soft drink parlors. Not only were they seeking links to liquors sales but they also documented the locations of slot machines and other gambling equipment. Not satisfied with simply arresting the local bartenders, Hanson wanted to apprehend the owners of the buildings where alcohol was being sold. On his list were John Rowatt, James

Hannan, Dan Neary, Tom Hickey, and Sherman Cole, who owned the building where his tavern was located. Other building owners including Andrew Hebel, Johanna Fitzgerald, Rose Madden, and Anna Hanley were also sought. (12)

On December 4, injunctions were handed down by Judge Harry Reck to close down the five Utica saloons. Rumors were circulating that H. Ward Conde, a local Ottawa car dealer, was actually the head of the Secret Service unit in the area, and he was working closely with Hanson. When questioned about his link with Hanson, Conde would neither confirm nor deny any connection. Hanson took a similar position when confronted by local reporters. (13)

Something of a friendly competition arose between Hanson and Sheriff Welter. Not to be overlooked in his efforts, the LaSalle County sheriff also made significant arrests. More stills were seized in December. One operation at the home of V. Benningo in Streator was in full production. It had a capacity of 25 gallons and was boiling away when the sheriff and his deputies searched the cellar. Five gallons of moonshine were taken as evidence. Another Streator raid was at the home of C. Corsinia. The still was of similar size as in the previous raid, and there were six barrels of mash nearby. A third location the sheriff investigated was the soft drink parlor of John Menall. There they found two quarts of moonshine. (14)

In spite of Hanson's apparent successes, he suffered a setback in his ambitions to close down the buildings where the soft drink parlors were located. It was his goal to shut down all activities, illegal or legal, in any building where a saloon was actively selling liquor. However, Judge Reck refused the request of the new state's attorney. He explained, "In cases where the buildings are of more than one story, the court did not go so far as to restrain the sale of liquor in the whole building but merely made the order to apply to the main floor." At least that was the temporary position of the court until the January 1925 hearing. At that time, the judge said that he might consider closing the buildings for as much as one year. If Hanson's request had been carried out, Lee Browne, the defense attorney for Thomas Hickey and Andrew Hebel, argued that as many as 300 buildings in LaSalle County would be closed. This would prohibit their use for legitimate business practices. (15)

Apparently it wasn't just the Illinois Valley that was feeling the effects of prohibition enforcement authorities. A small item from the Chicago newspapers stated that although good whiskey and rare wines from St. Louis were plentiful, "beer is at the vanishing point." The paper attributed the drought to "the closing down of practically every brewery in northern Illinois." (16)

Hanson continued to close as many saloons as possible. On December 16, injunction proceedings were begun against 20 of Streator's soft drink parlors. Hanson brought into the court bottles allegedly secured at each establishment. Each one was corked and sealed with wax marked with the accused's thumbprint. One of the saloons was located in the Plumb House hotel (right). In this case, Hanson did not seek the closing of the entire hotel but just the room where the drinks were being served. He brought forward

witnesses who testified that they had paid 25 cents for drinks in the hotel bar.

The Fred Trapp saloon at 112 S. Park not only sold liquor but also was a gambling den according to Hanson. Five witnesses came forward to testify that they had purchased moonshine in half-pint bottles for 75 cents each on November 18 and November 23. Other places that were being charged were located at 120 South Park, 423 E. Main, 410 E. Main and 202 N. Sterling in Streator. (17)

The Trapp bar in Streator, which dates back to the 1890's, was located at 308 E. Main. The bar closed in the 1970's, and the Rockwell Inn in Morris bought the back bar. Streator Historical Society.

Chapter 9
1925
Hanson's Raiders Take Charge

With the opening of the January session of the court, State's Attorney Hanson was handed the decision he had long awaited. Judge Edgar Eldredge ordered that three of the buildings in Streator, for which Hanson had won temporary injunctions to be shut, would now be permanently padlocked for one year. The buildings were located at 525 S. Illinois, 101 W. Main, and 508 Adams. Now Hanson could seek the closing of other buildings. (1) On January 14, he began proceedings against a tavern in Seneca owned by Tom Norem and the building located at 1033 Fulton in Ottawa. (2)

Next, he went after a bar operated by Steve Quay in Leonore just north of the post office. Three of Hanson's Raiders, Dave Cooper, M.R. Smith of Streator, and Stan Farrell of Marseilles, actually conducted the 8:30 p.m. raid. Farrell went in for a time and played the slot machine, which paid out 60 cents on a nickel spin. Smith found that the pool table had a secret shelf holding several bottles of liquor. When confronted with the evidence, Quay admitted his guilt and said it was time to get out of the business. He even praised Hanson admitting that the state's attorney was "doing the right thing in waging a campaign to put bootlegging establishments out of business." Quay made a full confession saying that he bought the whiskey for $10 a gallon; hid the bottles under the pool table; and sold the whiskey in the same bottles that were seized for 75 cents a glass. Quay went on to say that the owner of the building in Leonore was Henry Hoerner's Star Union Brewing Co. of Peru. They also owned all the bar fixtures. The slot machine, which he had installed 2-3 weeks previous to the raid on Jan. 12 and paid as much as $1 on a nickel bet, was actually owned by Archie Haskins of LaSalle who got one half of all the proceeds. Quay pled guilty to all charges.(3) Hanson immediately proceeded to seek an injunction to close Quay's building and named both Quay and Hoerner as defendants. (4)

The Ajsters soft drink parlor in LaSalle was next on Hanson's hit list. He sent special agent M.R. Smith with another man to the business on 3rd and Chartres in LaSalle. During the raid, Anton Ajster tried to dump a pitcher of alcohol down the drain. At his hearing, Joe Ajster simply paid a $300 fine plus court costs. Hanson was not satisfied and filed to have the saloon closed for a year. Judge Reck ordered that the Ajster place be locked up and that a notice be posted that it was going to stay closed for a year.

Hanson began a new legal tactic - applying the county nuisance laws to saloons. The first of these cases to be heard involved Andrew Kozlowski who owned a tavern at 1157 First St. in LaSalle. The Feb. 11 hearing went without any challenge from the defendant. Investigators Cooper and Smith had searched the place and found seven gallons of moonshine and another 50 gallons of home-brew. Kozlowski paid over $500 in fines and court costs. This was an important victory for Hanson who now felt that he could apply the principle to other pending cases and close many more of the buildings that housed saloons. Only the day before, another raid had been carried out at Joe Metzger's saloon at 213 Main in Ottawa. Pressing on, they went after Dominick Rinando and his wife, former Granville residents, who now owned a store in Naplate. (5)

Later in the month, the raiders went to 8th and Crosat to search the parlor of Fred Block. Cooper and Hanson came back to Ottawa with three gallons of "moon" they had found in Block's rear room, along with smaller quantities found behind the bar. Appearing before the judge, Block excused his actions by claiming that he didn't sell any moonshine but merely gave it to his friends. If the judge bought that argument, Block would have gotten off with only a possession charge, which usually resulted in a smaller fine. In any case, the man was held over for trial.

Ottawa's "Hit and Run" saloon was also raided later on the evening of March 2. Walking into the establishment at 509 LaSalle Street, Utica officer L.D. Holland and Investigator Smith announced that they had a search warrant. The bartender, Harry Schafer, made a quick move to grab the pitcher by the sink. Smith jumped over the bar and tried to wrest the pitcher from Schafer's hands as the bartender was pouring the contents into the sink. Smith succeeded in saving a small portion of the liquid in the pitcher and put it down on the counter. Just then, the owner, R.W. Kelly, walked in and went straight for the pitcher again trying to empty the remaining contents. Unfortunately for Kelly, a stopper was in the sink so the contents could be retrieved and saved for evidence. Although the contents of the pitcher were diluted by several gallons of water in the sink, the liquid was sent to a lab for analysis.

The third raid of the night came at 11 p.m. This time, Hanson, along with Harold Butters and two other men, proceeded to the Seneca saloon operated by Louis Scarini. There, they confiscated six gallons of moonshine and a gallon of wine. Under a gunny sack in the basement, they found a trap door. Scarini had constructed a 4' x 4' pit in which he had hidden many gallons of wine and moonshine. He admitted his guilt without further argument. Scarini spent the night in the Marseilles city jail since he couldn't put up the $1000 bond. (6)

Special Investigator Smith was heading more of the operations after Cooper resigned from Hanson's force. On Saturday night, March 7, the raiders first headed to the "Tin Building" saloon located at 1301 First Street in LaSalle. As soon as Smith, Holland, and a new man, Charles Walling, entered the business run by Joe Galinski, a woman ran to the back and disappeared. The sound of breaking glass triggered the investigators into a dash, but it was too late. The woman was gone as was the contents of the glass jug whose fragments were scattered around the floor with the liquid contents seeping into the floorboards. A few glass shards were collected for evidence since no other containers of booze could be found.

Next, they decided to see what they could find at John Guggenberger's place at 2301 Main in Peru. Behind the bar was a bottle of wine, but the real jackpot was discovered in a shed behind the bar. After securing the key for the lock on the shed from Guggenberger, they found barrel after barrel of wine. Not having a truck to remove the evidence, Smith and his men first took samples from each barrel and then rolled each barrel over to the gutter and pulled the plug to let the red liquid pour into the sewer. Guggenberger finally had his day in court in March and paid $365 in fines and court costs.

Having good luck so far, the team headed to 357 Third Street in LaSalle. They had a tip that John Essl had some moonshine on the premises. Bartender Joe Hybki tried to hide a small bottle of "moon," but Smith grabbed it in a brief struggle. It was a good night for "Hanson's Raiders," but things were about to get ugly. (7)

The high profile image of M.R. Smith as Russell Hanson's chief investigator almost cost Smith and his family their lives on two occasions. The first incident took place on March 10, 1925. Around midnight, an unknown individual planted a black powder bomb next to the foundation at the rear of their house. When the bomb went off, the six-room bungalow located in Streator at 302 W. LaRue was badly shaken. Dense black smoke filled the house. A hole was blown in the wall, and all the windows on the north side were broken. Shattered glass covered the kitchen floor. Damage was estimated at $25. Fortunately, the bomber was probably only trying to scare Smith, because the bomb had not been placed near the bedrooms where he and his wife and two young children were sleeping at the time. Most of the blast energy was lost because the bomb was only half under the supporting beams. Perhaps it was intended as a warning.

The special agent reacted immediately; saw to the safety of his family; and after quickly dressing, armed himself with his revolver and searched for the perpetrator outside on the street. Finding no suspicious characters wandering through the neighborhood in the early morning hours, Smith contacted the state's attorney and Sheriff Welter to explain the situation. Streator Police Chief John Hopkins offered his assistance. There hadn't been a bombing in Streator since 1908, and it was the first experience the police chief had had with this type of crime.

Streator Police Chief John Hopkins served the city from 1911 until 1926. He was born in Holley, N.J. in 1863 and joined the Streator police force in 1889. He died on Feb. 1, 1927 in the arms of the mayor of an apparent heart attack while he was still on duty. Streator Historical Society.

Rumors spread of one suspicious character, who was seen boarding a northbound Yellow bus carrying a satchel and getting off the bus at LaRue Street. The following day, the Streator Chamber of Commerce posted a $500 reward for the capture of the bomber. Threats against law enforcement officers were not taken lightly. Davis Cooper, the former Marseilles Chief of Police and investigator for Hanson received several "black hand" letters threatening the man with violence if he did not stop his enforcement of the prohibition law.

Smith had no doubt created many enemies as he helped to close many area saloons in recent months. The Streator *Free-Press* speculated that a local element was at work. "Smith has recently been operating in LaSalle, Peru and Spring Valley territory, which is considered by authorities as the stronghold of whiskey distillers, beer runners, and violators of prohibition laws." (8) But anyone who thought they would scare off the determined law officer was badly mistaken. In an interview with a LaSalle reporter, he said, "This only makes me want to go after the bootleggers stronger than before. They can't scare me with bombs or bullets. I only regret though to have the lives of my family endangered by such cowardly tactics." Smith's wife said that she wanted her husband to continue his activities against the bootleggers regardless of her personal safety. (9) A few months later Smith's life would again be in jeopardy.

The excitement in Streator did not sway the efforts of other law enforcement officers any more than the Smith family. In one of the biggest raids in the Spring Valley area, revenue agents from Peoria and Chicago swooped down on the Bureau County towns of DePue,

Seatonville, Ladd and Spring Valley and arrested 30 saloon operators and bartenders. Trying to secretly conduct such a large raid over such a large area was difficult at best. As soon as word spread that a raid was in progress, owners phoned each other so that evidence could be hidden or destroyed. At the Frank McCooey Bar in Spring Valley, the bartender, Henry Martin, was seen exiting the building with a large bag of bottles just as the investigators came in the front door. Throwing away bottles, one after another, he ran for three blocks with the police in hot pursuit. Finally they caught him when he fell. By that time, all of the bottles had been pitched. Of those arrested, 4 were from Ladd, 13 from Spring Valley, 1 from Seatonville, and 7 more from DePue. A Tobler truck was brought to the area to haul the accused back to Peoria. (10)

The name of Andrew Kozlowski had been on the court docket back in February. In March, he was once again answering to charges of selling intoxicating liquor. The saloonkeeper had been arrested again by Hanson's Raiders at his saloon at 1157 First Street, LaSalle on March 29. When the officers walked in at 6:00 p.m., they only found a glass smelling of liquor. Proceeding outside, they spotted distinct tire tracks in the newly fallen snow. The telltale lines led directly to another part of the building where there was a hole in the foundation. Probing into the cavity, Officer Virgil Holland found two gallon-bottles and a quart-bottle, all containing moonshine. When confronted with the evidence by Investigator Smith, Kozlowski denied any knowledge of the material saying that someone else must have hidden it there. (11)

The soft drink parlors were obvious targets for Hanson's Raiders, but that didn't mean that the state's attorney was limiting his investigations to the most likely targets. Many tips came into his office. One of those informants led Smith and Holland to the little community of Rutland where Angelo Calvetti had a bar in the basement of a two-story building. Walking down the stairway, the men found a loose board in the ceiling. Behind it Calvetti had stored a quart of moonshine. As in the Kozlowski raid, Calvetti denied ownership of the bottle. He said he didn't even know there was a secret compartment in the ceiling. Nevertheless, he was brought back to Ottawa where he posted the $500 bail and was released pending a court hearing. (12)

Sometimes tips came from unlikely sources. Peter Lynch, a Granville resident, was sitting in his parked car with the lights turned off when a Peru patrolman stopped to investigate. Lynch was quite intoxicated and was brought to the Peru jail. He was initially charged with DUI and being in the parked car without lights on at night. While under interrogation, Lynch admitted that he had bought five drinks at the bar owned by Sam Hariminch at 1621 Water Street and then went next door to Nick Brabender's saloon at 1615 Water Street for another drink.

Lynch signed complaints against the two establishments, and the state's attorney responded quickly. In the raid that followed, both owners were arrested for possession of moonshine although only Brabender admitted selling liquor. When served with the warrant by Peru Police Chief Joseph Potthoff, Hariminch denied selling Lynch any alcoholic drink. Lynch received a $2 fine for parking without lights. The DUI charge was dropped since technically he wasn't caught driving. (13)

When a customer came to a local bar in LaSalle and asked for a drink, one would think that the bartender would be cautious, especially with strangers. But on March 23, Felix Wasilawski was feeling friendly and gladly poured a stranger first one drink and then another. The man had ten cents and even bought a beer for his friend. Then another man came into the bar at 1235 Fifth Street, had a 20-cent glass of whiskey drink and even told Wasilawski to pour himself one as he threw a half-dollar on the bar. Without waiting for his change, the man started to walk away but motioned for the bartender to come down to the end of the bar for a private conversation. In a secluded area, the stranger introduced himself as Mr. Smith and he also introduced his friend, Mr. Holland, investigators for State's Attorney Russell Hanson. They then produced a search warrant; Wasilawski realized he was caught. A search produced a pop bottle with a small amount of moonshine and a pint-bottle containing whiskey. The saloon owner's only defense at his hearing was that he and his wife had six children and were expecting another one. He even asked Hanson to be the godfather to which the state's attorney agreed if the saloonkeeper still wanted that after the trial. (14)

The Rathskeller was one of the popular soft drink parlors in Ottawa. Investigators Smith and Holland walked into the bar owned by T.J. Nertney. Just as Smith placed his hand over a filled glass at the bar, the bartender Ed Connelly tried to knock it away to spill the liquid. When that failed, Connelly grabbed a pint of whiskey and broke it on a brick on the floor to destroy more evidence. Then the bartender grabbed a pop bottle and tried to smash it over the head of Holland. Smith jumped over the bar and grabbed the man's hand. As they wrestled behind the bar, more of the evidence spilled until only a small fraction was left. But that was enough evidence. Connelly was charged with resisting arrest and interfering with an investigation. Analysis of the remaining liquid found it to be 100 proof alcohol. Bond for Connelly and Nertney was set at $1000.

Another raid at a private home at 1215 Walnut the same night resulted in the seizure of a ten-gallon wine barrel, five gallon-bottles of wine, and six half-pints of moonshine. The homeowners, Mrs. And Mrs. Charles Engel, were released after each posted a $500 bond. Later in the evening, a third Ottawa raid was conducted at Mat Bayuk's saloon at 530

W. LaFayette. Hidden under a trap door in a closet, Smith and Holland found six half-gallon bottles of wine and 15 half-gallon bottles of moonshine. At a meeting with State's Attorney Hanson, Buyak in a seemingly defiant proclamation stated, "I intend to keep on selling moon!" But in a whimsical clarification, he quickly added, "I'm not going to sell any more moonshine. I'm going to sell Moon automobiles instead. I've just secured an agency." (15) *[Note- Moon automobiles were introduced in 1905 by Joseph Moon as a luxury car costing $3,000. The plant in St. Louis Mo. run by Stewart McDonald, Moon's son-in-law, hit a peak production of 7,567 cars in 1924. The company went out of business in 1930.]*

Bootleggers and saloonkeepers tried every trick imaginable to hide their merchandise from the prying eyes of the authorities. Secret panels, trap doors and covered pits were all used with varying degrees of success. But Hanson's men continued their unrelenting search. Simon Micavich was found in the basement of his cousin's house at 215 Sterling in LaSalle. Washing a few dirty pop bottles seemed innocuous enough, but spotting three pop bottles filled with a clear liquid and other bottles covered with mud made Hanson's Raiders suspicious. Securing a shovel they probed the dirt floor. The metal shovel made a distinctive sound as it struck glass only a few inches from the surface. The investigators carefully cleaned away the dirt from a gallon jug of moonshine. Micavich and his cousin, Mrs. Blascavitch, were both arrested. (16)

Tavern owners realized that if the prohibition agents couldn't confiscate any evidence, the owner could not be charged. So they constructed all sorts of devices and methods to dispose of any evidence. Smith and Holland uncovered one novel device when they entered John Kenny's saloon, which was located in an alley north of Main Street running between LaSalle and Clinton Streets in Ottawa. Kenny had rigged a rod to push all of the incriminating evidence off the bar with a single kick from the bartender. Trying to prevent the destruction of evidence, Smith grabbed the bartender's hands, but much to the officer's surprise, the bartender managed to kick the pusher bar into action. All of the bottles were swept into a hole in the floor at the end of the bar. One by one, each bottle fell to the basement and was smashed so thoroughly that there was no way to save the "evidence." Kenny could not be arrested. (17)

A more successful raid was conducted on April 18 at the saloon operated by Leonard DeGroot. Wine and whiskey in the amount of 450 gallons was uncovered in the establishment located at 1701-1705 Water Street in Peru. (18)

It took some time, but one by one, the LaSalle circuit court closed the raided bars. On April 10, the bars at 233 First St., 1157 First St., 1235 Fifth St., 1058 Eighth St., LaSalle and 2301 Main St., Peru were ordered to be closed. Additional court orders were pending to close the "101" Ranch in Marseilles, the "Hit and Run" Saloon in Ottawa, Erickson's Saloon in Ottawa and Wantland's saloon in Sheridan. (19) In addition to the closings, the court handed out numerous fines. On April 20 alone, the aggregate of fines was $1,200. (20)

In rare instances, the court imposed a jail sentence. Such was the case against Carl Gugis of West Wenona who was arrested following a domestic disturbance with his wife. The intoxicated condition of the man prompted Hanson to conduct a raid, which netted a still and some moonshine. Since Mr. Gugis was charged with manufacturing and possession of a still, Judge Reck sentenced the man to six months in the county jail. Mrs. Gugis, who was severely beaten by her husband in the altercation, admitted to assisting her husband in bootlegging. At the hearing, Judge Reck commented, "I believe you have been punished enough." The charges against her were dropped. (21)

While most of the offenders offered minimal resistance to a search, there were few cases in which the owner of a saloon was more cooperative than John Gorgorich of LaSalle. The entire raid was incidental to an investigation at the Retzel grocery store at 135 First Street. While Smith and Holland searched and later found a gallon of wine, Gorgorich came into buy some cigars. Smith approached him and asked his name. Then Smith said, "You're just the fellow I'm looking for. You've got booze at your house haven't you? And you've got a still? Come on over and show me where it is." Gorgorich just laughed and said, "All right." They went into Gorgorich's basement where the man had a still, nine barrels of mash, a ten-gallon cask with five gallons of moonshine. "Any more?" Smith inquired. "You bet." Gorgorich replied. Returning upstairs to the bedroom Smith was shown 5-6 gallons of moonshine. The search warrant was read to Gorgorich as a technical matter before he was escorted to the Ottawa courthouse. Ironically, Frank Retzel, the owner of the grocery store being investigated, was not arrested in spite of the discovery of the gallon of wine. (22)

The little coal mining village of Cedar Point was the scene of a major raid on April 27, 1925. The large raiding party of 20 officers left Ottawa in ten cars and arrived around noon. Russell Hanson led the convoy personally. Undercover agents had already made several "buys" in order to justify the issuance of search warrants. Totally surprised by the prohibition agents, there was no time to hide the evidence. Ten saloons and two homes were searched. Vincent Curry, one of the bar owners tried to bribe the agents offering Smith $70 and saying "Now just forget about it." The incorruptible Smith gave his partner Harold Butters, the Assistant State's Attorney, the money and arrested Curry for attempted bribery. Another one of those arrested was Quinto Ossola, a saloon operator and police officer. Entering his home, the investigators found a 20-gallon crock cooking on the stove. Evidence seized at the Julius Farnetti saloon included home brew, moonshine, and wine. Similar products were found in the taverns run by Recordo Seghi, Alfred Turki, Vincent Biolchini, and the homes of George Mursatti, Tom Champley, and Joe Buffo. The later residence had served as a saloon at one time. Here they found two stills and a thousand bottles buried in the dirt. Mrs. Buffo said that the stills and bottles were not owned by her husband but rather belonged to a border who had left them there a year before. A total of eight men were arrested, and four stills and a truckload of liquor were hauled back to Ottawa. This was the largest bust Hanson's Raiders had made since the State's Attorney took office. (23)

The following day, Smith and Holland arrested Joe Tomasello at his hot dog restaurant in LaSalle. The two agents, who were enjoying their lunch at the restaurant on North Main St., became suspicious of certain carry out "orders." Strange things like "shoelaces" were asked for but not found on any menu. Tomasello told customers with these unusual requests that he just ran out of the requested item. One man, who brought in an empty pop bottle and asked for a refill, was taken aback when the owner said, "You know I don't do anything like that." Smith and Holland finished their meal and returned a short time later with a search warrant. They found a half-pint of moonshine behind the lunch counter and many empty bottles smelling of liquor.

Later in the day, the investigators stopped at the home of Charles Rizzo. But the man was not home. He had been arrested by Livingston County authorities for carrying 30 gallons of moonshine in his car and was incarcerated in the Pontiac jail. The LaSalle authorities searched the Rizzo house and found four 50-gallon barrels of wine, which were taken to the Streator police station. (24)

While enforcement of the Volstead Act was the motivating force behind the majority of the raids in the Illinois Valley, there were occasions when gambling equipment rather than illicit liquor was the object of search warrants. Hanson learned that a variety of illegal gaming material could be found at the Waszkowiak saloon at 1059 Ninth St. in LaSalle. Smith and Holland again took charge of the raid. As soon as the men walked in, Waszkowiak dumped the contents from several glasses. Although no other liquor or beer was uncovered, there was a large number of gambling devices in evidence. This included punch boards, baseball pools and Kentucky Derby tickets. This was the first time the state's attorney's office tried to clamp down on gambling in the county. (25) Similar raids were made in LaSalle at the California Fruit Store at 606 First St. and three Streator establishments. No arrests had been made for punchboards or pool gambling in previous raids so those arrested were surprised by this development. The penalties could be very severe; heavy fines and up to a year in jail could be handed out by the court.

On May 8, a series of raids were conducted in Marseilles. Smith, Holland, and six other officers conducted simultaneous operations. Ferdinand Bollatta, Mike O'Brien, Anton Pomatto, and Henry Schultz operated the saloons being searched. At the Bollatta saloon and residence they seized 55 gallons of wine. The other locations were also sources of either moonshine or wine. (26)

During the summer of 1925, Smith led numerous raids. East Wenona, which had separated itself from "West Wenona" when prohibition went into effect, had one particular bar that was uniquely located in both LaSalle and Marshall Counties. The front porch was located in LaSalle County. Before searching the place, it was necessary to determine which county had jurisdiction. The deciding factor was to see who taxed the property. Since it was on the LaSalle County tax roles, Hanson's office had jurisdiction. Holland and Carl Robinson from Dimmick entered J.R. Kane's business in mid-July and conducted a search. They turned up some gin behind the bar and a pint of bonded whiskey under one of the tables. In a shed behind the building, they found an additional 25 pints of moonshine and five gallon cans of "moon" that later tested at 188 proof! There were also bottles of coloring and flavoring. On July 14, Kane was in the South Ottawa court for his hearing. (27)

Hanson followed with a raid at 1401 First Street, LaSalle, a bar operated by Joe Pienta and another search on July 21 at Joe Albert's saloon (117 N. Vermillion) in Streator. On July 30, four more saloons were hit in LaSalle. These included those operated by Joe Cigolle (1026 First), Joe Goresek (1101 Third), Fabian Ciganovich (1101 Fifth) and Anton Mahnich (1153 First). So many gallons of moonshine and wine were confiscated that it was necessary to destroy most of it on the spot. But always a small sample was taken from each container and marked for evidence. (28)

Another Smith raid on two Streator bars made front-page news on August. 3. Andrew Guitilla offered investigators a hundred dollars to overlook the home brew that they found in his soft drink parlor. The men promptly arrested the owner for bribery and selling liquor. The total bond was set at $3000 because of the attempted bribery. The same day, Smith and Holland also searched the establishment operated by Albert Shortell. The man had a miniature brewing operation. Some 3,000 bottles of brew had been produced. To wind things up for the day, Hanson's men took a short trip to Rutland where they arrested William Brunner, who had in his possession a quantity of home brew. (29)

In spite of the numerous arrests made by Hanson's Raiders, the locations of alcohol production in the Illinois Valley seemed limitless. No sooner had one still been shut down than one or more new ones were put into operation. In fact, when the liquor investigator Holland made a evening visit to the home of Jacob Sczepaniak at 403 E. Ninth in Peru, he found two stills in full production and another one ready to be set up.

The investigation at Sczepaniak's was a typical sting operation. In order to gain evidence, Holland offered to buy a pint of moonshine. After the deal was completed, Holland announced his real intentions. During the interrogation, the bootlegger admitted that he had been in business for six months making $4 on every gallon of moonshine he produced. In the basement, the lone agent found 40 gallons ready for the demanding clientele. Near the stills were 14 barrels of mash ready for the boilers. Sczepaniak even went into detail explaining how he used the large bags of rye grain and sugar to make the brew. The evidence being too bulky to transport, was simply destroyed. The Peru man was taken to the state's attorney in Ottawa where he admitted his guilt. At the bail hearing, he told the judge that he was "done with the game." (30)

The cat and mouse game and frequent raids encouraged the bootleggers to become innovative in their attempts to destroy evidence. Pasqualli Vinnochio of Ladd thought he had come up with a foolproof system. Two Bureau County officers, Deputies Len Spaulding and Jack Applen, finally exposed it. Armed with a search warrant, they broke in. Initially, the men could not find any contraband in the Ladd bar. However, they did find a long board attached to the floor running at the base of the bar. The owner had it set up so that if the place was raided, he could easily tip the jug of liquor he had near the center of the bar. The jug would then roll into a hole in the floor and be shattered on a pile of rocks in the basement. Wanting to catch Vinnochio in the act, they placed a serving tray under the rocks and departed the saloon. They returned at 7:30 p.m. and were greeted by the cordial bartender who leaned against the bar triggering the device. Within seconds, there was the sound of shattering crockery. The three men went down to the basement where Vinnochio was shocked over the sight. The serving tray under the rocks and broken crockery was filled with liquor. There was a bit of mutual admiration exchanged at the hearing the following day. Spaulding commented on the "pretty slick rigging" the Italian had constructed. To which Vinnochio replied, "Yes, but that was a slicker one you had. I guess I got to hand it to you. You're just a little bit smarter than me." (31)

Meanwhile over in LaSalle County, more arrests were made in Marseilles and Seneca. Two men were found to be selling liquor. At Tomasello's coffee shop at 523 S. Illinois in Streator, the owner and a 14-year old bartender were arrested in a third bust. This location had been raided five times already, and in every case, liquor was confiscated. (32)

In mid-August, a minor skirmish in the war on gambling was fought at the Kaskaskia Hotel (below) in LaSalle. The cigar counter

salesperson in the hotel was selling chances on a punch board that was hidden in one of the cigar boxes. Holland and Constable Carl Robinson from Dimmick township thought it was unusual that customers were paying money but never walking away with any cigars. The hotel manager, Eric Korb, was arrested for operating a gambling house.

The two men also went over to Oglesby and caught Mrs. Laura Bichini serving liquor in the bar at 445 Walnut Street. After she poured some wine and moonshine for the investigators, they announced that they were the law and she was under arrest. (33)

From time to time, the business of law enforcement during the 1920's became dangerous. Officers tended to be complacent about making arrests. However, Spring Valley officers became more wary after an incident on August 13. The case began when Mr. Barney Sack noticed a Cadillac with three young men sitting inside parked on the road between the Dalzell Road and Delaney's hill. He contacted the Spring Valley Police Chief Anton Ponsetti, who called in Patrolman Raldo Ranieri to assist him in the investigation. When they came upon the scene, the chief ordered the young men, all of whom were about age 21 and thought to be Sicilians, to follow him south back to Spring Valley. Instead the men took off to the north.

During the attempted getaway, the men fired several times at the pursuing officers. One bullet almost grazed Ponsetti's head and three more rounds hit the police car. While speeding down the road, the fleeing men smashed into a lumber wagon being driven by Sam Sack. Their Cadillac was disabled so they pointed their guns at Sam and forced him to take the wheel of a Ford that was parked nearby. Sack tried desperately to start the car, but it stalled. Just then, the Spring Valley police came upon the accident. The trio then fled into the nearby cornfields with the police and several farmers in close pursuit. One of the fleeing suspects suddenly turned and fired three shots at the officers but missed; their ammunition was exhausted. After running for several minutes through the cornstalks, the fleeing men were cornered in the field and arrested.

1925 Cadillac

Once in custody, the Spring Valley authorities tried to determine why the three Italians, who identified themselves as Sam Mondeli, Joe Ramono, and Jim Pinto, were just parked out in the country. According to the suspects, they had come down from Chicago at 1 a.m. to guard a bootlegger's Dodge truck. While they parked outside the city, the load of whiskey was driven to another location while they stayed on the country road. They were supposed to escort the truck back to Chicago when it returned, but they would not say where the truck was supposed to take its cargo. But the Dodge truck never returned and no trace of it was found in the Valley. In spite of their insistence that they were from Chicago, the police chief felt that they were really associated with the rum-running coming out of the St. Louis area. (34)

At their hearing in Spring Valley, it was revealed that the Cadillac was stolen from a St. Louis address. Judge Simpson ordered that they be sent to the Princeton jail. It was not long before "friends" from Chicago traveled to the county seat to post the $25,000 bail. Eventually they were freed after paying a $250 fine. (35)

One of the biggest raids of the year occurred on August 21, 1925. Hanson together with his lieutenants, Smith and Holland, and 21 other officers blanketed LaSalle and Peru in a huge dragnet. Simultaneously at 9:30 p.m., teams of officers struck at nine homes, all but one of which were on Second Street in LaSalle. The LaSalle *Daily Post* reported how Hanson attempted to "Mop Up" the West End of LaSalle and shut down the wholesale liquor business. The paper listed the names and address of the bootleggers. Those arrested included Joe Ajster (20 Second St.), who had a still and hundreds of gallons of mash. At the Yerkes residence (42 Second St.) there were three stills, one of which had 20 gallons of brew cooking, more than a barrel of wine and six barrels of rye mash. Lefa Juresec was found with three stills and 20 gallons of moonshine. Pete Bodra (58 Second St.) had 250 gallons of mash waiting for use in his two stills. There were also 15 gallons of moonshine, bottling equipment and 20 barrels. Joe Gende (70 Second St.) had eight cases of home brew from his two stills. There were also 110 gallons of wine ready for distribution. Andrew Borisek (82 Second St.) had 700 bottles of wine ready in cases. Matt Starovasenik (110 Second St.) was arrested for having seven cases of home brew and a bottle of moonshine. At 136 Chartres, Tony Meznaric was picked up. In his house the investigators found a still, over six gallons of moonshine and a couple of cases of home brew. And Joe Puntar (318 LaSalle St., Peru) was also arrested after a search discovered five cases of home brew and a gallon of moonshine. Hanson's Raiders had netted a total of 13 stills and hundred of gallons of wine, home brew, and moonshine. (36)

Hanson's men had put a dent in the local operations. At the end of the month, Judge Reck ordered the destruction of property seized in 17 other raids during the month. Raids had not only been conducted in LaSalle-Peru and Ottawa but also in Cedar Point, Oglesby, Sheridan, Marseilles, and Mendota. The illicit liquor consisted of mostly whiskey and wine. Beer was found only in one of the locations, and even then, the officers only found six bottles. (37) Perhaps the reason for this was that near beer was still being produced locally. It also took huge vats to make profitable amounts of beer on a commercial basis. The closure of the local breweries in Peru and Ottawa stopped most production. To make matters worse for those who drank near beer, a fire destroyed the Star Union brewery on August 27, 1925.

Star Union workers noticed a small fire in the brewery cupola above the ice room about 9:30 a.m. Firemen from Peru and LaSalle were quickly on the scene and crowds of onlookers soon gathered. The greatest fear was that an explosion would rupture the ammonia tanks. Walls began to collapse endangering the firemen and workers who assisted them. As one area of the fire was brought under control, smoke began to pour from the central tower, windows, and roof. Timbers supporting the roof collapsed sending debris to the top floor.

While the cause of the fire could not be determined immediately, fire and plant officials speculated that it started from spontaneous combustion in the cupola above the ice room. The fire spread quickly and was out of control before Peru and LaSalle fire departments arrived. Almost everyone escaped unharmed. However, Nis Ellberg of the Peru Fire Department was standing near a small ammonia pipe which burst pouring the liquid and fumes over him. He passed out but was soon revived when he was taken outside to fresh air.

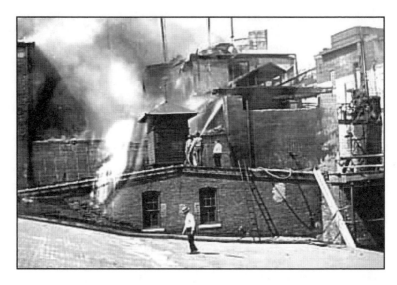

The fire was believed to have stared in the ammonia room of the ice manufacturing department. The 1925 fire at the Star Union brewery was under control within two hours. Peru Library collection.

The LaSalle fire department left the scene at 12:15 p.m. The Peru firemen stayed on the scene continuing to flood the smoldering embers.
Peru Library collection

Inspecting the remains of the brewery, Rudolph Bender, plant superintendent, described it as a "total ruin." He added, "If it were to be rebuilt today, it would cost many times the original building amount." Another company official said that at least a portion of the damaged building was covered by insurance. Besides the manufacturing equipment, a boxcar of sugar located next to the building, and 365 bags of sugar inside the brewery were destroyed. Although the ice-making machine was damaged, it was not beyond repair. Fortunately, the plant was constructed with concrete firewalls that stopped the spread of the conflagration. (38)

The uncertainty of reconstruction was lifted the following day when company officials held a news conference to announce their decision on the future of the plant. The ice operation was very important to local businesses. In spite of the gutted appearance of the structure, Star Union was back in ice production, if not beer production, the afternoon of the fire. (39)

The excitement of the fire lasted for a short time and was quickly replaced by stories of continued raids led by M.R. Smith. The operations were not as earth shaking as the Second Street raids were only a week before. The local paper referred to the raiders as the "sponge squad." The raid on the Yednach farm only turned up a couple of pints. Several gallons of wine and moonshine were taken from the Tony Rigazio saloon in Oglesby. In the little village of Kangley near Streator the raiders only found a few wineglasses and some home brew at Mike Venegoni's bar. Smith was a little more successful at the Sabino saloon in Streator where he found over a gallon of moonshine, five gallons of wine and five cases of home brew. (40)

Smith's efforts in September resulted in the arrest of Joe Sherman (314 Eighth, Peru) for having a still, 11 gallons of moonshine and four barrels of mash. Another still and 20 gallons of moonshine were found in the home of Tony Tomsha who lived at 147 Tenth St., LaSalle. (41)

A few days later, Smith was pounding on the door of Frank Bregar (1408 N. Creve Couer, LaSalle), who was a local tinsmith. Noting the pile of copper scraps when the Bregar house was searched, Smith came to the conclusion that the man was manufacturing stills for sale. Not only did Smith find a brand new standard size copper still, he also unearthed a miniature still, a model measuring 6" x 3". The Volstead Act said nothing about making copper boilers, but the six barrels of moonshine in the Bregar basement were definitely illegal.

Then Smith went to the home of Anton Katushek (35 Sixth Street, LaSalle) where the suspect had hidden seven gallons of "moon" and half a dozen cases of home brew. There were also about 20 empty mash barrels. Katushek said he was out of the business and only purchased the barrels for kindling. The man said, "You might as well take all I've got while you're here. Look in the garage and you'll find some more." Smith took the man at his word and began to search for more contraband. From the basement, Smith proceeded to the chicken house, which had a trap door. Descending into the concrete basement, he found seven 50-gallon barrels of moonshine- 350 gallons! Katushek gave his permission to destroy the barrels. Smith added some poison to the liquid just in case anyone had the bright idea of trying to salvage moonshine from the flooded basement.

Another raid was carried out in Leonore at the Katanich saloon. The brew they found on the premises registered 3.5% alcohol.

Hanson and Officer Holland picked up a traveling salesman from Chicago outside of the Modesti soft drink parlor in Naplate. The man appeared suspicious and was carrying a parcel wrapped in newspapers. The man walked toward his Buick touring car and then disappeared. When Holland approached the car, a large, snarling German shepherd in the car greeted him. The man, later identified as W.N. Wing, reappeared; grabbed the package; and threw it to the ground shattering the glass container and splashing the contents on the pavement. The distinctive odor of moonshine encouraged Holland to sponge up enough contents to fill half a pop bottle. Later it was analyzed and found to be 9.6% alcohol. Wing was bound over for a hearing by the grand jury. (42)

Looking back over the last few months, there were so many raids that Smith was involved with, any number of people might have wanted him dead or at least intimidated sufficiently to leave the area. While most saloonkeepers tended to take the periodic raids in stride and accepted the fines as just another cost of doing business, undoubtedly there was at least some resentment to the routine harassment they experienced. However, the unflagging efforts of M.R. Smith, Hanson's chief liquor investigator, were producing more than resentment. The bombing of Smith's residence in Streator in March in no way deterred the man from enforcing the law.

On May 24, he was in harm's way again. While driving alone in his Ford town car from Ottawa to his home in Streator in the early evening, he began to pass a Chevy touring car near the road leading to Leonore. Immediately he identified the driver as Joe Latino, who was wanted by the law. Smith had been searching in vain for the man for the last two months trying to serve a warrant on the Italian. He shouted for Latino to pull over. Instead, Latino responded by firing three shots from his automatic. The first round narrowly missed the officer's head. A second round hit the door of the Ford. Finally, the third round ripped through Smith's leg just above the knee. Wracked with pain, Smith lost control of his car crashing into a ditch so badly that one of the wheels was ripped from the axle. In spite of the intense pain and profuse bleeding, Smith pulled his revolver as he leapt from the smashed Ford and fired off six rounds at the fleeing attacker. Fortunately, a Streator druggist, came upon the scene and transported the bleeding law officer to St. Mary's Hospital in Streator. Smith was in the operating room for 55 minutes while the surgeon closed the severed artery.

Other law enforcement officials were immediately notified of the shooting. Hanson, Smith's immediate supervisor, raced to the Streator hospital from Chicago. An all-points bulletin was issued for the assailant. Latino had moved from Streator to Ottawa so the Ottawa police completely surrounded the house at 1514 N. LaSalle in Ottawa and all the streets were blocked off. But no one entered or left the residence. Mrs. Latino, who had also been in the car with their children, was brought in for questioning. She claimed that Smith fired first. She said that her husband drove further down the road and then got out of the car and told her to go home. Mrs. Latino told the police that she had been at the Streator residence at 203 W. Broadway since Saturday night.

Chief Hopkins revealed on May 26 that Latino's car was discovered in Streator. It had one bullet hole located in the back. The angle of the entry confirmed Smith's story. He had fired from the ground as the vehicle was speeding away. Later a Streator *Free-Press* reporter found a .25 caliber bullet on the floor of the Chevy behind the driver's seat. (43)

From his hospital bed, Smith was able to give a description of the shooter. Latino who was in his thirties, weighed about 200 lbs., stood 5'5," and had bushy hair. The wounded officer told the press Latino had been peddling moonshine throughout the county and probably had a load in his car.

Before the police arrived to stakeout the house in Ottawa, an eyewitness said they saw a man entering the Latino house and leaving with three suitcases. Later, investigators determined that it was not Joe but rather his brother Nick Latino who had been visiting from Chicago.

What motivated Latino to take such deadly action? Hanson knew that a raid was being planned on the Joe Gapinski saloon in LaSalle. It was also known that Latino and Gapinski were good friends. So maybe that was the connection or perhaps it was a deep-seated hatred for Smith's efforts to dry up the county.

The shooting of Smith was not going to stop Hanson. The action at Gapinski's was carried out not only to confiscate illegal liquor, but perhaps Hanson thought he might also apprehend Latino. The 7 a.m. search netted a large quantity of wine and several bottles of champagne which was locked in a safe, but Latino was not there. He had been arrested and found guilty several times for liquor violations and was still on the run. (44)

In spite of Smith's close encounter with death, he diligently continued his work for Hanson. But on September 13 there was another attempt on his life. Once again, a bomb rocked his Streator residence. This was similar to the device used in March but much more powerful-probably dynamite. The blast hole under the house was 2½' deep. The explosion broke windows in the Smith home, in neighboring houses, and three large windows at the Grant public school. Authorities theorized that it was a drive-by bombing by assailants driving down Jefferson Street.

Fortunately, Smith and his wife and children and a male guest were uninjured. The bomb went off only ten feet from Smith's bedroom. Had the dynamite been positioned under the front part of the house close to the bedrooms instead of under the closet, everyone would have died.. Local residents joined Smith in a search for suspicious characters but none was found. His son, Robert, age 9, was eager to help his father. Little sister Catherine, age 5, told the press, "Every night I pray for my daddy and ask God not to let the bad men hurt him or us."

Talking to reporters, Smith recounted his experience. "I was awakened by the deafening crash, and found myself standing between the bed and the dresser. Dressing hurriedly, I rushed through the house. My wife and children were crying hysterically. It was difficult to see, so dense was the smoke. I knew well enough just what had happened, and I could see lights from the street through the gaping hole torn in the northeast wall of the house. Outside the house, about a block away I saw a shadow and then a form of a person fleeing. Shouting for it to halt, and not being obeyed, I fired. My shot did not strike the fleeing figure."

It was later learned that the figure was a 17-year old Streator High School student, George Duder, who was walking home. Duder explained to the police, "I was walking home and when I neared the Grant school I was knocked off my feet by the force of the explosion. Stumped, I did not know at first where it was or anything, by recollecting my sense, I fled to reach my home a short distance away. I heard the shot but was not touched by the bullet." (45)

While the first bomb only caused minor damage, this incident was estimated to cost $2,000 in damages to the house and another $1,000 to the contents. The entire back porch of the house was demolished. Wooden planks were found scattered in the yard and high in the tree branches. The house itself was lifted off of the foundation. Plumbing was ripped from the walls. Crockery and 300 quarts of canned fruit were scattered on the floor. (46)

M.R. Smith's bombed home in Streator at 302 W. LaRue. Original photo by Foldenauer Studio, Streator. Reprinted from LaSalle *Daily Post-Tribune* Sept. 15, 1925.

At the same time as efforts were being made to solve the attempt on Smith's life, the LaSalle County Board of Supervisors met in a special session. At that time, they planned to raise the reward for the unknown bomber and for Joe Latino. Also under consideration was the hiring of full time guards for the homes of Smith, Hanson and other liquor investigators.

Hanson later emphasized the need for secrecy by not divulging the names of any of the special investigators he hired. The state's attorney told the press, "If the names of my special investigators became generally known, it would permit the lawless element to go after them and intimidate them. These men are engaged in hazardous work-as the attempts made to kill Smith indicate-and I intend to give them all the protection possible. The best work can be done when secrecy is maintained." (47)

Smith continued to lead raids such as those in Ottawa at John Kelly's tavern and the Carl Savage saloon in Streator. In Marseilles, at the Louis Fanoglio ice cream parlor, they found a barrel of wine. Two hundred barrels of home brew came from the home of "Chippy" Costello, and a search of the August Bolatto home resulted in the seizure of 72 bottles of beer and a quantity of moonshine.

The sheriff was also busy with a raid in Peru on Sept. 30. Nick Burman thought he had put one over on Welter and his deputies by dumping all the alcohol in his Pulaski Street saloon. But Burman's grinning composure turned sour as the investigators took their search to a pile of corncobs behind his house next door. In a few minutes, the police exposed a barrel buried in the ground. A piece of hose dipped into the barrel so that its alcohol contents could be siphoned out as needed.

Another smiling tavern owner, Tom Johnson, who ran a business on North Bloomington in Streator, thought he too had fooled the sheriff. Johnson said the officers could do all the searching they wanted. Indeed, there was no booze to be found anywhere. But then one of the investigators spotted a large heap of coal ashes that looked like they had been disturbed recently. Kicking through the heap, one man struck a large crate. Inside they found 500 beer bottles and seven quarts of moonshine. Johnson had a date with the judge the same day. (48)

The next day, October 2, Smith found a barrel of wine at Frank Retzel's grocery store and 30 gallons of beer at the home of Joe Gorisik (237 Second St., LaSalle). Frank Zank was another LaSallean breaking the law. He was caught with 36 cases of home brew and another 20 gallons of alcohol cooking in his still. Joe Potekar was ready to make some moonshine before Smith confiscated a barrel of corn mash at his residence at 32 Second St., LaSalle. The fifth suspect arrested that day was Joe Baboroni, who had five gallons of moonshine. (49)

After the massive raid in Cedar Point, one would have thought the bootleggers would have been out of business in the small mining town. Unfortunately all law officers were not beyond reproach. One of those arrested by Hanson's men was the local constable, Quinto Ossola. The man had his own soft drink parlor and was caught with seven cases of brew. Not wanting to be charged with the sale of liquor, he protested to Hanson's men that all 168 pints were for his personal consumption. This was Ossola's second offense so he faced the loss of his job as well as a fine or imprisonment. Another second offender was Recordo Seghi who had in his home 50 gallons of wine and 16 cases of home brew. However, nothing was found in the Seghi saloon. The raid also produced seven stills. James Serina had two of the units, one of which was in use at the time of the raid. It was a rather large operation - 95 gallons of moonshine produced and 15 50-gallon barrels of rye mash. Another 22 barrels of mash were in another Cedar Point location also said to be owned by Serina. The old James Markus store had been converted into a distillery where investigators found 16 barrels of mash and 30 gallons of moonshine. George Mussatto was running two stills at the time of the raid at Cedar and Fifth Streets. Mussatto had brewed little more than a gallon of moonshine. There were 15 barrels of mash ready for use. The stills, pressure tanks, coils and stoves were hauled away as evidence. (50)

In another first in LaSalle County, Constable Holland raided a tent saloon in West Ottawa on October 4. As the officer approached the tent, he heard the clanking of glass bottles. Upon entering, he found a customer purchasing a quart of moonshine. The proprietor, Paul Etinne, and the customer were taken to the Ottawa jail.

In other raids of the day, Welter's men found liquor in two more Ottawa locations, a home at 1511 W. Main and the Lakin saloon at 800 Jackson. The proprietors of the Wilkerson saloon at 111 Main, Streator and the Vincent Urbino saloon at Third and Chartres in LaSalle were also taken into custody. (51)

Although it wasn't said, it appeared that the stress on Smith and his family probably took its toll. On Oct. 7, Smith announced his decision to resign from Hanson's Raiders. Neither the state's attorney nor his chief liquor investigator would elaborate on the resignation other than to say there was a disagreement. Smith told reporters, "There will be no break-up in the friendship between myself and State's Attorney Hanson." Virgil Holland of Utica was slated to take over the raids. (52)

Bureau County officers were just as determined as those in LaSalle County to keep the pressure on the bootleggers. The court was getting tougher too. Ambrona Mozzini was picked up in his home in Cherry for possession of intoxicating liquor - specifically wine and moonshine. When the man went to court, Judge Prichard fined him $600 and sent him to jail for another 60 days. Why was Prichard so tough? After all, Mozzini even offered to pay a $1000 fine rather than go to jail. But Prichard was fed up with Mozzini's constant violations of the law. He had just gotten out of jail after serving 60 days for the same offense. Apparently he had not learned his lesson. The defendant tried to explain that he had a wife and four kids and could not support his family on miner's wages. Prichard didn't back down and ordered the jailer to take him away.

Prichard was ready to throw the book at another bootlegger, Mike Mapaki, a Spring Valley resident. It was the man's third offense. So Prichard handed him a $700 fine. Since the state's attorney couldn't prove the Mapaki had sold any of the booze, there was no legal way that Prichard could sentence the man to jail even though that's what the judge thought he deserved. (53)

The big breweries were gone in LaSalle County, and the men longed for their favorite ale so there was a definite demand for real beer. Authorities had known for some time that beer was coming into the area in large quantities, but until now they could not find the source. To fill that "need," three men, including a former brewmaster from one of the

Peru breweries, set up shop on a farm owned by Gus Pinter and located a mile north of Ladd. They found an old slaughterhouse where chickens had been processed. There were still the old cattle pens and a few chickens and hogs on the property to make it appear authentic. The shabby appearance camouflaged an operation with the most modern equipment available. The bootleggers had attempted to conceal their operation by only producing the alcohol at night.

On Sept. 14, federal agents descended on the operation. Thousands of locals from Ladd and Cherry, many of whom had suspected the existence of an illegal still, milled about watching the agents at work. With eight wooden vats to destroy, five additional federal agents were brought in from the LaSalle office to speed the destruction of the equipment. (54)

The Ottawa *Daily Times* reported that the raid led to the arrest of John Stauch, Charles Link, and Rudolph Bender (brewmaster). Confiscated in the raid were 200 barrels of beer. A large truckload was ready to be shipped. The brewers were freed on $3000 bonds. Pinter, who rented out the farm, claimed no knowledge of the distilling operation. (55)

Bootleggers were often told simply to appear the next day before the court for sentencing instead of being hauled off to jail after a raid. One individual who had become well known by county police was Frank Retzel. His grocery store was raided on Oct. 21, and he obligingly showed up in Ottawa the next day. However, he knew the routine so well he simply by passed the courtroom and reported to the jailer. He knocked at the door and stated, "Here I am. I am ready to start my term." The astonished jailer asked Retzel if he had seen the judge. The unabashed Retzel retorted, "No I didn't see no judge. Hanson's men raided my place yesterday and so I supposed I had to go to jail. Open that door so I can get it over with and go back to my store!" The jailer responded by saying he couldn't let him in until the judge sentenced him, and he should go see the State's Attorney. After visiting Hanson's office, the 50-year old grocer was sent to the courthouse where he admitted his guilt of alcohol possession before Judge Reck. But he refused to admit that he sold any liquor, and the raiders had not caught him actually selling any. He also took exception in the charge that he was operating a "soft drink parlor." He insisted he was a grocer. Commenting on the state of affairs in the community, Retzel pointed out that in almost all of the stores in LaSalle when you pay your bills, "They ask you to have a little something." After hearing the man's arguments and his plea for leniency for the sake of his wife and young daughter, Reck sentenced the bootlegger to 15 days in the Ottawa jail and fine of $100. Upon hearing the judge's decision, he expressed his thanks and reported to the jailer. (56)

By the end of October 1925, there was a huge amount of evidence being stored in the Ottawa jail. Even the samples of liquor that were confiscated were taking up much space in the facility. Finally on Oct. 30, Judge Reck ordered that all of the evidence that was used in previously concluded criminal hearings be destroyed. Hanson took charge of the operation. Of the 12 stills, four were copper wash boilers. Hanson's men used blowtorches to cut off the tops so that the bottom portion could be donated to the Salvation Army for distribution to needy Ottawa families. Hundreds of gallons of wine, whiskey, moonshine and various other alcoholic concoctions were dumped into the sewers. (57)

No doubt one of the oldest Valley residents to be arrested for operating a still was Joe Kulpa, age 85. The senior citizen who lived on Ninth Street in Peru was collecting welfare payments of $6 a month from LaSalle County. At his hearing, Sheriff Welter recommended that the man be required to pay a fine for operating the still. Judge Reck asked Kulpa if he could pay the $130 for the fine and court costs. Kulpa replied, "Yep, I guess so." Pulling a large roll of singles from his pocket the defendant counted out the required amount and paid the clerk. Kulpa offered no protest. He still had about $10 left to support himself and his 86 year old wife. (58)

State's Attorney Hanson was finally having his way. Former bars, stores, and restaurants that sold liquor or served as manufacturing sites were being closed. In LaSalle County, 21 buildings were padlocked for six months. Another 19 homes had restraining orders placed on them. Additional violations of the anti-liquor laws could result in the additional charge of contempt of court and a second charge that would likely result in a prison sentence. Every major city and village in the county was affected by the writs issued by Judge Edgar Eldredge on Nov. 5, 1925. (59)

Closing a large number of saloons did not dissuade LaSalle bootleggers sufficiently. The LaSalle sheriff confiscated over 1000 gallons of mash and two stills in only two LaSalle raids. One was at Mike Mura's home at 436 Sixth St.. The largest quantity of mash, some 700 gallons, was found at the home of Tony DiGianni 428 Sixth St. A total of 35 gallons of moonshine was also seized.

The state's attorney's men led by the new chief investigator, Virgil Holland, worked from 8 p.m. until midnight as they searched Oglesby saloons and private residences. The first stops were at the Joseph Ferrari saloon at 139 Walnut and the John Ingagnoli bar down the block at 253 Walnut. At both locations, a quantity of wine was found. Private homes included those of Jim Skerzton (258 E. Florence), Jake Alaszus (317 E. First), Joe Langlis (243 E. Second) Frank Marzis (131 N. Spring Ave.) and Stan Karkiess (318 E. Florence). In each search a still, large quantities of mash, and dozens of gallons of moonshine and were found. Each of the owners was ordered to report to the Ottawa court for a hearing the following day. (60)

Apparently news of the raids traveled slowly in Oglesby, or saloon operators thought that additional raids would not be coming again very soon. Nothing could be further from the truth. There were so many enforcement officers that it was difficult to recognize the lawmen. Only a few days later on Nov. 20, Officer Stan Farrell from Marseilles stopped by the drinking establishment of Hugo Corsini. Farrell asked if the bartender had any hooch. According to reports, Corsini said "No, but I have some mighty fine wine." After Farrell bought a couple of drinks, Holland and another officer walked in to serve a search warrant. It wasn't too hard to find the two quarts of wine that Corsini served patrons. (62)

The LaSalle state's attorney took a hand in closing down saloons. With court order in hand, he personally began the process of padlocking buildings. The first of these was in the little town of Ransom, located about ten miles east of Streator. William Brunner, the owner of the soft drink parlor was selling again in spite of the injunction posted on his front door. When undercover investigators came into his place, they asked him about the paper on the door. His reply was, That's an injunction, but you notice I'm still doing business." The owner didn't sell the officers anything more than cigars and pop when they asked for moonshine. However, even that was illegal under the terms of the writ. There was to be no business of any kind allowed. Hanson came in and told Brunner to take any perishable merchandise. With that, Brunner took his stock of soda, tobacco, and turned off the lights. Hanson attached a hasp and padlock to the front door. Now Brunner's place was going to definitely be closed for six months. (62)

Looking back on 1925, it appeared to be a year filled with frustrations, excitement, and danger from the perspective of law enforcement authorities. The fire at the Star Union plant in August and the increasing numbers of raids coupled with the threats and bombings aimed at agent Smith made it one of the most unforgettable times in the annals of prohibition enforcement thus far in the Illinois Valley. But the incidents faded quickly as even more exciting days lay ahead .

Chapter 10
1926
The People Voice Opinions

The Ransom bar owner wasn't the only one ignoring the court injunctions. On Jan. 7, Holland and Cooper raided Valentine Cigolle's saloon located on First Street. Like many of the soft drink parlors in LaSalle, the family lived in the room behind the barroom. The court had ordered the front door be padlocked and restrained Cigolle from using any part of the building for the manufacture, sale, or storage of alcohol. When the inspectors searched the place they found 500 gallons of wine in the basement. So now Cigolle faced an additional charge.(1) The officer's next stop was on Ninth Street in LaSalle.

Rare interior view of the LaSalle tavern at 959 Ninth St. It was operated by Joe Manicki (1922-1926), Marion Sment (1928-1929) and Paul Waszkowiak (1929-1934). Built in 1883, it is one of the oldest continuously operating establishments in LaSalle. The Brunswick back bar was installed in 1903. Its mahogany and cherrywood carvings, stained glass and mirrors are still in perfect condition.

In the afternoon, Joe Manicki's saloon (959 Ninth, LaSalle) and the residence of Frank Zank (137 Second, LaSalle) were investigated after the state's attorney's office received complaints about the sale of liquor. At each location, the complaints were justified; quantities of moonshine and mash were discovered. (2)

January was a busy month for inspectors. At 8 a.m. on the 9th, a four-man team from Hanson's office entered the De Kowski saloon (856 Third St., LaSalle). At first, the officers only found a single glass of whiskey. Knowing there had to be more somewhere, the search continued until they found two one-gallon jugs of whiskey. It was concealed in the rear of the building. Boxes of pop bottles had been stacked over a trap door leading to the cache. (3)

Nothing seemed to change in LaSalle County. Booze was still being manufactured and sold in ever larger quantities, and the authorities tried in vain to dry up the county. The bars operated by John Charley at 1101 8th Street and Stan Gapinski on First St. were raided. Two quarts of whiskey were picked up at Charley's, and three cases of home brew and a gallon of moonshine were found at Gapinski's. (4)

The local raids continued at the Julius Burtash saloon (1400 Fifth, LaSalle), a bar that had been raided only a few weeks earlier. The evidence seized included a two-gallon bottle of moonshine and a gallon jug of whiskey. At 1212 First Street, officers arrested Mrs. Elizabeth Dvornicki, the former wife of Fabian Ciganovich, who had two gallons of wine. To serve her customers she used a couple of coffeepots, one containing a pint of moonshine and another filled with wine. They were color-coded, one blue and the other white, so that there would be no mistake when serving customers. She hoped a $20 bill would sway Officer Cooper, but he refused the offer. But she insisted, so Cooper accepted the $20 and immediately turned it over to the state's attorney. At her bond hearing on January 14, Mrs. Dvornicki was charged with selling liquor and attempting to bribe a law officer. Each offense required a $1000 bond. Another raid was carried out at 202 North Sterling in Streator. The bartender saw the men coming and attempted to dump any possible evidence down the drain, but there was enough left to make an arrest. Wrapping up the raids on the 13th, Holland and Cooper visited the Louis Barla soft drink parlor in Seneca. The raid produced a half-pint of moonshine and a pint of wine. (5)

The violations in Cedar Point continued in spite of two previous raids, so Hanson ordered another mopping up operation on the morning of January 27. The houses searched included Domonick Bioliemi's where Officer Holland found a half-ton of sugar, 20 barrels of mash, and 16 gallons of moonshine. At John Bartolini's, they seized 400 gallons of wine stored in eight barrels. Two other houses had operating stills in the basements. A total of 50 barrels of mash were destroyed before they left. (6)

On February 11, there was another raid in LaSalle. For the second time, the establishment at 1313 First Street was searched. Felix Malandrino, the owner, was found to have over a half-gallon of moonshine. (7)

By 1926, there seemed to be a nationwide rebellion against the provisions of the Volstead Act. The courts were swamped with cases involving the liquor law. So the NEA Service, a feature syndicate of 700 newspapers, decided to have a poll of Americans to ascertain the mood of the country. Each of the participating newspapers printed a "Prohibition Ballot" which listed three attitudes about the law:

PROHIBITION BALLOT

Prohibition Editor,

The Tribune

La Salle, Ill.

I have marked below, with a cross, my position on the prohibition question.

I favor keeping the prohibition amendment as it now stands, with strict enforcement. ☐

I favor repeal of the prohibition amendment. ☐

I favor modification of the prohibition law so as to allow the sale of light wine and beer. ☐

Signed ....

Street address ....

City ....

Ballot reprinted from original printed on March 10, 1926 LaSalle *Daily Post*.

The 40 million people who read the papers were given a week to return their signed ballots to their local newspaper, who in turn sent in the results to the NEA for tabulation and eventual submission to Congress. The initial returns to the LaSalle *Daily Post* after two days were very revealing. The paper concluded that their readers favored either modifying the law to allow for light wines and beer or to completely repeal the Volstead Act. Of course, only 342 readers had taken the time to reply; so to be fair the paper ran the ballot every day and encouraged readers to participate. Another unofficial survey had been taken a few years before this, but the trend was the same 10-1 in favor of the "wets."

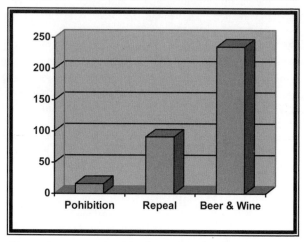

Results of LaSalle *Daily Post* prohibition Survey - March 13, 1926

Two other papers in Illinois were participating in the survey, the *Rockford Morning Sun* and the *Elgin Courier.* The early reports in those regions showed significantly different results. The respondents in the Rockford and Elgin areas indicated similar preferences – being evenly divided between a continuation of prohibition or in favor of modification to allow beer and wine. However, LaSalle readers had indicated a distinct preference to repeal the law or to at least allow beer and wine to be served. Those who favored strict enforcement of the Volstead Act were in the minority.

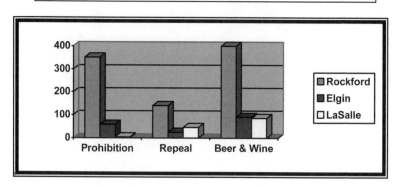

Prohibition attitudes by Rockford, Elgin and LaSalle newspaper readers.

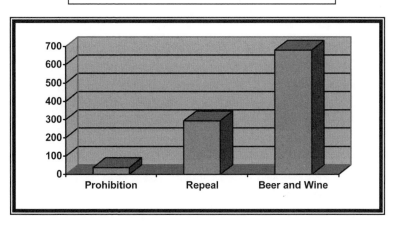

Final results of LaSalle *Daily Post* prohibition survey

The final local results were published in the LaSalle *Daily Post* on Mar. 19, 1926. A total of 1,010 people participated in the survey. Only 4% of the participants wanted to keep the law as it stood. Of the remaining people, 67% wanted the law to be modified to allow for beer and wine and 29% wanted outright repeal of the law. According to the paper, the names signed to the ballots represented a cross-section of men and women and a diversity of ethnic groups and social classes. The LaSalle area was clearly in favor of amending the law or doing away with prohibition entirely. The statewide results showed similar but not as strong feelings against the law. There was still a large portion of those responding to the survey (almost 30%) that wanted to have strict enforcement of the law.

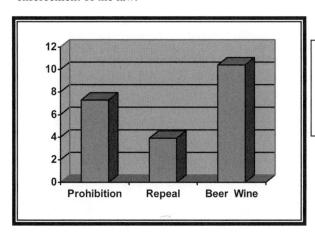

Illinois statewide poll results
Mar. 20, 1926
LS Daily Post
Nos. in 1000's

One product of the national breweries was called "tonic beer." It wasn't something that was palatable to any degree. According to officials of the Anheuser Busch Co. in St. Louis and the Pabst Brewing Co. of Milwaukee, the extremely bitter liquid was almost black in color and had about 25% solid material floating in it. It wasn't a new product. Anheuser Busch had been producing it for 30 years, but when prohibition became the law, they had to drain the fermentation vats. In March 1926, however, the federal government decided to allow production to begin again. According to Fred Pabst Sr., "It is palatable but could not be drunk as a beverage." However, the Milwaukee brewer pointed out, "It will have great value to convalescents and persons afflicted with cancer." Local druggists were allotted five cases of the "medicine" each week. The chief prohibition chemist, J.N. Doran, said that the malted barley drink was "something of a cross between beer and molasses, but it certainly does not taste like beer." Some people felt that this was at least a beginning to breaking down the strict prohibition laws and a victory for the "wets." It was expected to go on sale in mid-May 1926.

Manufacturing of the product was to be carried out under strict government controls. The drink containing 3.75% alcohol could only be advertised as a medicine. Druggists and grocers were also allowed to sell sherry and port wine but only for medicinal or seasoning purposes. (8) Tonic beer was certainly no substitute for the fine products produced before prohibition by Star Union, Peru Beer Co., and the Ottawa Brewing Association, so it was business as usual for both bootleggers and law enforcement authorities.

While much of the alcohol being consumed in the Valley was produced locally, there was also a small amount being imported from other regions. Three young men decided to go into the bootlegging business by bringing in liquor to the Valley from Aurora. Having received several complaints, Officers Holland, Cooper, and Farrell began a stakeout at the DeLagneau farm located northwest of Ottawa on April 29 at 11 p.m. Finally at 2 a.m., the lights of a Nash touring car appeared coming up the road to the farm. The occupants, Walter Thompson and Joe Moe, were arrested.

A 1926 Nash Model 261. The company offered 24 different models in 1926. This is the 5-passenger touring car, which sold for $1,375.

According to the *Daily Post*, "In the rear seat were two 20-gallon kegs, one containing rye moonshine whiskey and the other corn whiskey." Thompson and Moe admitted that this was their third run from Aurora. They were marking up their $2.50 a gallon investment by 100%. Their associate William Wise was their distributor in the local area but had not accompanied them on this trip. At. 5 a.m., Cooper went to Marseilles and arrested Wise. The law provided that the impounded Nash could be confiscated and sold with the proceeds going to the county treasury. (9)

Miranda warnings were unheard of in the 1920's. Many individuals got more jail time than they bargained for because they

incriminated themselves. One such instance involved the case against John Hall of Streator. Standing before the bench of Judge Reck (at left), he admitted that he was "doing nicely" before Sheriff Welter raided his place and spoiled everything. Hall challenged the sheriff's claim that there were 5,000 bottles waiting to be filled with moonshine. Hall retorted, "There wasn't more than 3,500." When the judge commented on the large number of bottles and asked Hall if he didn't think that was a lot, Hall added, "If the sheriff would had let me alone, I would have had more than that."

Ordinarily bootleggers were only given a $200 fine, which Hall was ready to pay. But Judge Reck was fed up with the smug attitude of the bootleggers he had seen. Confronting the accused, Judge Reck said, "I am satisfied that a fine wouldn't do you any good. For that reason I am going to send you to jail. I sentence you to 60 days imprisonment in the county jail." The stunned bootlegger complained that it was a "dirty deal."

As he was being taken away by the bailiff, Hall yelled out that the equipment he used wasn't even his. It was his father's, Luke Hall. Judge Reck then turned to Sheriff Welter and ordered, "Better get a warrant for the father too." (10)

Rural stills were constantly being discovered. A little more than a mile northeast of Ottawa was a two-story building near the Fox River. It was owned by W.C. Bracken and known to be a gambling and drinking establishment. Investigators Holland and Cooper conducted an 8 a.m. raid that resulted in the confiscation of two slot machines and 50 bottles of moonshine, gin, and wine. Bracken had hidden some of the moonshine under the coal bin. The rest of it was concealed in a secret compartment in a concrete wall. Bracken was taken before Justice L.L. Thompson for his hearing. (11)

In mid-July, two Oglesby bars were raided after two LaSalle boys confessed that they had purchased liquor at the locations and stole a car to go joy-riding. One of the businesses was owned by Mary Seminzi (159 Walnut). The other soft drink parlor was known as the "Music Hall" (439 Walnut). Mrs. Seminzi made no attempt to conceal any of the gin, moonshine and wine that was available. But the "Music Hall" had several secret locations in which to store illegal liquor. Officer Holland found a shelf behind a hollow place in the wall. One of the panels in a cupboard could also be removed. That led to the basement where four barrels of wine were stored. (12)

Ten days later, the headlines in the LaSalle paper proclaimed, "Hanson Squad Mops Up Again On Creve Coeur." A distillery located along the alley of Creve Coeur Street in LaSalle and owned by John Preano was found in full operation. The raid netted 65 gallons of moonshine, 1,650 gallons of mash being stored in 33 barrels, a still, and a stove. The quantity of mash was too large to handle so it was dumped down the sewer. This was the same location that was operated by Joe Tomasello only two months earlier. Tomasello was currently out on bond. (13)

Cedar Point bars had been raided numerous times, but certain individuals seemed determined to keep the production of moonshine going no matter how many times Hanson's men took away their equipment. But these individuals were more than annoyed. Finally it sounded like it was becoming a "Little Cicero" as Hanson made one of the largest raids to date. It was August 12 when Hanson's Raiders struck with 16 men at 10 a.m. The eight cars did not come up Route 71, as would be expected, but rather took a dusty gravel road up from the south by way of Tonica. The town was wired with a series of buzzers to notify bootleggers of an impending raid. The system worked to a degree. Many of the buildings were found abandoned but had stills in operation. Some of the buildings were saloons, and others appeared to be abandoned residences.

As Officer Holland entered one of the wooden buildings, he spied five stills in full operation. Just then there was a tremendous explosion that sent flames into the face of the officer badly burning him. The initial detonation then triggered successive ones with concussions that could be heard for miles. The alcohol fueled the flames until the building was nothing more than a pile of ashes. In minutes, the flames spread to the neighboring building also containing large quantities of mash and alcohol. It was gutted in short order. (14)

Later, it was uncovered that Henry Hoerner, the owner of the Star Union Brewery, also owned the two buildings that were destroyed in the fire. Hoerner told reporters that he would "welcome an investigation that would assist him in finding out the names of the persons who were connected with the wholesale manufacture of moonshine in the two buildings in question." (15)

Fires from exploding stills were not an uncommon occurrence in Cedar Point. As a precaution, bootleggers had fire extinguishers hanging in every building where stills were in operation. Along with four stills, three barrels of moonshine and hundreds of gallons of mash, suspicious papers were found in a building owned by Charles Benedetti and rented to Pete Cavaletto. Two unknown occupants had made a hasty retreat only taking time to turn off the fire under the stills before the raiders struck. In a coat found hanging on the wall was a small notebook detailing certain incriminating evidence against unnamed police officers. It was interesting to note that Cedar Point had no police force. The LaSalle *Daily Post* published the following transactions:

June 1 – police got ten gallons
June 3 – police got ten gallons
June 6 – police got twelve gallons
June 7 – police bought ten pounds yeast.

The profits from sales were also recorded.

June 22 – $33.73
June 24 – $35.20
June 26 – $61.80
June 27 – $45.00
June 28 – $50.00
June 29 – $55.60

Authorities speculated that there were three gangs operating out of Cedar Point. Two of the leaders were believed to be Joe "Blacky" Pedrone and George "Shorty" Mussatto. Six men were eventually captured. John Rich surrendered without a fight. In his place, officers found 46 barrels of rye mash and 126 gallons of alcohol. Dominic Thera and Joe Begani also surrendered without a fight. August Bernardi appeared to be cooperative telling Officer Cooper, "I'll show you where I have the stuff." But as they proceeded down the stairway, Bernardi punched Cooper in the face. The smaller officer struck back with a punch so hard that Bernardi was sent sprawling over one of the two stills in the basement. After being handcuffed, Bernardi offered Officer John Tryon of Brookfield Township a $20 bribe just to drain some of the moonshine and add water to the barrels to dilute it. When Tyron refused the bribe, Bernardi allegedly picked up a newspaper and showed the officer an article describing the gang killings that were so commonplace in Chicago. Bernardi furiously threatened the officer. "That's what we do in Chicago, and that's what we ought to do here." (16)

Some of the bootleggers successfully fled in automobiles down the country road going south of Cedar Point. Mussatto and Pedrone ran into a nearby cornfield but surrendered when the pursuing officers fired several shots over their heads. The house where Pedrone and Mussatto were staying had three operating stills and 60 barrels of rye mash. The hundreds of barrels of mash and moonshine along with kegs seized in the raid were destroyed in Cedar Point, but it still required two trucks to haul samples of evidence and equipment back to Ottawa. (17)

A few officers were left behind in Cedar Point to see if any of those who fled would return to the scene. The next afternoon, Hanson and Holland found everything much as it had been. Doors were ajar and there was no evidence that anything had been touched. They did search the home of Tom Ricco. Two stills, 40 gallons of moonshine and 15 barrels of mash were uncovered. (18)

Hanson returned to the mining town on August 20. It was the fifth time the state's attorney had the town searched. Hanson told reporters that he was going to keep Cedar Point "under close surveillance" with the aim of eliminating the wholesale liquor business there. (19)

While Hanson was busy at Cedar Point, Sheriff Welter had also been very successful. The basement of the Ottawa jail was filled with evidence that finally was to be destroyed in November. The sheriff used an ax to demolish a dozen stills and a gambling table he had stored. A large cache of beer and liquor bottles was also destroyed. The contents flowed down into the Ottawa sewer system. (20)

The public mood against prohibition was having an effect in the Nation's Capital. On Dec. 29, 1926, General Lincoln Andrews, the Federal Prohibition Administrator, announced a policy change regarding the manufacture of "home brew." Speaking at a convention of 300 malt syrup manufacturers, Andrews asserted, "I see no reason why a householder should not be able to make his own beer in his own cellar." Certain guidelines were established in new legislative proposals. There would be no labeling or advertising indicating the manufacturer of a prohibited beverage. No trade names associated with breweries could be used. And all warning labels to prohibit the use of the product in beer manufacturing had to be removed. (21)

Chapter 11
1927
The New Sheriff Cracks Down

A new sheriff, Floyd Clark, had taken office in LaSalle County following the November elections. He would soon prove to be as effective as his predecessor. In a raid at the home of Joe Langles, Clark confiscated all the equipment necessary for manufacturing moonshine. There was a still, coil, five-gallon container of moonshine and a similar one filled with whiskey. In addition, the sheriff dumped a barrel of mash and six cases of beer. Mrs. Anna Langles took the responsibility for the operation. (1)

Just as Sheriff Welter had done in past years, Sheriff Clark began cracking down on speakeasies. On Jan. 5, he was back at Dvornicky's soft drink parlor on First Street in LaSalle. It was the same old story; moonshine and beer were available again. The Twin City Park Saloon owned by Nick Herakovich was next on Clark's list. There he found a dozen cases of beer. Later in the evening, John Srnik's place in Naplate was raided. Then Clark went next door to the home of Eva Scurtie. In both locations Clark seized moonshine and large quantities of beer. (2)

No one was exempt from Clark's investigations. One prominent citizen was found to have a pint of whiskey, five cases of beer, and ten gallons of wine in his home The individual was Joe Madic, a candidate for city commissioner in Oglesby. When Madic was charged with the sale of liquor, the politician claimed it was all strictly for medicinal purposes. He had made the wine on doctor's orders for his ailing wife. Clark told Madic that he could tell it all to Judge Thompson. (3)

Floyd S. Clark was elected sheriff by the voters of LaSalle County and served from 1926 to 1930 during the most active period of prohibition

Spring Valley was noted for many years as a mining town with a large number of bars. Always suspicious that these locations were not always serving near beer and grape juice, a federal investigation was authorized. Undercover agents disguised as employees of Illinois Power had gathered evidence for weeks before a raid in late January. When it finally came, almost every tavern in town was to be searched. But only in four cases were arrests made. Most of the buildings were padlocked, and the owners were nowhere to be found. (4)

A month later, on Feb. 24, 1927, there was another federal sweep through Spring Valley, Hick's Junction, Cherry and Ladd. Of the 62 warrants, 40 were served in Spring Valley, 2 in Hick's Junction, 13 in Cherry, and 7 in Ladd. A hearing was held in Peoria to handle the "greatest mop-up in the history of liquor law enforcement in the district." (5) A deputy U.S. marshal and the chief prohibition officer together with eight men had visited almost every drinking establishment in the four communities. The entire investigation had been going on for two months using agents dressed in overalls and muddied work clothes. The agents would not discuss the arrests with reporters pending court hearings. (6)

Federal agents out of Springfield made another raid on one of the largest "wildcat breweries" in Illinois on March 24. The raiders swooped down on a building in the heart of Arlington, Illinois only ten miles north of LaSalle. A four-man team of Treasury agents arrested Harvey Peart, John Skeffingtonan, and Frank Flannagan. The arrests, according to investigators, were only the tip of the iceberg. The building itself was the property of J.D. Prentergast, and there was a long list of owners for whom arrest warrants were issued.

From the outside, the building appeared to be a deserted and dilapidated hardware store in the heart of the town. But inside, there was a modern brewery with ten vats capable of holding 1,000 gallons. In addition, there were cooling rooms, a refrigeration plant, and all the other equipment necessary to turn out 50 barrels of beer every day. The wholesale operation had been in business for a number of years, and there had been no attempt to conceal the operation other than to maintain the appearance of an abandoned building. In reality, it was a $50,000 brewery. (7)

While federal agents were trying to clean up at Spring Valley and Arlington, the LaSalle sheriff continued his vigorous enforcement efforts in Oglesby. The south side of Walnut Street was lined with numerous soft drink parlors that were serving a lot more than sodas. On Mar. 8, 1927, Clark and Deputies Walter Kerney, Art Mason, and Leonard Orr searched the business owned by Mrs. Baima at 433 Walnut and found a quantity of wine. She was ordered to appear in the Ottawa court the following day. When she failed to do so, the three deputies went back to her business, found more wine, and immediately brought the woman to the Ottawa jail. Then Clark went to 139 Walnut to search the saloon of operated by Mrs. Joe Ferrari. There too, the officers found wine and a quantity of moonshine behind the bar. (8)

The following month on April 21, Clark carried out three more successful raids in Oglesby. The operators of the Rigazio, Herrick, and Dusac soft drink parlors were arrested after wine and moonshine were discovered. Rigazio's had been raided five times and, in every case, an arrest was made. The largest raid was at Frank Dusac's place. The evidence invoice listed one five-gallon jug of moonshine, two one-gallon jugs of wine, two quart bottles of moonshine, three pint bottles of liquor, two pitchers of wine. (9)

Clark's next major effort was in Ottawa. Arriving at the Kelly and Haley speakeasy on Main Street, Deputy Orr hefted a 16-pound sledgehammer and bashed in the locked door of the upstairs room. The large raiding party stunned the confused patrons with their sudden appearance. It was reported that some of the 28 people arrested tried to jump from windows to escape. Poker cards, chips, and a few bottles of liquor were collected as evidence. They were all charged as "inmates of a gambling house." A preliminary hearing was scheduled for Tuesday, May 3, at South Ottawa's Turn Hall. (10)

East Wenona was the scene of a June 30 raid by Clark. One of the largest crowds was on hand to witness the sheriff's work since a concert was in progress in town. When the sheriff and his men entered the soft drink parlor operated by Matt Yare Jr., the proprietor tried to dispose of the evidence. A deputy grabbed Yare by the collar of his shirt thwarting his efforts. During the raid, the officers found some home brew and four quarts of moonshine for some post-concert business. In the meantime, the musicians lost their audience at the park as the crowd rushed to Yare's business to learn why the sheriff was in town. (11)

On August 17, Sheriff Clark decided to take a little trip to the southern end of LaSalle County. First he stopped once again in East Wenona. At Pete Mezzeni's saloon, he found wine in pint, quart, and gallon containers. Four cases of real beer were dumped on the spot. Continuing his search in the village of Dana, Clark found 13 cases of beer in the soft drink parlor of E.J.McGrew. Both Mezzini and McGrew were taken into custody. (12)

The summer of 1927 was a busy one for Sheriff Clark as he continued mopping up raids in Ottawa, Earlville, and Streator. In Earlville, William Hugh, a prominent citizen was arrested. The wealthy 60-year old had become a regular beer runner in the area. He didn't need the money but simply enjoyed the thrill of evading the law in his journeys between Streator and Earlville. Unwittingly, Hugh drove his beer-laden car right into a raid being carried out at one of his customers, William Meade, who was found with nine quarts of wine and two quarts of moonshine. Then Clark forced Hugh to retrace his route back to the Streator residence of Albert Shartell at 512 Illinois Street. It turned out to be a medium-sized brewery with 40, 28-gallon vats of fermenting beer. Thirty-six cases of brew had been bottled - ready for the next shipment. (13)

LaSalle and Peru continued to be sources of a variety of illicit liquor products. Judge L.L. Thompson had heard every hard luck story and excuse imaginable, but Mary Mickiwick's tale no doubt caused the judge to shake his head in disbelief. Clark and his men had conducted a search of her home on the corner of First and LaHarpe in LaSalle on July 13, 1927. The officers had found 25 cases of beer and another 120 gallons of beer not yet bottled. Incredulously, she had complained to the prosecutor before her hearing, "I asked them (the sheriff's men) to leave me one case of beer but they wouldn't do it." At her arraignment before Judge Thompson, she explained that it all belonged to her divorced husband, who had moved out and should be the defendant. But it appeared that the beer had been brewed in recent days. So bond was set, and Mary Mickiwick was out of jail until the trial.

Across the street, Clark also visited Pete Massock, who ran a speakeasy across the street. Massock's inventory included two cases of illegal beer and two quarts of moonshine to quench the thirst of his customers. But they went thirsty since Massock was detained in jail.

The LaSalle sheriff made another large haul the same night in Peru at 115 Tenth Street. Anton Castelie had a 150-gallon still in his home. It was identical in every way to one the sheriff had uncovered in a recent Streator raid. The boilers were so big that they would not even fit into the evidence storage area of the Ottawa jail. Dozens of 55-gallon barrels containing mash and five gallons of the finished product were also found. The Wednesday night raid had been very productive. (14)

Federal warrants served in Bureau County may have embarrassed Sheriff Jack Applen into more vigorous action. On Wednesday, August 25, the sheriff took deputies Gross, Flaherty, Dahlgren, Ryan, and Cowenburg to search speakeasies in Spring Valley, Ladd, and DePue. Apparently the raid by the federal authorities had at least scared the local owners into either finding better methods of concealment or in shutting down liquor sales until the heat was off. Applen's men searched seven different establishments over the course of several hours. Their reward was limited to a couple of bottles of moonshine found in Paul Gurdini's establishment in Ladd. The DePue and Spring Valley taverns got a clean bill of health. (15) The sheriff was suspicious, however, knowing the reputations of many tavern owners. On Saturday night, Aug. 26, liquor violations were charged against August Krano who owned a business at Howe Station. On Sunday night, a young man from Peru reported that he had been robbed in the Location. Applen took Deputy Flaherty and made an inspection of the business run by Maxine Kersoda and Joe Sanchez. After a brief interrogation, Applen charged them with violating the liquor law, assault with a deadly weapon, and conducting a house of ill fame. (16)

The LaSalle County sheriff was also busy over the Aug. 27-28 weekend as he made three raids in Utica. Two raids were conducted on Saturday night, one at Tom Keenan's soft drink parlor and the other at the Brennan bar. Keenan tried to use a now-familiar liquor disposal system of dumping the bottles to the basement where they would smash on rocks. However, Clark was able to salvage enough liquid to prove his case. There was only a small amount of liquor at Brennan's, but it was enough to arrest the bartender, E. Zubowski. It was because of such tactics that the newspapers referred to the sheriff's prohibition task force as "The Sponge Squad." Clark waited until Sunday morning for his third raid of the weekend. He drove down to William Nagle's place in Ransom and once again procured enough evidence to make a case. (17)

In another first in the history of local prohibition enforcement, federal agents from Chicago descended on downtown Ottawa to raid a drugstore on September 3. There were many laws allowing the prescribed use of certain medicines containing quantities of alcohol, but in this case the store was a front dispensing illegal alcoholic "prescriptions." The agents were tipped off that liquor was being dispensed from the Gapen drug store on LaSalle Street. The local rumor mill had it that there were about 20 men walking the streets of Ottawa selling liquor. The federal agents tried to make a buy inside the drugstore, but the proprietor was suspicious of the strangers and refused to sell them anything. The agents decided to stake out the Ottawa pharmacy. They observed customers entering and leaving the store until they finally spotted a customer, John Berry, hide something under his shirt as he left the drug store. The agents ran after him. Just as they were about to catch him, Berry pulled the concealed object from under his shirt and threw it down shattering a glass bottle and splashing its contents over the sidewalk. Under questioning, Berry lamely explained that the bottle was full of turpentine not liquor. The agents then returned to the Gapen pharmacy and showed their badges. When the proprietor, C.E.Gapen, protested that they didn't have a search warrant, they explained that they didn't need one; they would only take what was in plain view. The seized evidence amounted to 25 quarts of moonshine. Every type of bottle imaginable, even infant nursing bottles, were used to store the liquor. A large curious crowd was milling about outside the drug store. To prevent any trouble, one of the two agents secured assistance from Sheriff Clark's department only three blocks away. The next day, Mr. Berry and the evidence were taken from the city jail to Chicago. Gapen could not be arrested, according to his attorney, because the store was searched without a warrant. (18)

In spite of all the best efforts of federal, county and local law enforcement officers, it was obvious that there was still a large quantity of beer and moonshine flooding into the Illinois Valley. The main breweries in Peru and Ottawa had been accounted for, and the raid in Arlington had certainly curtailed supplies, but somewhere there was an unknown source in operation. Finally on September 21, 1927, Sheriff Applen made the discovery. Early on Wednesday morning, Applen together with six deputies drove from Princeton towards Spring Valley. Proceeding to the Pulaski Park, the men entered the Petroski building at the Location and found the largest wildcat brewery in northern Illinois.

The facility was modern in every respect. In the basement there were six 300-gallon vats. Upstairs was a 200-gallon still, which was producing pure alcohol from a combination of sugar and yeast. Unfortunately, the raiders were unable to confiscate much of the production run since it had been shipped out earlier. However, there was more than enough to bring back over four gallons of liquor as evidence of the operation. Josef Skinner, the Bureau County State's Attorney, came on the scene at about 1:00 p.m. to assess the situation and to assign a guard to make sure that nothing was removed. Further investigation revealed that the plant had been in operation for the last two years. (19)

At the end of September, another large moonshine operation in LaSalle was put out of business. John Luzar was accused of manufacturing large quantities of a variety of products. In a search of the residence at 128 Chartres, two LaSalle Motorcycle Patrolmen, Bob Fritz and Frank Krueger, stumbled upon the operation in an unrelated theft investigation. As the officers walked down the stairs into the basement, they immediately spotted a huge copper still. Three barrels were being used to age 150 gallons of peach mash in one corner of the basement. The officers also found 15 cases of beer. After taking samples for evidence, kerosene was used to destroy the remaining mash.

The discovery of a still by the local LaSalle police on Sept. 27 was a first for the department. They had confiscated moonshine before but not the equipment used to make it. (20) Bootleggers always thought they had the perfect hiding place for their hooch, and for many years much of the supply flooding the local market was safe from prying eyes. It often required a confession by a purchaser to get the necessary information for a search warrant. Such was the case when a raid was conducted at the home of Mrs. Amelia Cristo, a widow living in Cherry. The warrant was read; the officers knew exactly where to look.

An informant described the procedure for making a "buy." They would drive into the Cristo garage behind the home to make a purchase. The building was equipped with a secret underground room that was entered through the garage. Applen's men documented the illegal material: five barrels of wine, six cases of beer, one 20-gallon crock of fermenting liquor, seven gallons moonshine. The sheriff told Mrs. Cristo to appear at the Princeton Courthouse on Monday to answer the charges against her. (21)

It must have seemed like a hopeless battle for the county authorities. No matter how many places they searched and no matter how often, the fines and other penalties were not making an impression. Neither the distillers nor the operators of the speakeasies gave up. The only notable change was that the quantities being seized were increasing.

Anyone who wanted a drink in Oglesby could find a soft drink parlor on the south side of Walnut Street in Oglesby. *[Note: No taverns were allowed on the north side of the street in Oglesby since T.T. Bent, coal entrepreneur, had bought the land and demanded that provision in any property he sold.]* And if you lived in LaSalle, there were over two dozen places on First Street alone where a purchase could be made. Tavern owners, like John Sabol in LaSalle, simply kept the moonshine in common water pitchers so as not to raise suspicion when a stranger walked in. (22)

The weekend seemed to be the more opportune time to conduct a raid. What the sheriffs really needed to do was to hit the small time distillers, who usually operated in their basements, as well as the larger distilleries that were later found in rural areas.

During a series of evening raids on Friday, Oct. 29, 1927, Sheriff Clark was able to plug a few holes in the law enforcement dikes holding back a flood of beer and moonshine. Three homes located at 414 Canal, 147 Tenth, and 133 First Street in LaSalle were found to be the sources of much of the illegal booze. The evidence filled an entire truck. Frank Sevrenski had 15 cases of beer, three 20-gallon crocks of beer, one gallon of moonshine, and two gallons of wine. Charles Tomsha and Mrs. John Gerboric had complete distilleries with all the necessary attachments, stills, coils, hoses, boilers, stoves, whiskey tester, whiskey coloring. The raw materials included 300 pounds of sugar. Over a dozen barrels of mash were also found. Tomsha and Gerboric had dozens of gallons of moonshine wine ready for sale. (23)

It wasn't merely the lowly bartenders and widows who were accused of Volstead violations. As time went on, the money to be made from the manufacture and sale of alcohol corrupted respected citizens, city officials, and local law officers. Fortunately, they were few in number according to the arrest reports, but it was still a shock and embarrassment to law-abiding citizens. Henry Chandelier was a Republican precinct committeeman who owned one of the numerous soft drink parlors in LaSalle. It was almost Halloween, but there would be no treat for the bar owner after Clark made a surprise raid and found five quarts of whiskey, a number of cases of beer and a slot machine. (24)

A few days later, a retired LaSalle police officer, Vince Hetherington, was picked up at his saloon at 1202 First Street. He was well stocked with gin, wine, whiskey, and beer.

More often than not, it was just ordinary people who got involved in the business and couldn't make enough money selling grape juice and near beer in their soft drink parlors. Dominic Renaudo made that point after the police took 20 gallons of whiskey and ten cases of beer at his LaSalle Street place in Peru. He pleaded with the deputies, "I've got no money to pay a fine." One of the arresting officers replied, "Well you will have to go to Vandalia (penal farm) then." (25)

Restaurants were sometimes found to be serving more than menu indicated. On Saturday afternoon, Nov. 12, the sheriff visited the Farrell and McElroy restaurant in Ottawa. It was located north of the Illinois-Michigan Canal Bridge on Columbus Street. The establishment was found to have almost two gallons of moonshine on the premises. In an investigation of the eatery of Ed Grosch in Mendota, Clark found a similar amount of illegal liquor. (26)

Making an arrest in the Illinois Valley was usually conducted without incident or violence. At most, a brief scuffle might occur. Those arrested knew they had broken the law and, after being confronted with the liquid evidence, they went peacefully to jail. For that, local law officers could be thankful. The nationwide enforcement of prohibition was much more dangerous. On November 16, Seymour Lowman, the Assistant Secretary of the Treasury, released the casualty figures in what was quickly becoming a war between organized crime and the government. While the numbers of victims did not soar into the thousands as claimed by Senator Edwards of New Jersey, they were nonetheless alarming. The eight years of enforcement of the Volstead Act had cost the lives of 175 persons – 125 citizens and 49 prohibition agents, all "killed in action," according to Lowman. He did point out, however, that those figures did not include those killed in gang wars that were becoming more common in the turf battles between rival mobs. (27)

The local pattern of raids, arrests, and fines continued unabated and relatively uneventful. In spite of the numerous successful raids at Cedar Point, a number of raids on the local stills were repeated in December.

The series of pre-Christmas raids continued on Friday night December 17. The officers went to downtown Oglesby and made arrests at 251, 333 and 407 East Walnut. Joe Minni, Andrew Kravich, Emile Moalli, and Emma Perino were ordered to appear before the Ottawa court for a hearing the following day. At each establishment, officers found real beer, wine, and moonshine. (28)

On Saturday night, December 18, the bar of Pete Doukezas at 1005 Eighth Street in LaSalle was raided. "Moonshine" Pete was said to have his source of booze in Putnam County. Several gallons of moonshine and a quart of wine were the only illegal drinks on hand. A much larger haul was made at the Four Corner's in Peru. John Yohn was concealing 28 quarts of moonshine and 42 cases of beer and wine at his soft drink parlor. The sheriff said it was "one of the largest stocks of liquor ever seized by him in a soft drink parlor." (29)

At 6:30 Sunday morning, the homes of Emo Justie, Geno Justie, Richardo Seghi, James Claudie, Eugene Fornetti and Paul and John Maggi were raided. All had contraband. It was alleged that Justie offered a deputy a $75 bribe to call off the raid. So he was also charged with attempted bribery. (30) The Seghi place was loaded with not only a still but also 41 cases of beer and 60 gallons of beer in crocks, most of which was destroyed before the raiders left the village. Farnetti had made ten cases of beer, more than ten gallons of wine, and five gallons of moonshine. Among the supplies he was using were ten cans of malt syrup and a box full of hops. (32)

Ads for various brands of barley malt syrup appeared in the LaSalle *Daily Post* from time to time. This Budweiser ad appeared in the March 28, 1927 edition. Some of malt syrup was available without the hop flavoring.

Claudie had a small shack where he was operating three stills. Apparently he didn't learn from his mistake. Six months later, he was arrested again in Cedar Point in a rented home with two new stills dripping moonshine until he had accumulated 13 gallons. (33)

It should be noted that every raid did not produce the evidence that was thought to be at the location. During the Sunday night Cedar Point raids on the homes of Pete Quincy, Roman Kotecki, Louis Bragini, and Mary Jennings, not a trace of alcohol was found. Nor was there any evidence that distillery equipment was being used on the premises. (33)

Chapter 12
1928
The Quiet Before the Storm

Bootlegging arrests rarely made the front pages of the local newspapers in 1928. However, a large cache of 140 gallons of moonshine was found in the home of Ray Miller. But the man was too sick to be taken to jail. (1) One *Daily Post* story described an Arlington raid. Sheriff Applen of Bureau County arrested Frank Peart who had 50 quarts of wine, four cases of beer and three quarts of whiskey in his car ready to be transported. Peart had been cleared of federal bootlegging charges, but the sheriff had been suspicious of the man for over a year. (2) Most of the other raids in January were rather petty affairs involving small quantities of moonshine.

But in mid-February, it was time for another look at Cedar Point. To no one's surprise, stills were found throughout the town. However, only two men were arrested, Caesar Salsi and Angelo Fachieni. Other occupants vacated several of the residences indicating they had been tipped off recently. The owners left behind 50 sacks of corn sugar, 16 sacks of rye and 34 barrels of fermenting rye mash. Their kerosene fuel tanks had just been filled, and two stills were still cooking on the stoves when Clark and his men arrived at 7 a.m. Sunday morning, February 12. (3)

Ottawa was not left out of the search pattern of the sheriff, but the seizures were rather small. The cigar store and soft drink parlor of Fred Redlich at 630 W. Lafayette yielded only six cases of beer and a small quantity of moonshine. A home in Naplate occupied by Barney Gregori netted four gallons of liquor. Frank Corrigan was arrested for possession of a gallon of moonshine, a quart of wine, and a few cases of beer. These were certainly not the types of arrests that were going to dry up the county. The law enforcement authorities knew that there had to be a larger source in the area but they couldn't pin it down. (4)

Normally the fire department isn't called out on a liquor arrest, but on April 27, LaSalle Fire Company No. 1 was sent to North Tonti Street near St. Hyancinth's church. Arriving around 7:30 on Sunday morning, they found a new Olds coupe engulfed in

1928 Olds Coupe

flames. After a half-hour of hosing down the gutted car, the firemen returned to their station, and investigators went to work. It was discovered that the car was packed with 50 one-gallon containers of alcohol. It was concluded that one of the leaking cans had dripped its contents onto the hot muffler. LaSalle police could not identify the owner from the license plates since the plates were brand new and not registered locally. (5)

Efforts to dry up Bureau County were going no better for Sheriff Applen. A series of raids were made in DePue on March 11 by federal authorities out of Peoria, and five men were served with warrants. Applen followed up with a raid of his own and arrested the owners of the Gold and Kazolier saloon for the sale of liquor. Eli Gold pleaded guilty and was sentenced to four months at Vandalia. Kasimir Kazolier pleaded not guilty; posted bond; and traveled to Peoria for a federal hearing. (6)

In June 1928, Clark decided to check out some rumors about gambling in the Ransom Hotel. State's Attorney Russell Hanson had padlocked one of the small town's soft drink parlors in December 1925, but since then not much had been heard about any violations.

The Ransom hotel still exists on the main street.

The laws didn't even allow for a poker game if money was involved. So when Clark found three men playing cards and money on the table, he had to make an arrest. The owner of the hotel, Roy Bayless, was also arrested when a search produced six cases of beer and a gallon of wine in the hotel kitchen. Clark also checked out the Weyand soft drink parlor across the street and found six cases of beer and a gallon of whiskey. When Clark reported his finds to the state's attorney, Hanson sought to have both establishments padlocked. (7)

Clark was much more successful in a summertime raid at William Ferguson's soft drink parlor in Ottawa. The owner was arrested and Clark's men began the tedious job of popping the caps on 500 bottles of beer and pouring the ale down the sewer drain. Apparently, Ferguson had been brewing his own private stock and also kept a small amount of moonshine whiskey and gin on hand for his customers. (8)

Federal agents were active in shutting down soft drink parlors in in Grundy County during July. The Rev. Henry Rompel, sometimes referred to as the "two-gun" preacher, had requested federal intervention in Morris to curb the drinking in that city. Agent Brice Armstrong led a 12-man team to eight soft drink parlors. John George, Henry Briscoe, John Mitchell, Patrick Whalen, Ed Brady, Joe Olsen, Fred Johnson, and Maurice Ferry were cuffed and taken to Chicago. Additional warrants were issued for R. Kay, Nick Palowski, Judge Ryder, Bill Seillisy, and Frank and Ed Black.

Everything went smoothly until the agents walked into the establishment of Cash Baker. A Morris patrolman in the bar, Martin Enger, shouted, "You can't do this!" The federal agents immediately relieved the patrolman of his gun and his badge, and he was handcuffed. A bystander, Howard Burden, who resisted arrest, was also taken into custody. The agents initially took the saloonkeepers and men who interfered with the raid to the Morris jail. Then they were moved to Joliet and finally to the Cook County jail. In this single raid, the government had successfully wiped out the majority of the distribution outlets in Morris. (9)

The beer and "moon" raids continued into August. Tom Walsh was arrested in his Ottawa business at LaSalle and Marquette for having three slot machines as well a small quantities of whiskey and gin. Six cases of beer were found at Gattano Guttilla's parlor at 116 E. Main. Clark also paid another visit to Ransom after hearing that Tom Berry and Jim Connell had opened another drinking establishment on the second floor of the building that was closed in June. The rumors proved to be true, but the sheriff could only find a pint of liquor. (10)

No place, not even the local barber shop, was safe from the long arm of the law. At the end of August, Sheriff Clark drove to the LaSalle County border town of Welland about five miles northeast of Mendota. His long trip was rewarded with another arrest. Mr. McDonald, the resident barber, had in his possession a dozen quarts of alcohol, three gallons of moonshine, and several cases of beer. The barber was offering his customers more than hair tonic. (11)

Clark drove south to Dana five days later and raided Ray Reynolds' restaurant 11 p.m. Thirty-seven men were involved playing poker and dice games when the county officers broke down the door to the gambling room in the basement of the restaurant. Those arrested came from LaSalle, Streator, Pontiac, El Paso, Wenona, and Dwight. Deputy Sheriff Arthur Mason seized a gallon of moonshine, a half-gallon of wine and two cases of beer. The poker chips and dice were also seized as evidence.

Since there were so many individuals under arrest in this case, Clark called the Streator bus company. Shortly after midnight two buses arrived and the prisoners were boarded for the ride back to Ottawa. After their hearing in "night court," the buses took the men back to Dana to pick up their cars. The $10 fines and costs for the gamblers seemed hardly worth the effort. Mr. Reynolds paid several hundred dollars in fines and costs. But when all the fines were tallied, the county had an additional $1,100 (12)

A more satisfying raid by Clark took place in Streator on November 22. The home of Claudio Sabino at 901 Everett was found to be a virtual arsenal of weapons ranging from police and army pistols to shot guns and a 30-30. There was also plenty of ammunition for all of the guns. But all of this was perfectly legal since they were not carried as concealed weapons. Sabino had fled his residence leaving behind an operating still and seven 55-gallon barrels of mash in the attic. Deputy Sheriff Kemery discovered another distillery hidden by a false bottom in a large cupboard. A stairway led to a basement room in which a still was kept.

Down the block at 808 Everett was the residence of Lorenzo Maniglia. Another secret room was found when Deputy Arthur Mason moved a large table on the first floor. After rolling up the carpet and the underlying linoleum, he exposed a trap door and stairway that led to a still. Another section of the basement contained an operating still and six 55-gallon barrels of mash. Five gallons of whiskey were located near the still. Across the street at 805 Everett, Frank Menio, the owner, was arrested when the officers found yet another still, six barrels of mash and fifteen gallons of whiskey. (13)

The year ended with a few more raids of a similar nature. A few more gallons of moonshine and wine were taken out of circulation. But nothing of consequence was accomplished to stem the rising tide of liquor in the Illinois Valley. Even New Year's Eve was celebrated with little concern for the law. According to the LaSalle *Daily Post*, "This year's celebration was perhaps the wettest the city has seen since the advent of prohibition. Liquor of every make and description was to be had at almost every bar in the city. No raids were made by police or the sheriff." (14) But all of that was about to come to an end as federal agents under a new chief investigator descended like vultures seeking to devour every source of alcohol in the Valley.

Chapter 13
1929
The Water Street Distillery Raid

January 9, 1929 was a landmark date in the war on liquor in the LaSalle-Peru area. On that Wednesday afternoon a swarm of federal agents swooped down on the largest waterfront distillery in the region and perhaps even the biggest operation in Illinois. This was much more than a symbolic raid that would net a few barrels of mash and a few gallons of moonshine. Even the raids in Cedar Point paled in comparison to what the prohibition men had discovered. It was the culmination of a two-month undercover investigation in LaSalle and Bureau Counties by federal agents. The illegal Peru distillery was located near Water Street and the Old National Bank. Nearby ran the Rock Island railroad, which brought in much of the ingredients and supplies. The complex of several buildings on the 1500 block of Water Street was valued at $150,000.

Those arrested included Ugo Ferroni, a Peru resident and one of the alleged ringleaders. Candino Piccoli from Mark was accused of being the cooker at the distillery. Lino Tonioni, a Peru resident, and Julius Bolleli of LaSalle were also charged. The only worker who did not live in the Valley was a Davenport man, James Green. But the workers at the plant were not the real targets of the federal agents. The arrests were made without resistance. Bolleli thought he might avoid arrest by hiding among the sugar sacks on the second floor of the plant. When found, he protested his arrest claiming that he had only been hired to unload the railroad carload of sugar.

The charges would eventually implicate one of the most prominent individuals in the Twin Cities. The investigation would even implicate the most notorious gangster in Chicago, Al Capone.

An editorial in the Ottawa *Republican-Times* cast an ominous shadow over the law enforcement officials of Peru and LaSalle County. The editor pointed out that the plant was not hidden as some were. Nor did the police fail to conduct raids. They merely got the retailers; the wholesalers were ignored. It took federal agents from Chicago to capture, "the biggest outfit ever taken in the Chicago area." The editor went on to observe how remarkable it was that since the raid, every soft drink parlor in Ottawa suddenly closed. (1)

In the days that followed, other names were added to those being subpoenaed to testify before a Chicago grand jury. Most prominently mentioned was Frank Urbanowski, a Peru wholesale grocer who owned the buildings on Water Street that housed the huge distillery.

The Peru businessman said that he was going to testify in Chicago without being summoned. Urbanowski maintained, "I have had no connection whatsoever with the illicit plant or the operations of the plant. Containers and sugar that have been purchased from me were done so in a businesslike manner in the wholesale business in which I am engaged. This sale is no more than the business that I conduct with other firms and retail establishments in Peru and surrounding communities." (2)

Above are two samples of the actual 100-pound sugar sacks used at the Water Street distillery. One is from the Clinton Corn Syrup Refining Co. in Clinton, Iowa, and the other came from Anheuser-Busch Corp. in St. Louis. According to Jeno Bonucchi, in a conversation between his father, Bartolomeo Bonucchi, and his uncle, Dominick Bonucchi, it was related that Dominick worked for the bootleggers and unloaded the sugar from the Rock Island freight trains. The unopened bags were put on a ramp and slid directly into the vats. They would sink to the bottom of the vats, and the sugar would dissolve while still in the sacks. The burlap bags would then float to the top of the open vats and were raked off and burned. Bartolomeo, a truck farmer, asked his brother to save a few of the bags for his business in Granville so he could store corn, chicken feed, potatoes and other vegetables. His brother agreed and brought him some of the bags. The authenticity of the sacks is assured because they are still sewn shut.

Incriminating evidence also surfaced when it was discovered that the Peru "industry" and Ugo Ferroni's name appeared on the books of the alcohol syndicate that was exposed in Chicago Heights.

Another individual being sought was Andrew Comyns. According to Victor LaRue, the Assistant U.S. Attorney in charge of the case, Comyns was Urbanowski's sales manager. Before the conspiracy bill was filed, the names of Gaetano Orlandini, Louis Orlandini and Jack Collins were also added.

The main distribution plant was located at 1513 Water Street. Here 391 gallons of whiskey were already packed and ready to be loaded. A Cadillac and a Reo Speedwagon were found parked near the plant when investigators arrived. Another smaller building was constructed to house the large fermentation vats. Four large stills were in full operation. The largest vat held 1,000 gallons, and the three smaller vats had a capacity of 500 gallons. On the premises, the agents found 700 gallons of the finished product. Federal agents spent the night smashing the gallon and five-gallon sized containers of the alcohol. The contents were poured into the sewers that fed into the Illinois River.

During the inspection of the facilities, it was reported that the condensation coils were covered with a type of green poison called verdigris. It covered the copper pipes and polluted the alcohol. Federal agents told reporters that the bluish-green growth was characteristic of the conditions in many of the distilleries that they had raided.

The fires under the boilers were kept burning to warm the agents who remained to guard the plant. Additional federal agents were sent Friday evening from Chicago.

On Saturday, January 12, the federal agents began the process of dismantling the distillery. The accused "cooker," Candino Piccoli of Mark, assisted the agents by instructing them in the proper techniques for pumping the mash out of the vats. It was estimated that it would take a day to empty the 25,000 gallons of sugar mash. About 345 gallons of the remaining alcohol was carried to the banks of the Illinois River and set afire. The copper cookers were smashed. Holes were burned into the iron boilers to render them useless. The metal cookers and vats were cut up and turned into approximately 5,000 pounds of scrap. In an auction that followed the demolition, Hyman Ramenofsky, a LaSalle scrap metal wholesaler, was awarded the contract to purchase the metal. Although the buildings would have been padlocked for one year, as had been the custom, James Harrison, chief federal agent in Peru, said that structures that housed any distillery would be sold, and the proceeds would be deposited into the "miscellaneous fund" of the United States government. The money collected more than paid for the cost of prohibition enforcement.(3) Harrison added that the federal agents were also investigating the large number of retail outlets identified as "soft drink parlors." In Harrison's view, "There are too many here to make a livelihood from the sale of soft drinks. There are about 15 such places in LaSalle and about 23 in Peru."

The local Peru police were also being investigated. Peru Police Chief Joseph Potthoff claimed, "I did not know anything concerning the operation of a liquor plant in Peru." He told reporters that no one had made any complaints to his department.(4) By January 13, federal authorities were holding eleven individuals in connection with the distillery case.

As LaRue's investigation expanded, the role of the Capone organization was revealed. The alcohol produced at the Peru distillery, which was owned by the Urbanowski Grocery Company, was shipped to Davenport. From there, it was shipped back to Chicago. The syndicate extorted a fee of $2 on every gallon of whiskey and $5 on every barrel of beer. Bribes were passed out to keep a lid of the whole affair, but State's Attorney Hanson and Sheriff Clark vehemently denied taking any graft. Certain high officials in LaSalle County government were also rumored to be involved, but LaRue withheld the names of those suspects.

When the grand jury convened on January 23, LaRue grilled Potthoff and four of his officers. Regarding the "beat" cops who regularly patrolled the waterfront, LaRue claimed, "None of these men can conscientiously say that they did not know of the presence of the distillery." When the federal agents raided the distillery, LaRue said, "They could smell it several blocks away."(5) The officers claimed that they could not smell the 200,000 gallons of mash on the premises because the odor was hidden by the strong smell emitted from vinegar barrels in front of the Urbanowski warehouse. When Potthoff was quizzed about the presence of so many "soft drink" parlors in the city, the police chief explained that since they were not licensed by the city, it was not a matter of police business to investigate their operations. Even though Potthoff was aware that his department was responsible for the enforcement of the prohibition law, the chief excused his department by claiming that no one had made any complaints, and he personally knew of no violations of the law. The men in his command were instructed to inform him of any violations, but no reports were ever made. (6)

The subject of graft in LaSalle County was also brought before the grand jury in Chicago. LaRue claimed, "The County has been wide open for some time and bootleggers have been garnering fabulous amounts with the knowledge of the officers who have accepted large sums in consideration of protection of traffickers." The U.S. Attorney claimed that he had evidence showing that one unnamed county official purchased a $100,000 building in Chicago, a ranch in Texas, and a palatial residence in Ottawa. The syndicate allegedly made annual payments of $268,000 as hush money.(7) LaRue claimed that practically every drinking establishment in the Tri-Cities (LaSalle-Peru-Oglesby) and Ottawa and the other towns of the county was selling openly and brazenly because of the graft being paid. Later, one of the federal officials boasted to reporters, "When we are through with our investigation of conditions in LaSalle County that county will be as free of bootleggers as Hades is of angels." (8)

The Capone connection was also explored in the grand jury testimony. LaRue told the press that 90% of the alcohol from the Peru distillery was shipped to the Capone mob. Using a circuitous route, the gang had the booze shipped first to Davenport, which served as a clearing house, and then Dubuque, Iowa. From there it was trucked back to Rockford, Illinois and then to Waukegan and entered the Windy City's north side thereby evading the federal agents in South Chicago and Chicago Heights.(9) When it arrived in the Capone warehouses, the alcohol was labeled as "Genuine Canadian Liquor" before being distributed to Chicago speakeasies and sold at exorbitant prices.

In order to maintain the Peru distillery, it was necessary to have a vast quantity of supplies. LaRue called Mike Linsky, a coal dealer from LaSalle, to explain the 740 tons of coke that he sold to Ferroni in 1928. Lew Conway, also a LaSalle merchant, testified that he had sold large quantities of yeast to the same gentleman but had no idea of why he needed such large quantities as the orders requested. (10)

The Peru distillery investigation was overshadowed by the shocking news of the St. Valentine's Day Massacre on February 14, 1929. Capone was vacationing in Florida when members of the Bugs Moran gang were gunned down in Chicago. For days, the newspapers ran stories of the most notorious mob hit in American history.

The Chicago hearings about the Peru-Chicago alcohol operation were also moved from page one with the explosive news of another major raid in Putnam County on Mar. 27. While the distillery operation was not nearly as large as that found in Peru, it was significant nonetheless. The coal mining town of Mark was the site of the latest revelations.

Agents from Peru arrived in Mark at 8:30 p.m. and broke through the locked door of the Mark dance hall and social center located on Hennepin St. The upstairs was devoid of any activity or contraband, but a distinct odor of alcohol wafted from the cellar. A team of agents went around to the rear of the building and broke the lock on a basement window.

Hennepin St. in Mark was the location of numerous taverns and the Mark social hall. View of south side of street looking east to the four-corners intersection. Circa 1900.

134

Initially, the place appeared to be quite ordinary with only a furnace and miscellaneous items being stored. But the investigators could still smell booze. Breaking through a panel of wood covering another window, they hit pay dirt, barrels and barrels of alcohol. A long passageway, 8' feet wide and running for about 35' long along a north-south line led to four stills, two 10-gallon, one 30-gallon and the fourth a 50-gallon unit. They were heated with small kerosene burners. The barrels and other containers in the tunnel contained about 600 gallons of moonshine. The agents proceeded to remove the stills and burners. Pulling the bungs from the barrels, a veritable flood of moonshine surged through the hallway. As the hundreds of gallons were emptied, a moonshine pond, 4' deep, began to fill the yard of a neighboring house. Armed with wrecking bars and hammers, the agents then pounded away at the stills and burners to make them totally unserviceable. The men finally finished the job and returned to Peru around 10p.m. (11) The agents planned another trip to Mark for the following day.

On Mar. 28, they returned to Putnam County by way of the bottom road, stopping briefly just before noon to inspect the farm property of Joe Engelhaupt. It had been reported that there was a distillery in a tunnel under the farmer's new hen house. The search proved fruitless since the structure was built on a concrete slab with no basement. Englehaupt's claims of innocence appeared to be true. (12)

After giving Engelhaupt "a clean bill," they drove on to search a residence only two blocks off the main street in Mark. The search could have been a dangerous raid for an over-zealous team. The federal agents battered down the doors but proceeded cautiously since these were not really entrances but rather "blind" doors. The owners of the distillery had removed the floorboards on the ground level of the two-story stucco house. An unsuspecting officer could have fallen 6' into the basement.

The operation with an estimated value of $15,000 was using three vats to process 50,000 gallons of mash. The vats were huge. A cypress vat, which had a diameter of 12', held 14,000 gallons. Two concrete vats measuring 18' x 12' each held 18,000 gallons. They towered from the basement floor 14' to the ceiling of the first floor. Everything was constructed of the best and most modern quality materials. Commenting on the product being produced, one agent said, "Alcohol turned out by the plant was of the highest grade possible under the conditions, and a product of 188 to 190 proof, by test, was possible. Alcohol of that proof is standard."

The *Putnam County Record* estimated that 2,400 pints were seized in the Mark raid. According to the paper, the numerous raids in LaSalle County led to the shift of operations to Mark since "no one would ever suspect imports into Mark." At the same time however, the soft drink places in Putnam County "had been expecting visitors and had cleaned up and cleaned out for the occasion, but anticipation was pleasantly disappointing since the federal mop squad failed to touch them." Indeed, little mention was made in the local paper of raids on soft drink parlors in Putnam County. (13) But this would not be the last raid on the Italian community.

The unsanitary conditions of the illegal Valley distilleries were almost as bad as the meat packing houses of Chicago as vividly described by Upton Sinclair in *The Jungle*. The LaSalle *Daily Post-Tribune* reported that open mash vats "made it inevitable that prowling rats and mice should fall in them." Large amounts of black grime formed a coating for the thousands of gallons of moonshine mash churning within the vats. "Dust, dirt and other refuse, even empty sugar sacks, formed a part of the foreign material in the swirling mash. No wood containers were provided for the reception of the alcohol as it came from the distillery." There was only a 15-gallon galvanized tub to collect the alcohol. "The still, column, condenser, and other paraphernalia connected with the distillery were grimy with grease and dirt and the place resembled a garbage dump." (14)

The afternoon raid in Mark did not result in any immediate arrests since the occupants had fled. Whoever owned the plant had taken every precaution not to be identified. The electric meter had been removed so the registration number could not be checked. However, the agents were able to locate the water meter, which had an identification number. The agents had their suspicions that a Spring Valley man was connected, and evidence did seem to confirm that theory, when they discovered hundreds of empty sugar sacks on the second floor. Incriminating evidence indicated that the sugar had been delivered from Iowa and billed to a Spring Valley resident. The brand on the sacks indicated that they had been delivered from the Clinton Corn Syrup Refining Company of Clinton, Iowa. They were identical to the sugar sacks found at the Peru distillery. In an outside shed, the agents found a half-ton of coke used to fire the boilers and a quantity of alcohol.

A second attempt was made that evening to catch the bootleggers, but when no one was found, all the agents could do was destroy the distillery equipment and seize a sample of the liquor as evidence. (15) Rumors persisted that the true owners of the Mark stills were either the Chicago gang or the Rockford gang. (16)

In the meantime, the Peru distillery case dragged on into the late spring. Al Capone was named as the buyer of the thousands of gallons of the Peru liquor. In a surprise move, three of the defendants, Ugo Ferroni, Candino Piccoli, and Jim Green, all pleaded guilty on April 22. Urbanowski and Comyns insisted that they would fight the accusations. (17)

Victor J. Dowd, who was assisting Victor LaRue in the case, testified on April 24 that Urbanowski had accepted a check for $2000 from Ferroni, the head of the distillery conspirators, on January 10, the day after the raid. The Peru wholesaler had been receiving $100 a month rent on the complex of buildings that he had purchased for $1,200. Urbanowski insisted that he had no idea that there was a distillery operating in his property that extended from 1501 to 1537 Water Street. Dowd also said that he had no trouble in finding the distillery. Even at the Peru Rock Island railroad station four or five blocks from the distillery, "The smell was so strong that I didn't have to know the address of the distillery to find it." One of the government agents, C.M. Simonson, testified that they could smell the odor of alcohol at all of the buildings. According to the agent, Urbanowski came personally to investigate the situation, and when he was leaving, Piccoli said, "That is the man who owns the distillery."

The government's physical evidence against the Orlandinis was weak. On the bottom of a 50-gallon whiskey barrel was a tag indicating that the barrel was purchased at Tri-City Hardware, which they owned. Louis Orlandini admitted that Ferroni had a small interest in their business. The only circumstantial evidence found at the distillery was a message concerning a phone call and an envelope dated May 9, 1927 from Peoria sent in care of the Orlandinis. (18)

The following day, Federal Judge Fred Wham reconvened the hearing at the Federal Building in Chicago. After LaRue made his closing remarks, the judge directed the jury to find Gaetano and Louis Orlandini and Andrew Comyns not guilty. The government simply did not have enough direct evidence to connect any of the three men to the illegal operation. (19)

LaRue's examination of Urbanowski on April 26 was grueling. The wholesaler admitted that he had gone to the buildings several times a month to check his stock but never smelled any alcohol. He also admitted that he sold large quantities of corn sugar and tin cans to Ferroni but denied that he had any knowledge of how Ferroni was using the merchandise.

Closing arguments were heard, and Judge Wham instructed the jury for an hour before sending them into the jury room. The jury reached a verdict within less than three hours. They found Urbanowski guilty of violating the Volstead Act. The other defendants, Julius Bolilli, Lino Tonioni, and Jack Collins were found not guilty. According to news accounts, Urbanowski was stunned by the verdict. (20)

On May 3, 1929, the defendants in the most notorious distillery case in northern Illinois were sentenced. Frank Urbanowski, the owner of the building, received a $10,000 fine and a year and a day in

Leavenworth penitentiary. Ugo Ferroni, the head of the distillery operation, received a similar fine but received a term of eighteen months in Leavenworth. Candino Piccoli, the cooker at the distillery, received the same sentence as Urbanowski. The lightest sentence, one day in the custody of a marshal, was given to Jim Green of Davenport. LaRue had recommended leniency because Green had cooperated and testified for the government. Only Urbanowski was visibly shaken by the sentence and seemed to be on the verge of collapse. He maintained, "I am going down to Leavenworth an innocent man." All of those sentenced to prison were eligible for parole in as little as four months. (20)

As things turned out, Urbanowski's good behavior resulted in a recommendation by the parole board for an early release if he agreed to pay the $10,000 fine within 60 days of his release. But Attorney General Mitchell overruled the parole board, giving an indication that liquor violators were going to serve their full term. So the release date was set for Feb. 27, 1930. Unfortunately, Urbanowski could not pay the fine; his prison sentenced was extended to Mar. 22, 1930. When he was finally released, his wife, two sons, and his brother, Vincent, and his wife drove to Leavenworth to bring him back to the Twin Cities. He had no comment for waiting reporters other than to say he was only interested in returning to his business.

During the period of imprisonment, Ferroni and Piccoli had been moved to the penitentiary in Alderson, West Virginia. Piccoli, who also could not pay the fine was finally freed one day after Urbanowski. Ferroni remained at Alderson since he had received an 18-month sentence for being the ringleader. (22)

Throughout the many months of the Peru distillery trial, very little had changed in the Illinois Valley as far as the patterns of liquor sales and raids were concerned. A new chief investigator, Victor Dowd, had led numerous raids when he wasn't engaged in providing testimony at the Urbanowski trial in Chicago.

Raids on local saloons and private homes never stopped but were overshadowed by the events in Chicago. Soft drink parlors on First Street in LaSalle continued to be a favorite target of local and county law enforcement officers. On Jan. 25, Chief of Police Peter Walloch received a tip that a decrepit house at 225½ First Street behind the Moose Buffet was being used as a storage and "cutting" facility. When the LaSalle police arrived, the house looked totally abandoned, but they did find one door with a heavy padlock. Breaking in, they found what they had come for, four barrels of whiskey and a five-gallon bottle of wine. The room also contained an auger to tap the barrels, rubber hose, a hydrometer, wood chips to purify the alcohol, tin funnels, and two bottles of Carmel coloring. A total of 85 gallons of illegal liquor was taken.(23) The investigation that followed implicated Gus Sutt, the owner of the soft drink parlor at 233 First Street. Sutt denied any connection with the operation other than to admit that he had sublet the building to "two other fellows" whose names he could not remember. (24)

Sheriff Clark was also responding to numerous tips. Frequently nothing was found. One successful raid was conducted on Thursday, Feb. 7 at 228 Water Street in Streator. Clark and Deputy Art Mason found two stills, only one of which was in operation. Five gallons of moonshine had already been made while 15 barrels of mash were being prepared. (25)

The LaSalle newspaper carried a few stories about activities in Grundy County, especially when they focused on Morris, Illinois. The old Gebhard Brewery had been out of business since prohibition began, so liquor dealers relied on independent producers. On Feb. 6, 1929, federal agents converged on the Morris Country Club and found a huge still measuring 26' in height and capable of producing 250 gallons a day. In order to house such a large still, the operators, who were not to be found, had removed the partitions of a two-story house on the property. Holes were cut in the first and second floors of the residence so that the entire apparatus could stand upright.

The agents were at a loss in their efforts to apprehend the bootleggers. Only a caretaker, Martin Tehan, was on the premises at the time of the raid. He refused to say anything about the people who were operating the still and only admitted that he had been employed there since July 1928. The owner of record was Sam Hoge, but he was not there. His wife said that he had rented out the house. The ownership of neither a truck nor a Buick sedan could be traced from the license plates since both plates had been stolen from other vehicles. The best the agents could do was to arrest Tehan and destroy the still and the tin containers used to store the alcohol. It was believed that this was one of the main sources of liquor production in Grundy County. (26)

It was business as usual in LaSalle County in February. Novak's soft drink parlor was raided after Deputy Sheriffs Charles Johns and Walter Kemery overheard some teens talking about how they bought liquor there. (27) Sheriff Clark destroyed two more stills, one operated by Joe Wrona and the other by Joe Kotecki. These were relatively small operations. (29) On Feb. 26, a raid at the Kandis grocery store at 1403 Fifth Street in LaSalle produced a small quantity of moonshine.(29)

Raids in Bureau County were more successful. Steve Pletkovich, referred to as the "King of the Bootleggers" was caught red-handed in Neponset making a delivery of ten gallons of moonshine. (30) Sheriff Applen also made a series of raids at the end of February. He found 12 kegs of beer and over 12 barrels of wine at Grossman's saloon. The biggest liquor dealer in the state, who made regular trips to Canada, allegedly supplied this bar. Cars with heavy-duty springs were used to deliver the heavy loads of beer back to Spring Valley. Grossman had a very interesting way of rationing his supplies. Different towns in the area had their special night to come down to the tavern. On the night of the raid, it happened to be "Wyanet Night."

Two other places were raided. At the Mayszak establishment, the sheriff found 180 pints of beer and found another 150 gallons ready to be bottled. Caveletto's saloon was loaded with 600 bottles of beer and ten gallons of whiskey and another ten gallons of wine. The speakeasies' requirement of a password and a key were well known to the sheriff who had no trouble making an entrance and arresting the lawbreakers. (31)

On Mar. 4, the sponge squad raided a speakeasy at 2nd and Spaulding in Spring Valley. As the raiders smashed in the locked doors, Matt Terasevich, the owner, proceeded to smash all of the beer and wine on the premises. However, enough evidence was sponged up to make an arrest.(32) Terasevich, who had been fined $300 in a federal court before on prohibition violations, was fined $600 for his current violation.

The cases before Judge Prichard seemed endless. On Mar. 5, the judge sentenced Guillio Morandi (Dalzell), C. Rainieri (Dalzell), Pete Actis (Spring Valley), Kit Ari (Bradford), George Meyer (Bureau Junction), and Hugh Rhyne (Tiskilwa). Penalties ranged from several hundred dollars to several months of incarceration on the Vandalia penal farm. Addressing the defendants, Prichard said that bootleggers would be driven from Bureau County. (33)

The LaSalle County sheriff was equally busy with raids in Streator at 717 E. Main, 202 N. Sterling and 1212 Plumb.(34) While these investigations discovered stills and moonshine, subsequent raids over the weekend were not as productive. In Oglesby, Clark went to Garzanelli's (750 Columbia) and Lorenzetti's (443 E. Walnut) and couldn't find any illegal beverages. But at Baima's (449 E. Walnut), the deputies did find a gallon of moonshine and a pint of wine. (35)

Undercover investigations set the stage for a federal raid in Ottawa on Mar. 9. The 40 agents came into town on a bus; then they fanned out and hit nine business establishments including a roadhouse in Naplate operated by Angelo DeVinti. Altogether 11 owners, bartenders, and patrons were picked up. Two taxi drivers were also arrested as they delivered alcohol to the speakeasies owned by William Ferguson and F.J. Krammer. Forced entries were required to gain access to the speakeasy operated by Jerry O'Conner place, which was located at the rear of the Moloney Building and the John Kenny place at 513 LaSalle St. One officer broke his revolver handle as he pounded it on the heavy glass in one door. Other officers suffered minor cuts from the broken glass as they forced their way into the bars. Three revolvers were seized at the

Naplate roadhouse. The agents were the same ones who took down the Peru distillery.(36) Ed McCormick, the bartender at Ferguson's was arrested again only two days later when federal agents walked into his soft drink parlor at 209 ½ W. Madison and found a glass of whiskey on the bar. McCormick claimed that he had just slept in the bar overnight because he had nowhere else to go. He said he had no idea that there was alcohol in the glass that was seized. Commenting on the raid, the chief investigator said, "We have just started with our clean-up of LaSalle County. We have obtained evidence against numerous places in Ottawa in addition to those raided on Saturday night. The alleged violators will receive official attention in due course of time." (37)

The biggest problem facing federal investigators, according to LaRue, were the tip-offs by members of the Bootleggers' Protective Association. He cited the examples of the Fox River Hotel on Route 7 and a building at 130 Marquette Street in Ottawa where they came out "clean as a whistle." A million dollars was amassed by the bootleggers syndicate to pay "hush money" to local officials. The federal investigator claimed that Al Capone's men were part of the organization that had its headquarters in Ottawa. He went on to say that he had tangible proof. "The protective association was the backbone of the LaSalle County booze syndicate."(38)

The Dowd raiders still made some progress. In mid-March, 28 individuals were arrested in LaSalle, Peru, and Oglesby. At the "Bridge Inn" at the south end of the Shippingsport Bridge, agents tried to arrest Louis Michelini who had escaped their search on Mar. 14. Working on a tip where he was hiding, they proceeded to see Mrs. Mattie Rinaudo, his mother-in-law, at 1202 First Street. But Michelini ducked out only minutes before the agents arrived. M. Bontani from Standard and August Querciagrossa of Granville were also implicated as owners of buildings where liquor was served. The plan was to padlock every establishment. Others taken into custody in LaSalle were John Thompson, a bartender at the John Essl saloon (Third and Bucklin); Angelo Monari (842 First St.); Steve Mueller (2301 First St.); Ed Waszkowiak (959 Ninth St.); Marion Sment (1000 Crosat St.); Frank Studzinski (1001 Eighth); and Fabian Ciganovich (1101 First St.). Mrs. Tomasino Bernardi and her son, Louis, were also arrested.(39)

The situation in LaSalle and Putnam Counties was so bad that the federal prohibition authorities decided to set up a permanent office. One agent said, "We had no idea of the true situation in this section until we actually got on the ground and began our investigation. The conditions here are startling and rival any yet revealed anywhere. It will take many months of tedious, hard work. We are going to the very bottom to clean this section." (40)

There was no difficulty in finding any number of places selling liquor. Usually, tips came from irate neighbors who were fed up with the boozers. Acting on a local complaint on Mar. 25, the "tea room" operated by Harry Shortland west of Cedar Point was investigated. Two men jumped from a second story window to avoid arrest. The owner was arrested, however, after a gallon of moonshine was found in a secret compartment on the second floor. (41)

The Retzel grocery store on First Street in LaSalle was a constant source of interest to law enforcement officers. In April 1929, federal agents inspected eight barrels of vinegar found in the cellar of the store. Retzel argued with the inspectors that he was simply making vinegar out of the apples and grapes he sold in his store. Unfortunately for the grocer, the chemical report showed an alcohol content in seven of the eight barrels was above the legal limit. So 300 gallons of the product was declared to be "wine." Retzel was charged accordingly. (42)

It was obvious that the paltry fines and short imprisonment terms were insufficient to dissuade bootleggers from their craft. Congress decided to up the ante by passing the Jones Act. Each infraction of the prohibition law could now result in a maximum penalty of five years imprisonment and a $10,000 fine for each offense. The first "customers" to fall under the provisions of the act locally were Frank Retzel and Frank Steinz, who operated a soft drink parlor on Pine Street in Peru. Dowd's men had found beer, moonshine, and wine in the bar. Samples of each liquid were retained as evidence; the rest was poured down the sewer. References to the "five and ten" law were being muttered across the Tri-County region. (43)

Apparently, bar owners in Bureau County had not been shaken by the news of the new law. "Rip" Riva and Ben Ballerine, owners of "Smoke Shop," and Fred DeFillipi were hauled off to Princeton by Sheriff Applen on Mar. 31. A search of the two Spring Valley saloons produced 19 barrels of beer and a quantity of moonshine. (44)

At 2102 Fourth, Peru, Chief Potthoff's men arrested Frank Krultz, the owner, and the bartender Ralph Woods for selling wine and whiskey. Otto Link, a customer, explained that he had only come into the establishment a few minutes before the raid. He claimed, "All I ever bought or all that I ever saw any one else buy there was soda and near beer." Since the officers did not have sufficient evidence, they released Link. (45)

Although the quantity of whiskey, beer, and wine being taken out of circulation by these raids at neighborhood bars was relatively insignificant, local authorities continued to pursue such investigations. On May 15, the LaSalle *Daily Post* announced that 50 more individuals had been charged with liquor violations, and federal marshals were on the way from Chicago to serve the papers. Prominent among those charged was Alex Galassi who had owned the saloon at 112 E. Fifth in Peru but rented it out to John Piecha. Joe Hybki, who owned a place at 517 E. Fifth, was charged along with his bartender. However, these charges were later dismissed due to insufficient evidence. (46)

One of the more significant arrests made by Dowd's federal agents was at the home of former Peru Alderman Teofil Twardowski. He was caught red-handed operating a 25-gallon still. In the basement, Dowd found four 50-gallon barrels of mash and five gallons of moonshine. Twardowski readily admitted his guilt as he came running out of the house when Dowd arrived.   The father of seven children claimed that he had to do it to help pay off the mortgage. Dowd claimed that this arrest would cut off a major source of moonshine in the east end of Peru. The former alderman was sentenced to 90 days in the Kane County jail in July. (47) Another well-known individual to get caught up in the liquor business was the former LaSalle Police Chief, Frank McInerny. He ended up in the Grundy County jail in Morris with a sentence of 90 days. (48)

Another raid by Dowd near the I-M Canal on River Street netted 47 cases of beer and 95 gallons of beer ready to be bottled. The shack they found was a miniature brewery stacked with large 20 and 15-gallon crocks filled with fermenting beer. (49)

Ethnic neighborhoods were a distinct characteristic of LaSalle. The homes along west Third Street tended to be occupied by Italians. Authorities had for some time suspected a distillery in the neighborhood but could not pinpoint the location. LaSalle police finally decided to search the saloon at 33 Third Street near the Chicago and Illinois Valley Railway car barns. A resident alien, Sam Scuito, owned the business. Federal Investigator Dowd and LaSalle Police Chief Pete Walloch headed up a three-car task force that surrounded the entire neighborhood. Somewhat apprehensive, the officers approached with guns drawn, as they searched through the apartments and the buildings at 33 and 27 Third Street. A large crowd began to gather in front of the bar as the investigation proceeded.

They did not find anything in the Scuito saloon, but in the building behind the bar, they did confiscate a large quantity of moonshine and two condensers hidden behind a pile of coke. Bootleggers frequently used coke because it gave off sufficient heat for boilers but little telltale smoke to tip off the authorities of the illegal operation. A hallway in the cellar of one building led to the saloon. However, there was no indication that the condensers had been in use for some time, and no other apparatus could be found. Besides sending Scuito to jail for having the liquor, Dowd also threatened him with deportation to Italy as an undesirable resident. Scuito had never applied for citizenship. (50)

Seldom did law officers find much more than a few cases of beer or barrels of wine. Tavern owners were very careful about not having much stock on hand in case of a raid. Sometimes a private still was discovered as in the case of Mike Polanski (523 E. Ninth, Peru), but these were small operations. In a LaSalle city council meeting, Commissioner George J. Dorman pointed out that "Four-fifths of the soft drink parlors have gone out of business." The city was getting more applications for ice cream parlors than soft drink parlors. (51)

Were the raids scaring bootleggers out of the business? Not really. While a few may have turned to other occupations, there were still plenty of soft drink parlors converted to speakeasies with more than near beer and grape juice to quench their customers' thirst. In late July, there were a series of arrests in Dalzell and Cherry. Sheriff Applen learned from his past mistakes that raids had to be conducted with the utmost secrecy to catch wary bootleggers. He organized his men into two raiding parties. A six-car detachment entered from the west and a two-car unit came from the east. There would be no time to sound the alarm. Both teams hit precisely at 8:15 p.m. The 26 officers entered the Dalzell pool hall, the residences of Julio Morandi and Louis Costelli and the soft drink parlors operated by Alfredo Bernardi, Julio Morandi, Angelo Balestri, Albert Tonielli, and L. De Gaglia. Other raids were conducted shortly after this in Cherry, Ladd and Arlington. The precision operation netted approximately 600 gallons of wine, 75 gallons of beer and a like amount of moonshine. Most of the contraband was found at the Morandi and Costelli saloons. The only places where no contraband could be found was the pool hall in Dalzell and the Columbia Hotel in Ladd.

Hundreds of visitors from LaSalle-Peru-Oglesby had journeyed to the remote village hoping to relieve their thirst and avoid the law, which had shuttered many of the drinking establishments in their towns. After the excitement died down, they left the Dalzell oasis, which they now described as "dry as the desert." (52)

The LaSalle police also made a major breakthrough two weeks later on the river front. An investigation led Chief Walloch and his men to the Frank Wirtz home at 358 River Street near the gas plant of Illinois Power. It took two hours for the officers to pull out 20 barrels of whiskey holding 800 gallons. A Tri-City Transfer truck had to be called in to haul away the moonshine. Wirtz, who was not home, was picked up later and fined $200. The brew was kept in the LaSalle municipal building while Walloch waited for a court order to destroy the evidence. (53)

The war on liquor sales in other towns in LaSalle County was not neglected. In November, Clark raided three locations in Streator.

Placed under arrest were Jerry Hogan, Mike Cannalle and Joe Galbot. Collectively, the raids yielded 30 cases of beer. The three men were accused of selling liquor to the husband of Mary Witko. This had caused family problems. So Mrs. Witko tipped off the police. (54)

There were endless reasons why people got into the liquor business, and the court knew them all. Earlville's notorious and wealthiest bootlegger, Will Hough, got himself into trouble with the sheriff's department once again when he smashed into another car. The 60 year-old Hough was traveling with his lights out on ice-covered Route 2 when he collided with another car causing both vehicles to careen into a ditch. Mendota police were first on the scene and found pieces of crockery scattered across the highway and moonshine dripping from the car. Seven gallons of liquor were found in the tonneau of the wrecked car. This was the third time that the wealthy landowner had been arrested for prohibition violations. (55)

While Hough engaged in bootlegging strictly for the thrill of it, another bootlegger, George Crank, did it to pay his bills. Standing before Judge Harry Reck on the charge of selling liquor, the Grand Ridge man pleaded, "I wasn't in this for a big profit. I was just trying to make a living." Crank tried to pay the rent and buy groceries by repairing cars but couldn't make it and turned to bootlegging as a last resort. The poverty plea may have influenced Judge Reck since he offered to put the man on probation if he could find five witnesses who would promise to turn Crank from a life of crime. (56)

Most people didn't peddle booze for the thrill like Hough but rather for the profit. In nearby LaMoille, another car accident resulted in the loss of a large quantity of Christmas "cheer." On Dec. 17, V.A. Howard, who was somewhat intoxicated, smashed his Chevy truck. While the Bureau County deputies were investigating the accident, they noticed something dripping from the truck. The liquid had a distinct odor, but it certainly wasn't that of gasoline or oil. Under the seat, they found 150 quarts of whiskey. Fifty of the

1929 Chevy Truck

quarts were genuine Scotch. Four of the bottles cracked when the car went out of control and crashed. It was surmised that because of the high quality of the cargo that it would be donated to the Princeton hospital rather than simply dumped as the homemade variety was usually handled. (57)

Chapter 14
1930
The Stills Were Everywhere

On Jan. 16, 1930, the government, if not the entire country, observed the tenth anniversary of the war on booze. President Wilson had been against the Volstead Act from the very beginning. Harding said it would be an issue for 30 years. Hoover simply called it a "Noble Experiment." The "drys" claimed that banning alcohol had worked, and the "wets" claimed that the law couldn't be enforced. Both sides were correct to a certain degree. It was expensive trying to keep a lid on alcohol. The country had spent over $264 million during the decade trying to enforce a law that was not very popular with the majority of the population. The enforcement war began with 2,000 government employees at the federal level. Ten years later, that number had risen to 4,664. Besides the monetary issue, there were other costs. The gang wars would forever brand the decade. Hundreds of people had been killed including 182 citizens and 68 government agents. (1)

Change was in the air especially in Washington. The nation's lawmakers began to evaluate the effectiveness and the popularity of strict enforcement of the Volstead Act. There was a growing realization that the government coffers at state and federal levels had suffered serious losses in terms of excise tax revenues. From this point on, there would be a serious debate developing over the possibility of revising or repealing the 18th Amendment. It was a hot political issue because certain areas of the country strongly believed in the need for prohibition while other regions wanted a change in policy.

The new year didn't immediately bring a change in terms of effectiveness of law enforcement nor the ingenious methods used by bootleggers to manufacture their products without detection. At the end of January, county and federal authorities had discovered three major distilleries. The first find in LaSalle was said to be one of the biggest illegal distilleries in the area, second only to the huge Water Street operation discovered in 1929. The LaSalle location at 230 Creve Couer was a humble four-room frame house with no indication of the activity within. When Sheriff Clark and his deputies arrived, they found no one was at home. It didn't take long to find the cooker, which could produce 200 gallons per day, and the 21,000 gallons of sugar mash fermenting in three huge concrete vats. They were large tanks measuring approximately 19' x 6' x 6'. Each vat had a capacity of 7,000 gallons of mash.

Surprisingly, there was only a small quantity of finished alcohol - about ten gallons. It was as if the still was just being set up for production. The all-copper cooler was located at the head of the stairway leading from the basement to the first floor. There was additional incriminating evidence in a shed behind the house including five gallon tin containers marked "Italian and American Wholesale Importing Co." Empty 50-pound sugar sacks and yeast boxes from Standard Brands of Joliet were also scattered around the shed.

It wasn't bad enough that the culprits were making illegal liquor, but they were also stealing from the city. Instead of paying for the water and gas, they diverted the utilities before the lines reached the meters. The vats alone required 23,000 cubic feet of water every time they were filled. It would take several hours to drain the huge tanks. The rest of the apparatus was disassembled and moved to the basement of the jail in Ottawa. (2)

Ad from May 2, 1930 edition of the LaSalle *Daily Post* extolling the uses of malt extract for food and candies. It also was used in brewing beer but that use was never suggested. Reflecting the typical German stereotype, the caption reads, "Look! Dot's Vat I Vant!"

Records showed that Mike Maura was the owner of the property. Although the lights were still burning when the authorities arrived, Maura was nowhere to be found. The man was definitely involved because invoices for the various supplies were found with his name on them. State's Attorney Hanson finally learned that Maura had gone to Rockford to be with his ailing wife. Finally on February 7, Maura turned himself in to the sheriff. Within the hour, he was arraigned before Judge Reck; confessed his guilt; and was sentenced to one year at the Vandalia penal farm. Maura was in total shock. He thought the judge would simply give him a fine or short jail sentence. The connection with the Rockford mob became stronger with every case. (3)

A second big distillery was found on the south side of Mark in a frame house west of the coal mine dump on Jan. 29. Two round, wooden vats on the first floor and three rectangular, concrete tanks in the basement were used to process 50,000 gallons of sugar mash. About 200 gallons of alcohol were found. Both the mash and the alcohol were dumped into the snow before the federal agents left. Edwin Eckerd of Mark, who was a young boy at the time, recently recalled how the agents took an ax to the vat, and the mash shot out like a "small fountain." The copper cookers and coolers were loaded into trucks and sent to Peoria. Certain similarities in the two distilleries convinced authorities that there was a tie to criminal elements in Rockford. (4)

Two men were arrested. Victor Bartolini, the cooker, was well known in Granville and Mark, and Joe Pinella was from Rockford. Bartolini was in charge of the distillery that was capable of turning out 500 gallons of alcohol every day. The men were turned over to Putnam County authorities, but Sheriff Turnbull was out of town during the raid. They spent the night in the Hennepin jail (right) before being transferred to Peoria. (5)

On Saturday, February 1, the Bureau County sheriff seized yet another distillery. This one, valued at $15,000 and large enough to make 250 gallons in a single batch, was located in a barn north of Seatonville. The sheriff had easy access; the large doors were unlocked. Four vats were found holding 40,000 gallons of mash. Whoever was running the operation apparently escaped just before the authorities arrived. They left 500 gallons of finished alcohol behind. The similarities in the distillery chain discovered in LaSalle, Bureau, and Putnam Counties only heightened speculation of a Rockford mob connection. (6)

Beginning in the summer of 1929, there had been a major structure under construction on the Joseph Engelhaupt farm. The new 60' x 40' barn constructed from heavy timbers and corrugated iron siding was finished with a concrete floor by Thanksgiving. In late April 1930, a federal agent and his wife were out for a drive along the Putnam County bottom road east of Route 89 when the odor of mash was detected. A follow-up investigation pinpointed the distinct smell coming from the Engelhaupt property. Deputy Administrator James Eaton from Springfield led a raid on the Engelhaupt property on April 30.

Inside the barn, they found the most modern, scientific brewery imaginable. This was no slipshod operation. Everything was "spic and span" according to the raiders. Eleven Cypress vats with a 51,000 gallon capacity for the mash lined the walls. Six of the vats were filled using water from a stream piped in from a natural spring in the side of the hill. The empty vats were soaked with water to swell the wood in preparation for the mash. Another pipe buried under rocks was used to drain the refuse water into a creek on the Engelhaupt property. From there, it flowed across the bottomland fields farmed by Engelhaupt. A 75-hp boiler, which extended almost 40' to the roof, sat in the center of the building. A ladder next to the vats was used to reach the copper cooling and condensing sections. The heat from the cooking mash was recycled to save money. The operators even installed cardboard sheets on the walls in an attempt to prevent the odor of the mash from seeping out. Obviously, that innovation had not been effective. Eaton said, "It far dwarfs the distillery taken in Peru last year. It is an exact replica of the old distilleries operated legitimately in the days before prohibition." According to the *Putnam County Record*, the plant was valued at $100,000, twice the value of the distillery equipment, which was found on the Flaherty farm in Bureau County in a raid the next day. (7)

Those arrested in connection with the raid at Engelhaupt's included Fred Gualandri, Cosmo Angilery, Tony Bartelino, and George Smith. The authorities believed that all of the men were Sicilians connected with the Rockford syndicate. Gualandri and Angilery were nabbed inside the building. The other men fled in a Ford truck loaded with three barrels of molasses and several gallon-tins of alcohol. They were caught after a chase of about a mile. Engelhaupt was not immediately charged because he claimed, "I rented the place to a Chicago man named John Miller on last April 15. He told me he was going to use it to store big trucks." (8) *[Note: His grandson, Joe Engelhaupt, who still farms the land today, said that all of the farmers along the bottom road had some kind of still in operation. But he staunchly defended his grandfather's motives citing how poor the man was stating that his only motivation was the paltry rent that the Sicilians paid. Perhaps for this reason, the judge only fined the elder Engelhaupt according to his grandson.]*

Ironically, Assistant District Attorney Victor LaRue and Special Investigator Victor Dowd had been duck hunting for several days on the Engelhaupt property in 1929. Dowd had made a fruitless inspection of the farmer's hen house in the summer. In neither instance was there any suspicion raised about illegal activities. The inspectors surmised that the brewery could have only been in operation for a week or more before the raid was made. (9)

Another major blow to the syndicate was dealt the following afternoon, May 1, 1930, when federal agents swooped down on the farm of Elmer Flaherty located one mile south of Ladd. Although it was a smaller operation having a mash capacity of 25,000 gallons and a daily output of 150 gallons per day, it had been operating for six months. The distillery itself consisted of three concrete vats measuring 6' wide by 16' long and 10' deep and three 10'- diameter Cypress vats 12' deep. Besides the arrest of Flaherty, two others, Joe Viglia and Jon Greno, who were believed to be members of the Sicilian syndicate, were also taken into custody. As in the Engelhaupt raid, Flaherty denied knowledge of what was going on in the large storage shed where the still, hundreds of bags of sugar and boxes of yeast were found. Flaherty said that he had sold the building to Chicagoans in October 1929, but he could not identify the men. Flaherty also rented land to William Maurer. Unnamed relatives and friends of Flaherty told the LaSalle reporter, "The building was sold to the men whom we do not know, along with a strip of land which took in the well. We never saw anything going on about the premises that would indicate that the prohibition law was being violated." (10)

Facing both Engelhaupt and Flaherty was the possibility of losing their farms. Engelhaupt owned 520 acres of Putnam County bottomlands and Flaherty was the owner of 208 acres along Plank Road. The U.S. Supreme Court had upheld such seizures of land in similar cases in Iowa. The federal charge against the two farmers was legally termed a misprison of a felony or in layman's language - allowing a felony to be committed without reporting it to authorities. A second count specified that all of the accused attempted to defraud the government out of the $1.10 per gallon in federal revenue tax. (11)

Then on Tuesday, May 6, the LaSalle sheriff took down a third major distillery. This one was located in East Wenona and had a capacity of 30,000 gallons. Two Springfield men, Antonio Senese and Andrew Litone, were found to be operating the still. It looked like another connection to the Chicago-Rockford syndicate. The operators had used the entire basement of a Wenona house to construct three 10,000-gallon vats

1930 Buick Sedan

that were filled with mash when the sheriff's men raided. The officers also seized a brand new Buick sedan that was hidden a block away near the Wenona coal mine. The men admitted that it was theirs, but refused to incriminate themselves any further. (12)

On May 10, Sheriff Clark found another major distillery in Streator. The still was found purely by chance because of the strong odor of fermenting mash emanating from a house on South Otter Street. When the sheriff entered the home, he caught Jack Tornabene filling a 5-gallon can with alcohol. His 20-year old son, Louis, was helping the 45-year-old Italian in the 30,000-gallon distillery. The two men confessed that they had been operating in Streator for some time but the real owner was a mysterious Fred King from Chicago. The two were hustled off to the Ottawa jail. In June, they were sentenced to 90 days in jail and fined $300. (13)

The sheriffs in LaSalle and Bureau Counties kept the pressure on the local speakeasies, restaurants, rooming houses and soft drink parlors. On May 17, Applen hit several Spring Valley locations including the "Smoke House," "Frenchies Place," "The Sandwich Shop," and the "Spaghetti Inn." In Ladd an inspection of the Columbia Hotel found no liquor but a slot machine. A trip to "Balestri's Place" in Dalzell netted both moonshine and beer. (14) A series of Streator raids at 111, 410, 502, 515, 715, 717, and 719 East Main Street as well as the Columbia Hotel and the saloons at 1113 Bloomington and 115 Vermillion brought the total count to 63 arrests in LaSalle County in May. The barroom raids only produced small quantities of beer, wine and moonshine, but it kept owners wary of the possibility of future raids. (15)

The discovery of major distilleries was causing serious shortages for local speakeasies. Small operations were discovered on May 28 in LaSalle at 1934 Crosat and 1373 Crosat. The first location was a still run by Adolph Karlosky. At the second stop, Deputies Orr, Cooper, and Kemery found George Mason with a small brewery and about 40 cases of beer. (16) In June, the Streator police led by Chief Mottershaw searched the abandoned Johnson Storage warehouse on East Main Street. The property owner, Ralph Johnson, claimed that the building had been rented out to an unknown individual who was responsible for the 1,500-gallon still and 5,000 pounds of corn sugar found on the premises. (17) However, Johnson was later implicated on June 25 when Battista Benning said that he was making alcohol for Johnson. (18)

On June 21, two more Streatorites, Tony Carbone and Charley Conti, were fined $1000 each for maintaining stills that handled almost 40,000 gallons of mash. The sheriff found them with 190 gallons of finished product. Charles Carbone, also of Streator, remained behind bars when he could not raise the $4000 bond set by Judge Reck for having one of the largest stills in the county. (19)

It was no wonder that so many speakeasies could still be selling liquor in spite of the many seizures of both small and large distillery operations. It seemed as though everyone had a still. On June 24, three more major stills were discovered and destroyed by Clark and his deputies. Charles Panno was found processing 30,000 gallons of mash at 215 Water Street in Streator. Then they went to 212 West Broadway and arrested Batista Brenning seizing his 250-gallon still. To complete the day, the sheriff's men only had to go next door to the home of Charles Ragusa where the found another 20,000 gallons of mash. The temperatures were so high in the crowded basements that the men could only work a few minutes at a time in breaking down the vats otherwise they would quickly be overcome by the intense heat of the boilers. The haul for the day was the confiscation of 141 gallons of alcohol; the dumping of 70,000 gallons of mash; and three more stills put out of action. It was an all-time record for a single day for the sheriff's department. (20) However, the outside influence was growing so quickly that neither the Streator police nor the sheriff's department had the manpower to close down the burgeoning number of stills that surfaced in such a short time. State's Attorney Hanson promised to send in additional men from his office to stem the tide. (21)

The raid, two days later at the William Miller home at 910 E. Eighth in LaSalle, was almost anti-climactic. Deputy Chief Charles Jones led the team as they proceeded to destroy two stills, 15 barrels of mash and 20 cases of beer. Clad in overalls and hip boots the men broke through a padlocked door in the basement and found another storeroom where four 5-gallon jugs of moonshine were hidden. (22)

The problem of small, home-based stills was becoming epidemic. In July, two more stills were found at the home of Sam Swartz who lived on Florence Avenue in Oglesby. (23)

In Putnam County, Sheriff John Turnbull swung into action with his deputies and investigated 15 locations in Mark on July 23. However, they could only find violations in four of the places. The following day, Rogio Piccoli and Vincent Donini pleaded guilty to possession of home brew. Guedi Bellesi admitted that he had a large quantity of wine and paid the $100 fine and costs. Although the DeFilippi residence was unoccupied at the time of the raid, the sheriff's men did find 35 gallons of alcohol in the basement. Mrs. Louis DeFilippi was arrested when she entered the house the next day. When she appeared before Justice of the Peace Earl Buhn on Friday, she was fined $100. (24)

Sometimes the bootleggers let their manufacturing process get out of hand. Such was the case on Aug. 23. On Friday morning, a deafening explosion ripped through the home of Joe Corso in Ladd. Sheriff Applen guessed that an illegal still had overheated. Returning to the scene of the demolished home, the sheriff attempted to find any evidence, but he learned that the still had already been taken to Buckman's scrap yard. (25)

Another ominous indication of the lengths to which people would go to be part of the bootlegging business was discovered in a note dropped over a farm near Sandy Ford, west of Streator, from a low flying airplane. The gist of the message was that the farmer should not make any revelations to the police about flights near the area. For some time, there had been rumors that cars would line up and turn on their headlights to illuminate a landing field to pick up cargoes of alcohol. The son of Pete Kallem had even been threatened at gunpoint when a plane landed on their farm near Newark. Clark thought that the planes might be taking the airborne freight back to Rockford. (26)

It was thought that with the exception of the few individuals arrested in July by the Putnam County sheriff and the closure of the big stills found earlier, nothing more would be developing for some time in the small county. Nothing could be further from the truth. On Friday Sept. 19, the *Daily Post* ran a banner headline, "Capone Booze Plant Seized at Mark."

Once again Deputy Administrator Jim Eaton sprang a trap. Waiting in three cars, the federal agents went into action at 1:30 a.m. at two Mark locations. The Cooperative Store on Hennepin Street and a residence located three lots west of the jail were targets. At both locations, they found men working at huge vats. A short time later, two more men drove up in a Ford truck with a Cedar Point license tag. It was loaded with 35 bags labeled "Corn Sugar Refining Co."

Then two more men arrived in a Chrysler sedan, which was registered in Rockford, apparently arriving to haul away a load of

1931 Chrysler

alcohol. Those arrested and taken to Peoria as listed in the LaSalle *Daily Post* included August Guisti, Ray Paganelli, Joe Tulini, Steve Faletti, and Joe Paganelli from Mark. Three others were from Rockford. A total of 700 gallons of alcohol were found along with bottles and labels for some of the old time popular whiskeys. Much of the alcohol was in plain sight on store shelves disguised in one-gallon cans, which were labeled Mazola cooking oil.

The next day, a large crowd gathered to watch the federal officers swing axes into the copper coils and condensers, and boilers. Children heading to the Mark elementary school watched in amazement as the alcohol was brought out to the curb and emptied into the gutter where it flowed eastward into the creek. When Mario Bazzani, the owner of the store and former mayor of Mark, came on the scene, he denied any knowledge of the distillery operation in the rear of the store.

Eaton said that with the seizure of the two Mark plants he "had curbed to a considerable extent the supply of booze within the Capone syndicate." He explained that "Scarface" Al had been pouring in liquor to Rockford, Chicago, Moline and other large cities in northern Illinois. The Mark alcohol was colored, bottled, and pre-dated labels were applied. The demand for the Mark product far outstripped the supply making it highly valued. The bottled products were picked up twice a day by trucks and distributed throughout northern Illinois. (27)

This building in Mark on Hennepin Street was once known as the Co-operative store and was the scene of a major raid by federal agents in September 1930.

Not every raid was aimed at finding a large-scale operation. A lifelong Mark resident, Corinne Eckerd, remembered when she was about nine years old, she was sleeping on the front porch of a girlfriend's house one hot summer night. Suddenly spotlights from the cars of federal prohibition agents illuminated a house on Bologna St. (Robert St. today) just north of the house where she was spending the night. The officers came up to them and told everyone to "stay put" and "not to come out of the house" while the raid was going on. Corinne ran home and found her mother and sisters were crying because their father, Guiseppi "Joe" Zagnoni, had grabbed a gun; went out the back door; and waited in the alley to see if he could help. Zagnoni helped his neighbor "just for the fun of it" in making moonshine. He took no money for himself.

Apparently, the neighbors were all asleep when the agents arrived in the early morning hours, but no one was arrested in this raid.

Rumors had been circulating for years that Al Capone and his men had frequently taken trips to the Illinois Valley. Unconfirmed reports had the gang enjoying musical performances in LaSalle County, dining in Bureau County, and going to the movies and duck hunting in Marshall County. The rumors were so persistent that Sheriff I.L. Davis of Marshall County was forced to investigate rumors of a fortress-like headquarters being established in a brick house near Lacon. The alleged reason for this move into the tranquil farming area was to establish a new base of operations in Lacon from which he could open additional speakeasies in Peoria. Davis said that he had visited the house in question and found no one around the residence. He asserted, "As far as I know, no gangsters have been establishing themselves in this territory. I have been checking this situation with aid from my deputies and we have found nothing that would cause alarm." (28)

This red-brick house, known as Wiffle Tree Place, is located near the junction of Illinois Rts. 17 and 29 in Sparland. It was owned by Mr. Jackson, a African-American who also operated two funeral parlors in Chicago and owned a stable of race horses in Indiana. From time to time, Al Capone and his men would leave the Lexington Hotel in Chicago and travel to this location for dinner and a relaxing day of duck hunting. They also would cross the Illinois River into Lacon to enjoy movies at the local theater.

The Capone involvement in the Illinois Valley was reinforced in December when indictments were announced in Peoria in the Engelhaupt (rural Putnam County) and Flaherty (Ladd) cases and the raid on Mark. One of the defendants from Rockford, Joe Plazalto, was linked to Frank Ingrassia, noted as the Rockford booze king. (29)

Eventually, indictments were handed down. Many of those charged listed their residences in Rockford. In the Flaherty case, two men from Ladd, Casmo Anfelari and Fred Gualandri, and one LaSalle man, Anthony Barceloni, were charged. Joe Cagaglia from Ladd and William Maurer from Spring Valley were indicted in the Engelhaupt distillery raid. The indictments issued in the Mark raids charged Steve Faletti, Joe Tulini, August Guisti, Joe Pagnelli, Ray Pagnelli (Mark residents) and Mario Bazanni (Granville). In May 1931, all of those implicated in the Mark raids pleaded guilty and received fines ranging from $300 to $1,000 and jail sentences of up to one year in Leavenworth. Although Victor LaRue planned to use a legal tool to confiscate the Flaherty and Engelhaupt farms from the men, he decided not to since it involved proving that those who held the mortgages were also involved in the distillery conspiracies. It was just too complicated to pursue the matter, and it was dropped. (30)

Prohibition enforcement was becoming more difficult as the mood of the country wavered towards a change in the law. Indeed, George Wickersham, Chairman of the Prohibition Law Enforcement Commision, had recommended to President Herbert Hoover in December 1930 that real beer (4%) and wine should be legalized. Illinois Valley brewers Andrew Hebel and Henry Hoerner were immediately sought out for their reactions to the news. The Peru Products owner stated, "We are all ready to start the manufacture of four percent beer upon short notice. It is great news and I am overjoyed." The plant was to be cleaned up over the next several weeks. As far as Star Union Products was concerned, Hoerner agreed that it would take a few weeks to make repairs to some of the equipment, but he too was enthusiastic in his reaction to the commissioner's recommendation. The two brewers had a huge territory to serve. The only other breweries were located in Peoria and Joliet. (31)

Chapter 15
1931
Agents Raid Town and Country Distilleries

The new decade opened with the same problems faced by prohibition officers as the year before, but there would also be some unusual discoveries. Cedar Point was targeted on Jan 7. A thousand gallons of mash was found in two houses, but the occupants had fled with the still cooking over an oil stove. (1)

Sheriff Welter's growing concern about a "Rockford connection" was reinforced with the seizure of two big distilleries on Jan. 15. Suspicion was first aroused during a raid on a LaSalle residence when Welter overheard Sam Saladino, a 15 year old Italian boy, who was on the phone, give a warning in Italian that the sheriff was in the house. After confiscating 50 gallons of whiskey and finding a large still hiding under some corn stalks in a shed, the sheriff questioned the boy and his mother. They said they were from Rockford. Welter also found some mail addressed to Raymond DeMar at 127 Second St., LaSalle, where he apparently picked up his mail. DeMar, who was from Rockford was arrested at 3 a.m. the next day and confessed to operating the LaSalle distilleries and selling the syndicate the alcohol for their Rockford speakeasies.

The bootlegger had been ingenious in hiding the equipment at 737 Hennepin St. The house had a large porch, and the dirt had been excavated under it to build a 15,000-gallon concrete mash vat. Two 500-gallon stills were found in the basement. On the first floor, 80 gallons of moonshine were being stored. (2)

Although it was always gratifying to catch a big "fish" in the river of alcohol that flowed though the Illinois Valley, the sheriff did not overlook the small time operators such as John Zupancic, operator of a small shoe repair shop at 1028 Third St. in LaSalle. He was found with 300 gallons of "green and aged" wine in his basement. Since there was no sewer in the basement, deputies were forced to carry the wine up to the first floor in small tubs. Two deputies dumped it on the floor while others used brooms to sweep it down the drain. The whole process took over an hour. Soon, the whole house and shop smelled with the distinct odor of fermenting wine. The shoemaker probably would have been ignored if only he hadn't been selling bottles of wine to his customers. (3)

Another small haul was made at Billy Baima's soft drink parlor in Ottawa at 326 Third St. It was a typical operation with a supply of moonshine, gin, and beer. (4)

In spite of this diligence, The National Wickersham Report branded the entire Illinois Valley with negative adjectives. "In LaSalle County there is widespread manufacturing of alcohol on farms and in surrounding coal mines. The state's attorney and sheriff are very lax. This (low-grade alcohol) is trucked into Winnebago County, where it is re-distilled into high-grade products. From there it finds its way into Wisconsin and Iowa." Putnam County was cited as "bad" with "much manufacturing by Rockford gangs." The state's attorney, Harry K. Ward, recently left the county for an unknown destination according to the government report, which concluded that "His work...was very lax," with regard to prohibition enforcement. Putnam County's newly elected State's Attorney, Lloyd Scriven, defended his predecessor saying that Ward had moved to his new home in Oak Park, IL. Scriven also justified Ward's early departure explaining that he "relinquished his office in a legal manner." Regarding Bureau County, the report concluded that the eastern half was bad, but the western half was "normal." "Spring Valley and Ladd communities had considerable liquor manufacturing and widespread bootlegging. Marshall County was described as "fairly normal." (5)

In spite of the report, Welter continued to conduct raids throughout the county. Two men were arrested at the Plumb Hotel pool room . Cliff McKee, a well-known druggist, and one of his clerks were picked up in Morris. (6) The following month the sheriff closed down the soft drink parlors in Streator at 811 Shabbona and 415 Illinois Street. (7)

In the spring of 1931, federal agents made several more raids on large-scale operations in rural areas of the Illinois Valley. Located a short distance from the Cedar Point school, the home of Roman Kotecki, was searched. The agents found a still and 21 gallons of whiskey ready for shipment in a pit under the garage and in an abandoned house adjacent to the property. Another 40 gallons of alcohol were being prepared. The authorities, who could not find the owner, believed that this was another distribution point for other local distilleries. (8) But these were minor successes compared to the discovery made by federal agents in the caves of the abandoned Blackball Mines at the end of May.

The spectacular find occurred on the same day near Happy Valley Farm four miles east of LaSalle. The distillery was found to be in an elaborate underground cavern known as the Blackball Mines, an abandoned limestone operation.

The equipment was very similar to that found on the Engelhaupt farm in Putnam County, but now, the distillers thought they had found a better way to conceal their activities. The federal agents proceeded to the site from Rt. 7 (*Later renumbered Rt. 6*) down a steep, but well-packed road to the cave entrance. The area looked much like the other limestone quarries along the Illinois River used by Utica cement companies. At the end of a 400' tunnel the bootleggers had installed a trap door with a lock. When the raiders broke in, they found a brightly illuminated cave extending for at least an acre.

Workers from Utica constructing the entrance to the Blackball limestone mines. Circa 1880's. Steve Shutt collection.

The 14 cypress vats, which held 70,000 gallons of corn sugar mash, were arranged around the boilers and stills. The agents could not even smell the fermenting mash until they entered the cave. The operators had a supply of 250 sacks of coke, a fuel they used because it produced very little telltale smoke. In order to vent the smoke from the cave, the operators drilled a 50' hole through the limestone. The smokestacks themselves only extended a few feet above the surrounding terrain. One of the stacks was covered by a corncrib. As the smoke rose, it was dissipated into an invisible vapor by the corn.

Authorities found this cave entrance that led to the still.

The moonshiners had plenty of supplies. Hundreds of sugar sacks, boxes of yeast, crates to hold the beer and alcohol, and hundreds of five-gallon tin cans to hold the alcohol were scattered about. It was a major production facility capable of turning out 300 gallons of beer and 1,500 gallons of alcohol daily.

It was estimated that it would have taken at least four men to run the distillery. Unfortunately, the agents could only find the sleeping tenant farmer, Earl Smith. He defended himself claiming that he had rented the cave to Angelo (a.k.a. Phillip) Conti from Aurora for $25 a month. One might ask why would anyone want to rent a cave. Conti had a perfectly logical explanation. He was going to grow mushrooms! When agents testified against Smith a few days later, they said that a water tank was filled by an artesian well and supplied the liquid needed for the distillery. There was no meter on the water line so there was no way of knowing that tens of thousands of gallons of water were being drawn for the mash vats. When queried about his high electric bill, Smith said that Conti was indeed using the same power line, but that the Aurora man always made up the difference from Smith's normal power bill so he never questioned why so much electricity was needed for the "mushroom farm." The agents speculated that horse-drawn wagons were used to haul the finished alcohol. They could have been driven through the large exposed mouth of the cave and 200' into the yawning cavern. The hard-packed road leading to the cave was additional evidence of the movement of the heavy loads to the highway. (9)

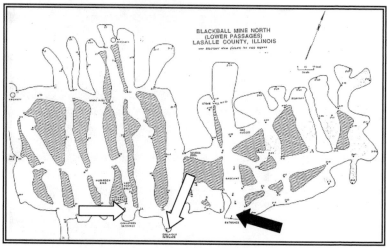

The complexity of the caves is indicated in the diagram above showing the passageways on the lower level. The upper level was even more complex. Source-Illinois Department of Conservation- Illinois Natural History Survey April 1, 1991. White arrows indicate collapsed entrances. Black arrow - main entrance. *Note: the cave is closed to the public due to the possible adverse affects on what has become a bat sanctuary.*

This rare, prohibition-era jug was recovered from the Blackball mine. The cork was still in the jug. This was not the typical container used by the bootleggers who poured the distilled alcohol into 5-gallon metal containers, thousands of which still litter the floor of the cave. Rather than waste ammunition to puncture the cans, the revenue agents used pick axes. Steve Shutt collection.

160

The next day, May 22, 1931, two more major distilleries were found. One was located four miles east of Seneca on a farm owned by William Hullerbach and Charles Donaldson. The other distillery was on the Ben Doll farm three miles north of LaSalle.

Dan Mahoney, who rented the property from Donaldson, tipped off Federal authorities to the Seneca operation. Mahoney, in turn, sublet the barn to "some fellows who wanted it for a hunting shack." He later recounted his involvement to an *Ottawa Herald* reporter. "Yesterday I walked over to the barn to make sure what was doing there because for the last two or three nights I had been watching it. I was met at the barn by a man who refused to let me enter the building, but I saw enough evidence that I went to Morris immediately to swear out a warrant." Once the warrant had been obtained, the Grundy County sheriff and his deputies proceeded to the farm where they found that federal authorities had already arrived and arrested one suspect, Phil Pecceuro, a Springfield man, who was tending the 300-gallon still. (10) He was out on bail for operating another still in Springfield, so he moved to set up a new operation in Seneca when it got too hot for bootlegging in central Illinois. The agents caught him red-handed filling five-gallon cans with alcohol. The nine 8'x10' concrete mash vats were camouflaged with bales of straw and located outside of the barn, which housed the 20-hp boiler and two condensers. He had only been operating for three days when the farm was raided.

The federal agents also caught three men at the Doll farm. One man acted as a lookout with a watchdog at the gate leading up to the barn. It was a similar operation to that found on the Donaldson property. The still was housed in a 75' x 100' low tar-papered structure. Inside were 14 cypress vats each holding 1,500 gallons of mash. There were also 65 hogsheads each of which held 450 gallons of mash. All told, about 30,000 gallons of corn sugar were in various stages of the fermentation process. A 35-hp boiler was used to heat the 500-gallon still. The operators, who authorities believed had been in business for more than a year, had 200 pounds of yeast for the fermentation vats and two tons of coke to heat the boilers. Water was pumped from a tributary of the Vermillion River known as "Shaw's Creek." In both cases the federal agents placed a value of equipment at the distillers at $25,000.

The federal agents arrested John Viola, Frank Rocchio, and Phil Scortino to the Ottawa jail. Two agents, who stayed behind, arrested a man from Kokomo, Indiana and one from Chicago as they drove up in their Buick to begin the night shift. Everyone denied any connection with the illicit operation.

Although it appeared that the Seneca distillery and the one on the Doll farm near LaSalle were part of a network run by the Rockford syndicate, the agents speculated that these were wildcat distilleries. They were operating independently of the other major operations found in the Valley in recent months. (11)

One did not have to search the countryside to find stills in the Valley. A few days after closing down the operations in rural LaSalle and Seneca, a brewery was found near Edwards and St. Vincent Streets in LaSalle. The operator, William Block, was thought to have been in business for about 18 months before being raided. Although his ale was not bottled, the raiders did find enough beer to fill ten barrels being chilled in a vat. The authorities had known ten days earlier that Block was in the beer-making business when they secretly broke into the long-abandoned building, which was allegedly owned by Block. The accused was the owner of the "Happy Corner" bar located in Peru at 4th and Schuyler. The Chicago agents waited until Block made his appearance before making an arrest.

The outward appearance of the brewery with its broken windows gave no hint as to the beer operation inside. The building also held empty vats, 13 half empty barrels, an old wine press, and a filtration system to clean the yeast and other foreign material from the beer as it flowed into the vats. The estimated value of the equipment was $2,500. (12)

The suspicion that Al Capone and his mob were connected to the Illinois Valley distilleries was foremost in the mind of federal authorities. They knew he controlled the syndicates with headquarters in Aurora and Waterloo, Iowa, but they could never find a direct link. When operators were picked up in the Valley, they consistently denied any connection with outside sources or conveniently had memory lapses as to whom they had rented their property.

The prevalent theory was that low-grade Valley alcohol was re-cooked into higher quality liquor that sold for $3-$4 a gallon. One of Capone's lieutenants, Mike Myers, confessed to a federal agent, "Except for one county, we've got the highways greased from Chicago west to the Mississippi River." The only area that the syndicate could not buy off was Lee County. Victor LaRue, the chief prohibition investigator for the Illinois Valley, had to admit, "LaSalle County has fallen off the wagon again." (13)

Although the syndicate continued to control the liquor business in northern Illinois, Capone himself was in trouble with the Internal Revenue Service. In June 1931, the federal government charged the Chicago mobster with 22 violations of the tax law. Anxious to stay out of jail until his trial, Capone posted $50,000 in bonds. His army of lawyers would soon have to prove that their famous client had not defrauded the government out of $215,080 as the IRS claimed. On June 16, Dwight Green, the Assistant District Attorney in Chicago, confronted Capone in federal court. "Did you violate the United States income tax laws in 1924?" To which the underworld chieftain replied, "Yes, I'm guilty." "Scarface" Al was now facing a possible 34 years in the penitentiary and a huge monetary fine. (14)

The indictment of the Chicago crime boss also had implications for the Illinois Valley. The government had also indicted more than 60 other members of the Chicago syndicate. Although authorities were able to round up about half of that number immediately, the others escaped the dragnet. Readers of the LaSalle *Daily Post* may have been shocked to read the headlines on June 19, 1931, "Hunt Capone Fugitives in LaSalle." An intense search was conducted in LaSalle, Peru, Ottawa, and Streator to apprehend the fleeing felons. According to one agent, "We are not here for any other purpose but to get these men and return them to Chicago to face the charges now against them." (15)

While the outcome of the Capone investigation captivated many, another aspect of the war on prohibition drew the attention of thousands of residents who lived near the I-M Canal. Rum runners operating on the Great Lakes apparently had been sufficiently checked by the vigilant U.S. Coast Guard. The government decided to move ten of their 36'-boats from Buffalo, New York to Lake Michigan and down the Illinois-Michigan Canal and the Illinois River to Peoria and Grafton. From there, the "fleet" was to head to New Orleans to patrol the Gulf of Mexico where rum running had become a more serious problem.

It was necessary to overcome a series of obstacles as the boats were moved through the 50-mile waterway. There was low water at Channahon causing the first delay for the small fleet commanded by Captain J.O. Anderson. Portions of the aqueduct at Seneca were damaged due to a June storm so that had to be repaired quickly. The boats could travel at 24 knots in open water, but it was slow going though the canal, and they never exceeded 12 knots in the waterway. Halfway to Morris, the line of gray- hulled wooden boats was halted as their keels began scraping the bottom of the canal. The 30 sailors who manned the boats tied up their craft at Aux Sable while additional water filled the canal.

On July 18, the lead boat ran into a sand bar three miles east of Utica. So the rum fleet tied up for the night at Lock 12 about four miles west of Ottawa. Another short delay was encountered when one of the boats got stuck in the mud because of low water east of the Rock Island viaduct. Some of the sailors put on bathing suits and jumped into the muddy water to help free their boat.

Arrangements had been made to have the boats sound their klaxons when they approached LaSalle. Mayor H.M. Orr said that the city would welcome the fleet with three blasts from the city's fire siren. The mayor also encouraged residents to fly the American flag from their homes and stores. It was a colorful sight as the "fleet" finally arrived in the evening with their green running lights illuminated. A tent was erected on the canal bank for the captain and any sailors who didn't want to sleep in the crew's cramped quarters. (16)

Rum fleet tied up at Morris to take on fresh water. Reprinted from *Morris Daily Herald.* July 17, 1931.

By morning, thousands of people had driven to LaSalle and lined the banks to catch a glimpse of the tiny fleet. Every vantage point was crowded along the Burlington and Rock Island tracks, on the banks of the I-M canal and along Canal and First Streets.

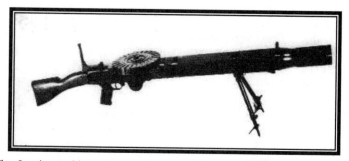

The Lewis machine guns were stowed below deck. When intercepting rum runners, the guns were mounted on the main deck. The crew also carried rifles and pistols. The Lewis machine gun was named for its American developer, Col. Lewis. It was used extensively in WWI, often mounted on biplanes. Its drum magazine held 47 rounds of .30 cal. ammunition. It was also used by the Army and the Navy and saw service into WWII.

The boats were refueled and by 10:15 a.m. on July 20 headed quickly into the open waters of the Illinois River. It was full speed ahead. Within five minutes, the rum fleet passed the banks of the Peru waterfront where hundreds gathered to wave to the sailors. Each boat sounded its klaxon as it approached the swing bridge at Peru. There was no need to turn the span since the boats had plenty of clearance. Within 15 minutes, the flotilla was out of sight and on its way to join other ships patrolling the Gulf waters. (17) The brief visit of the Coast Guard brought home the national scope of the prohibition effort to both visitors and local citizens alike.

The day to day problems of law enforcement sometimes became a spectator event especially in small towns. One embarrassing incident for the Toluca town marshal, William Lassen, occurred on July 24, 1931. Five federal agents had arrested Matteo Armadeo and Tony Sceatus in an 8 a.m. raid catching the bootleggers operating a $10,000 distillery in a two-story residence. After putting the men in the Toluca jail, the agents requested that Marshal Lassen return to the distillery to assist in its dismantling. They needed the extra manpower since there were three huge concrete vats filled with fermenting corn sugar mash. Empty sugar sacks and yeast boxes were strewn about the floor. News of a federal raid spread quickly. Soon, almost everyone in Toluca walked down to see the house where the still was located only two blocks from the business district. It wasn't until 5:30 p.m. that the work was completed, and four truckloads of parts were sent down to Peoria.

In the meantime, the prisoners were unguarded but securely behind bars - or so the marshal thought. Certain friends of the incarcerated men backed up to the jail with a truck; fastened a chain to the window bars; and pulled them out of the masonry wall. Sceatus and Armadeo then made their getaway in the truck. The Marshall County sheriff was immediately notified of the jailbreak, but the all points bulletin was futile. (18)

Such dramatic incidents in a small town life were overshadowed by the occasional large-scale invasion of federal agents. After months of undercover "buys" in the summer of '31, a determined effort was made to once again attempt to completely rid LaSalle County of bootleggers. A virtual army of agents descended on the area in a lightning raid on July 29, 1931. Drawing on manpower resources from Illinois, Wisconsin and Iowa, 185 agents struck precisely at 4:20 p.m. at 62 different locations. There was no time for the bartenders and owners to use what was called the "grapevine telegraph" to warn each other of the raids in progress. Victor Dowd, the Chicago special investigator, who was well known to local operators, was just one of the leaders of the raids. Deputy directors from the Milwaukee, Madison, Springfield, East St. Louis, South Bend, Indianapolis, and Chicago bureaus of prohibition enforcement also took part in the arrests of 78 persons. Every major city and town in LaSalle County was visited.

Some of those picked up did not have any illegal beer or whiskey at the time but were still arrested with warrants based on previous undercover buys. The majority of those arrested had a considerable amount of beer.

Two places in particular were of special interest to federal agents. At 329 Third St. in LaSalle, William Balma was arrested for operating a complete brewery. Agents discovered three vats, a large one of 750-gallon capacity and two smaller 175-gallon tanks. Seven barrels of beer together with 137 pint bottles filled with home brew along with some whiskey and wine were confiscated. Another brewery was found in Peru. At 1715 Water St., Julio Morandi was found in possession of 423 pints of beer, 44 gallons of beer mash, 128 gallons of wine, 33 cans of malt syrup, three gallons of alcohol and two gallons of ale. Another large cache was found at 829 Brunner. Frank Steinz had 50 gallons of beer mash and 23 cases of filled beer bottles and 2 ½ gallons of wine.

In Streator, the raids were numerous but less productive. A few of the speakeasies had a hundred or more bottles of beer, but many places had nothing or only a small amount of beer and wine. One exception was the operation at 501 West Adams where agents found 838 pints of beer, with 60 gallons of fermenting home brew mash, and seven gallons of wine. The impact was dramatic. (19)

Another federal task force of 60 agents returned in September. Thirty-one people were arrested on charges ranging from the sale of liquor to possession of gambling equipment on Sept. 25-26. Streator was especially targeted. The proprietor of the Gateway Inn, Sam Gracinto, and William Schmitz, owner of the speakeasy at 118 N. Bloomington, were out on bail from that raid and now faced a second charge. Twelve slot machines were taken back to the Ottawa jail after the raid. (20)

The county authorities continued to raid a few speakeasies and private homes. The only excitement in LaSalle came with the arrest of a retired LaSalle policeman, Mike Cilla. He was caught with 46 bottles of beer and a jug of wine in his home and roadhouse located three miles south of Peru. (21)

Rural farms were the ideal location for distilleries. Some were independent operations, but others were syndicate-controlled. The long lanes running up to the farm buildings gave bootleggers an opportunity to be watchful of approaching vehicles. Apparently "Moonshine" Pete Doukezas wasn't being too careful while tending 1,050 gallons of corn sugar mash. He was caught again in October operating two stills on the Norton farm 2½ miles west of Ottawa just south of Route 7. This was the third time that federal officers had apprehended the LaSalle saloonkeeper. At his arraignment, his bond was set at $7,500, a sum too large for the bootlegger to pay immediately, so he spent a night in jail. (22)

Federal agents were especially adept at finding stills that no one else could locate either in the cities or out in the farming areas. One such urban location was at 1520 Chartres in LaSalle. The two-story, frame house was the location of a re-cooking operation. Four men were eventually arrested. One of the bootleggers drove up to the house in his Lincoln limousine while the raid was in progress. In the back seat of the expensive car were 33 five-gallon cans of first-run alcohol ready to be refined into a better quality product that no doubt would have be re-labeled as bonded whiskey. (23)

1931 Lincoln - Model K. This was the year when Lincoln came out with their V12, 120-hp engine. Other changes included a lowered hood and roof. The price for the luxury car ranged from $4400 to $7400.

Organized crime also was suffering major setbacks. After pleading guilty to income tax evasion, Al Capone was finally sentenced on Oct. 24 to 11 years in prison and fined $50,000. He was incarcerated in the Cook County jail while his lawyers tried legal maneuvers so that the crime boss would not be sent to a federal penitentiary. A few days later, Al's brother, Ralph Capone, who was rumored to have been the purchasing agent in Putnam County, was also charged with tax evasion by the IRS. He too was headed for the federal lockup. Ralph had been indicted in Jan. 1930 and lost his appeal on July 24, 1931. On Nov. 5, he was sent to Leavenworth for three years. He was also fined $10,000. Al's lawyers dragged the appeals process out but lost at every level. Under heavy guard, "Scarface" Al was finally sent to the penitentiary in Atlanta, Georgia in May 1932.

The Chicago-based crime syndicate was reeling from the incarceration of the top bosses. Dozens of lieutenants were also jailed. But, while the mob was in disarray, the local distilleries and their outlets were still functioning. Streator Police Chief Tom Mottershaw tried to keep the bootleggers in check by tipping off the federal agents to Bill Sowerby's Streator operation. During their Nov. 3 raid, the agents were able to find 85 gallons of wine and over 800 bottles of beer in the Sowerby's residence. He had been arrested twice before for liquor violations but continued to defy the law. (24)

Bureau County Sheriff William Neil also kept up the pressure by arresting six men in Spring Valley on Dec. 4, 1931. The Friday night raid netted large quantities of beer, wine, whiskey, and gin at the speakeasies, most of which lined St. Paul Street. (25)

But the ultimate goal was to find the major sources of all of the contraband. As the new year approached, one of those sources was revealed. The Lee County sheriff's department, headed by Fred Richardson, was patrolling Route 70 six miles south of Rochelle. A deputy stopped a truck driven by Dominico Belle, a resident of Oglesby. At first glance, it looked like the man had a load of potatoes. The deputies couldn't help but notice that the cargo area of the truck was bearing down heavily on the springs. The officers became suspicious that perhaps Belle was carrying more than 15 bushels of potatoes. Under closer inspection, the deputies found burlap bags under the potatoes. Inside the bags were 634 one-gallon tins of alcohol. According to the police, Belle slipped a $100 bill into the pocket of one of the deputies as a down payment. It was implied that additional money would be forthcoming if the officers would simply allow him to continue his trip to LaSalle. The officers were not impressed with the ploy and took Belle and his load to police headquarters in Dixon. Under interrogation Belle confessed that he was carrying his load from Beloit, Wisconsin to a destination in LaSalle County. But he wouldn't divulge the delivery point. Belle was only mad at himself for getting caught. He said that he had gotten a late start leaving Beloit at 5:30 a.m. Usually he traveled earlier when there were few patrols to stop him. Here was further evidence of the Rockford connection and its effect on the Illinois Valley. (26) Belle got his truck back the next day but was furious when he realized that the government agents had also confiscated his load of potatoes.

Feeling the increasing impact of layoffs, these Streator men at the Streator Park in 1930 encouraged a return to pre-prohibition days. The legalization of beer would bring increased tax revenues to finance new jobs. Streator Historical Society.

Chapter 16
1932
Curtain Call For Bootlegging

One did not have to go all the way to Beloit to secure large quantities of alcohol. A large still was discovered in a vacant house in Ladd in January. Federal agents found a 350-gallon cooker, 75 gallons of alcohol, and vats holding 8,000 gallons of mash. Two men were arrested, Joe Zolli (a.k.a. Remigio Venturi) and Al Schwab, who owned a farm about two miles east of Ladd. When the agents went to the Schwab farm, they found over 500 gallons of alcohol in a machine shed. Schwab posted a $3,000 bond in Peoria and was released. Zolli claimed that he had nothing to do with the distillery but was still held in the Spring Valley jail since he couldn't post bond. (1)

Bars in Spring Valley were feeling the long arm of the law again in February. James Barto had located his bar behind a funeral parlor on St. Paul Street. John Mignone required the right password to gain entry to his speakeasy. When the feds came knocking at the door, the drinking ended abruptly. Not only did the patrons clear out, but each bar was literally cleaned out – lock, stock and beer barrel. The St. Paul Street businesses had plenty of beer, wine and whiskey. But after the federal raid, both bars were devoid of not only alcohol but also all of the fixtures, which were impounded. This was a new tactic used by the state's attorney to cripple the rapid return to business of the speakeasies after owners paid their fines. (2)

In March, Sheriff Welter closed down another still in Oglesby. Joe Coseglio and Tony Angelo had an operation that could conceivably turn out 700 gallons of alcohol every week. The 3,000-gallon mash vats were smashed to pieces with sledgehammers.(3) Another raid was conducted at 253 Walnut, but the raiders only came away with 15 pints of beer and a single pint of wine. (4)

These periodic raids seemed to occur less frequently and produced less contraband. It was not until May that there were major federal seizures in Streator, East Wenona and Cedar Point. Frank Panno of Streator was hiding a 100-gallon still in his establishment at 218 Water St. Mike DiMartini of 1312 S. Illinois had a very valuable hoard of 240 pints of "Old Colonel" bonded whiskey and 23 gallons of alcohol. In East Wenona, the stock was located in two separate buildings. One held 3 ½ barrels of beer and 164 pints of brew. The other soft drink parlor had a large amount of beer, wine, and gin. Agents also discovered that August Blum of Cedar Point was operating a Route 89 roadhouse where his stock consisted of 172 pints of beer. (5)

Popular attention no longer seemed to focus on the need for rigid enforcement of the prohibition law. So many other headlines were in the news in 1932. The Japanese had invaded China. Adolph Hitler was developing political influence in Germany. Charles Lindbergh and his wife were devastated by the kidnapping of their baby. Locally, the news concentrated on stories of armed robberies, car thefts and increasing poverty as the depression deepened.

But there was the occasional story of another incident related to prohibition. On May 31, there were two similar but seemingly unrelated stories describing trucks carrying alcohol through LaSalle County. In one case, a brand new Chevy truck suddenly erupted into flames near 5th and Pulaski at 9 a.m. Jim Welter the brother of the LaSalle Sheriff Ed Welter, was one of the first to spot the blaze coming from the cab of the truck.

Chevrolet turned out hundreds of panel trucks in 1932. This is an example of the body style used that year.

The fire department was quickly on the scene and doused the flames. As the smoke began to clear, the trunk box was opened exposing row after row of flaming tin cans containing alcohol. These too were quickly extinguished.

The whole incident was very strange. Jim Welter described how he saw the driver jump from the cab and remove the license plates before running down 5th Street. The sides of the truck were labeled "American Bakery." But there was no address. Others recalled that they had seen a number of the "American Bakery" trucks driving through Peru. The truck only had 266 miles on the odometer indicating that it was only recently put into service for whatever purpose. It was estimated that the cargo consisted of at least 600 one-gallon tins of raw alcohol. Without the plates it was difficult to trace the ownership. State's Attorney Hanson said that the truck would be put up for auction if no one stepped forward to claim it. The only real damage was to the seat cushions in the cab.

A similar truck had been stopped the same day near Mendota. It was carrying 450 one-gallon tins of alcohol. The driver, George Lewis, who gave his address as Burlington, Iowa, said he was heading to Milwaukee. During the interrogation by federal officers, Lewis slipped a $1,000 bill into the pocket of one of the agents. The rum runner implied that it was only a down payment and more would be coming if the agents would simply release the cargo valued at $2,500. Lewis was charged with transporting liquor and attempted bribery of a federal officer. The truck was also confiscated. (6)

The next month, attention was shifted to Putnam County. After observing a truck leave a farm, which was located off the bottom road ½ mile east of Rt. 89, every day at 2:30 p.m. Sheriff Milledge "Buck" Thomas (right) became suspicious. He decided to  have a closer look on Sunday morning, June 5, at 7 a.m. Joining him in the inspection were Wesley Kays, his son John, and Charlie Hynds. No one was at the farm when they arrived to check the barn, which had been constructed of old lumber about three months earlier. It was a typical structure measuring 50'x30'x30'. But there wasn't any livestock with the exception of a few chickens. Inside the barn, they found a complete, modern distillery valued at $6,000. The plant included six concrete vats measuring 12'x10'x6' holding 54,000 gallons of mash. Thomas estimated the plant could turn out 250 gallons of alcohol every day. A gallon diluted with 50% spring water could generate an income of about $2,500 a day! It appeared that the last shipment went out on Saturday morning since there was no finished alcohol to be seized. The Spring Valley bridge at Rt. 89 had been condemned as unsafe so no one even bothered to check the farms along the road for illegal stills. Thomas guessed that the hooch was being taken out by way of Peru.

The sheriff and his group spent most of the day tearing down the still, boiler and condenser. Then he smashed holes in the vats. It must have been quite a surprise for Granville residents as they left Sunday morning church services to see one of Hans Sandberg's big trucks driving down McCoy Street with the demolished remnants of the distillery. (7)

The Putnam County House in Hennepin was the scene of numerous prohibition hearings.

Who was responsible? The ownership of the property was confusing. Henry Maurer Sr. was a real estate salesman in LaSalle. His son, Henry Jr., had leased the farm for a time but then moved a short distance and began farming other acreage. Supposedly, the farm title had been transferred in April to the elder Maurer's daughter in Iowa. But the son was living on the property when the still was in operation. However, both the son and father claimed to have no knowledge of the distillery operation. The father finally claimed that he had rented the property to a Mr Hayes in Peru who wanted it for a "chicken farm." The father and son were both arrested since the sheriff was of the opinion that they both knew about the operation and that was a crime in itself. (8)

Change was definitely in the air regarding the Volstead Act. During the Democratic national convention in Chicago in the summer of '32, the platform committee argued over the adoption of a repeal plank. Some wanted an outright repeal of the 18th Amendment while others wanted a modification of the law. On June 29, the committee voted 35 to 17 in favor of an outright repeal of the amendment rather than limiting the manufacture and sale of liquor to only beer and wine. The Democratic presidential candidate, Franklin Roosevelt, promised to end prohibition if he was elected.

National politics not withstanding, Illinois Valley law officers were still trying to uphold the 1920 law. In July, Bureau County Sheriff Neill discovered a still operating in DePue. Together with DePue Marshal Herman Bansch, they arrested the owner of the two-story house, Pete Armaretta. In the basement, were three concrete vats for the mash. Each held 1,400 gallons. In order to avoid suspicion, the water had been diverted around the meter. Naturally, Armaretta denied any connection with the still. A routine follow-up inspection by the sheriff almost resulted in another arrest. As Neill was driving to the property, he spotted five men and two women apparently removing some of the blocks from the vats. As soon as they spied the town marshal, they fled. (9)

On the very same night, July 7, federal agents found a 500-gallon still operating in Cedar Point. It was located in the rear of a home owned by Kasimir Benedetti. In addition to the still, the contraband included a 10-hp boiler, 500 gallons of mash, a 14" column, a 25 gallon cooler, a 250 gallon receiving tank, 100 one-gallon tin cans, 3 barrels of colored alcohol, a 5-gallon jug of alcohol, an electric auger, and 25 sacks of coke. Benedetti was charged under the Jones "5 and 10" Act with three counts of prohibition violations and one charge of nuisance. He posted a $1000 bond in Ottawa. (10)

It was not until late August before any news of prohibition violations was in the papers. Even then, there was only speculation when there was a large explosion in an over-sized hog building on the Kern farm in rural Mendota. Many local residents guessed that another still had blown up, as this was not uncommon when alky-makers failed to watch the pressure gauges on the boilers. The sheriff searched through the smoldering ruins the next day and reported no evidence of a still.

It looked like the whole business of prohibition was coming to an end. Al Capone was in the federal penitentiary in Atlanta although his lawyers tried to have him freed in September. They claimed that their client had not been charged within the three-year statute of limitations for his crimes of tax evasion in 1925-1927. But it looked like he was going to have to serve his 10-year sentence. Even if Capone was incarcerated, there were others controlling the liquor business in the Valley.

For a time, it looked like a gang war might break out in the Illinois Valley. Two gangs in Peoria had combined to muscle in on the mob's turf that had extended its tentacles into Spring Valley. Apparently, two members of the Peoria syndicate began operating a still in a wooded area near Spring Valley. While they were turning out a fresh batch of alcohol in early September, 8-10 men with machine guns surrounded them. Rather than shoot the Peoria bootleggers, the rival gang forced them to finish the batch they were running and fill the empty cans. In the dead of night, a number of trucks pulled off the road and parked in the woods near the still. The Peoria bootleggers were told to load the cans into the truck and then "clear out and stay out." They were warned that if they came back they would be killed. As they ran for their lives, they heard the staccato firing of machine guns. Bullets riddled the still, boiler and tanks. The Chicago mob was not going to be driven from its lucrative investment in the Valley. (11)

One of the most popular weapons of the bootleggers was the Thompson submachine gun. It was compact and easily hidden and had tremendous firepower with a drum magazine that held 50 rounds of .45 cal. ammunition. At full automatic, it had a rate of fire of 700 rounds per minute. It weighed about 14 pounds with the drum magazine. Gangsters appreciated the weapon since the stock of the 33 3/4" standard weapon could be removed cutting the length to only 24". The so-called Tommy gun was also known by gangsters as a Chopper, Gat, or Chicago typewriter. They were perfectly legal and could cost between $1,000 to $2,000 in gangland.

There were more pressing issues for the local sheriffs. Bank robberies throughout the Valley were making headlines. Local officials were more concerned with Bonus Marchers and the joblessness that gripped the nation. Sheriff Welter had ordered that his Chrysler sedan be upgraded with more protective features as the war on crime became more hazardous in LaSalle County. In addition to adding bulletproof glass for all cars, the windows would be equipped with gun-ports so that officers would not have to roll down their windows in a running gun battle with felons. In addition, drop screens would protect the front tires, and a bulletproof louvered screen would protect the radiator.

The improvements were installed just in time. On Oct. 25, 1932, the sheriff and his men were engaged in a two-hour gun battle with six fugitives who had robbed the First National Bank of Ransom. The felons fled to Streator where they were finally captured. During the battle, a full range of firearms, including pistols, shot guns, and machine guns, were used on both sides. Fortunately, such shoot-outs were rare and less dramatic occurrences when bars and stills were raided in the Valley.

Note the improvements in the sheriff's police car: tire screens (white arrow) and bulletproof radiator shield (striped arrow).
Bulletproof glass windows and gun-ports protected the occupants.

Photos reprinted from LaSalle *Daily Post,* June 28, 1932.

The arrests of 54 individuals resulted from one last massive dragnet in LaSalle County on Oct. 17, 1932. In a very coordinated operation, 100 federal agents struck 46 establishments precisely at 4:45 on Friday afternoon. This was the third major "mop-up" in LaSalle County in two years. The previous two operations brought in a total of approximately 150 individuals.

The raids were conducted in LaSalle, Peru, Oglesby, Streator, Ottawa, Cedar Point, and Leonore. The most extensive operations were conducted in Streator where ten speakeasies were hit on Main Street alone. There were located at 102, 410, 414, 502, 619, 623, 709, 713, 717, and 812½. E. Main. Bars at 113 and 115 Vermillion, 114 N. and 415 and 527 S. Illinois, 118 Park, 810 and 811 E. Hickory, 116 S. Sterling, 811 N. Shabbona, and 1113 N. Bloomington Streets were also found to be in violation of the Volstead Act. Twenty-nine owners and bartenders were taken into custody in Streator. In LaSalle, raids on 11 speakeasies and restaurants netted 14 persons. There were fewer arrests in the other cities. In Peru, five places were raided, and five operators were taken into custody. The Oglesby raids on Walnut Street caught three proprietors. Only one person was arrested in Leonore, and another individual was taken in Cedar Point. According to the police, there was no resistance at any of the locations, but some of the bartenders did try to dispose of the evidence. However, there was so much alcohol that it was impossible to dispose of it before the seizures.

A few examples of the large stock of various alcoholic products on hand illustrate the problem the owners had in disposing of "evidence." In the LaSalle restaurant operated by Anton Trolia and George Koenig at 345 First Street, the contraband included 818 pints of beer, two gallons of "whiskey, " one gallon of uncolored alcohol and five gallons of wine. At Steve Miller's Peru grocery store at 2301 Main, agents found 24 pints of beer, 384 bottles of beer in 16 cases, 2 ½ barrels of beer and 45 gallons of beer mash ready for bottling. Miller was charged with sale, possession, and manufacturing of beer as well as maintaining a nuisance establishment. These were fairly typical of the quantity and types of evidence found by the federal agents. (12)

The processing of the 54 defendants was time-consuming as fingerprints and records of outstanding warrants had to be checked. Special attention was paid to the alien residents. Their prints were forwarded to the FBI in Washington, D.C. which in turn sent copies to the capitals of the countries from which the aliens emigrated. Those found with criminal records in their native countries could be deported as undesirable aliens.

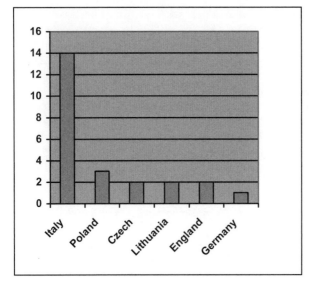

Numbers of alien residents arrested in the October 17, 1932 LaSalle County raids, who were threatened with possible deportation.

Federal operations in Bureau County were not nearly as dramatic. Two seizures were made at buildings located at 126 and 128 W. St. Paul Street. Agents destroyed two half barrels of beer at the 128 address. The other building was closed up so agents broke a boarded-up window in the basement where they found small quantities of beer and alcohol. No one was arrested. (13)

There were quite a few individuals making their own beer for personal use during the Depression. Authorities finally caught on to this practice by reviewing grocery reports. Using undercover buyers, the LaSalle Emergency Relief committee discovered that grocers were providing customers with malt for home brew but falsified the purchases as "beans." William Cummins, Chairman of the LaSalle Grocers Committee, sent out a warning that non-essential items such as malt could not be distributed to needy families. Grocers would be penalized if the practice continued. (14)

But this was a relatively petty matter as far as most people were concerned. Local authorities were more concerned with the WWI Bonus Marchers and the "threat" that they might pose. Another reason for the lack of concern about prohibition violations was the growing sentiment to repeal the Volstead Act and the 18th Amendment. Both at the national and state level, it was a hotly debated topic. For some time, Illinois lawmakers had been gathering momentum in the drive to abolish the search and seizure law regarding illegal alcohol as a method of effectively negating the federal mandate in the state.

The November 1932 election of Franklin Roosevelt and the Democratic Party pledge to repeal prohibition strengthened the resolve of "wet" legislators in the Illinois General Assembly. The implications of a change in the leadership at the federal level gave hope to local brewers. The President of Peru Products, Andrew Hebel Sr. said, "I am very happy to learn that the nation has elected congressmen who are pledged to legalize beer and submit the Eighteenth Amendment to the states for repeal or modification." He cautioned, however, that Illinois lawmakers would have to repeal the search and seizure first. The Star Union President optimistically predicted, "We should be able to start production within a few days after the law is repealed or modified." (15)

It seemed as though the country had lost all interest in prohibition. In December 1932, a local kidnapping story made residents realize that gangster interests in bootlegging were still active. On Dec. 9, Fred DeFilippi, a Spring Valley and Peru dealer in malt, wort, and sugar, was abducted from his Water Street business in Peru. DeFilippi had received a phone call from an unknown party who told him he wanted to place an order. While sitting alone at his desk, the door opened. Before he could even look up, a sack was thrown over his head. He later revealed that he thought 4-5 men had abducted him and hustled him off into their waiting car. This was the first kidnapping in the history of Bureau County.

In the course of the investigation, there were reported sightings of the abductors' car in Dixon and South Rockford. DeFilippi, it was learned, was actually being held in a hideout in Wisconsin. Newly elected State's Attorney Josef T. Skinner took an active role in the investigation and subsequent release of the Spring Valley businessman. Skinner had information identifying the 5-6 men, who were involved in the abduction. He sent word to them that unless DeFilippi was released unharmed by Christmas morning, warrants would be issued for their arrest. Such a release seemed to imply that the kidnappers would be immune from prosecution. But that was not true.

On Dec. 10, DeFilippi was forced to write an extortion letter that demanded $50,000 from his family. The kidnappers believed that there was a $300,000 inheritance from his father to be tapped. He told his abductors that they might as well shoot him then and there because there was no way that his family could raise that much money. The letter was postmarked "Chicago," but this was a ruse to throw off investigators and hide the true location of the hideout.

Everything was kept under tight wraps as the family used intermediaries to negotiate for a lesser amount or even give the gangsters the title to the DeFilippi residence on Cleveland Street in Spring Valley.

His brother, Tino, handled the secret arrangements. The family was cautioned not to go to the police.

Eventually, a deal was struck. A well-known Davenport bootlegger and two friends of DeFilippi's traveled to Chicago where they parked in front of the Lexington Hotel at 22nd St. and Michigan Ave. The hotel was associated with the Capone gang. The negotiators inadvertently parked directly in front of a police car. While the Davenport bootlegger left the car, another man walked up to it and asked the Spring Valley men if they were looking for him. The men in the car, shaking with fear, replied that they didn't know whom they were waiting for. Observing the patrol car, the Italian gentlemen then asked, "You got the law with you?" The Spring Valley men said that they had not come with the police, and the Davenport man could verify their story. As the inquisitive Italian turned to leave, he cautioned them that if the police were involved "there would be some shooting going on pretty quick." The Davenport negotiator returned; got in the car; and the three men drove a few blocks to a nearby speakeasy to wait. (16)

In the meantime, DeFilippi had been driven from the Wisconsin hideout 130 miles south to Chicago. As the kidnappers approached the metropolitan area, DeFilippi's blindfold was removed, and he realized that they were passing through Elgin. The ordeal for the 38-year old businessman was finally over. It was Christmas Day. Immediately after his release, he telephoned his wife who was overjoyed by this Christmas present for herself and their 4-year old son.

Fred DeFilippi, kidnapped Spring Valley-Peru businessman. Source-LaSalle *Daily Post*, Dec. 14, 1932.

DeFilippi later asserted that not a cent was paid in ransom. However, rumors persisted that between $3,000 and $5,000 was the actual amount that the abductors agreed to accept. They threatened DeFilippi with murder if the payment was not made. (17) However, it would not be long before investigators solved the case and brought the guilty parties to justice.

Chapter 17
1933
Happy Days Are Beer Again

The solution to the DeFilippi abduction proceeded swiftly. Joe "Zito" Bruno was picked up in Rockford as the owner of the Buick automobile that was used in the kidnapping. Bruno was suspected of ordering the Feb. 11 execution of Paul Giovingo, leader of a rival liquor syndicate. However, the police interrogation could not connect him with the DeFilippi kidnapping so he was released. (1)

It would not be until May that the federal kidnapping charges resulted in the convictions under the newly enacted Lindbergh Law. One of the accused, Victor Burman, a Spring Valley malt rival of DeFilippi, was charged with the kidnapping and extortion of both Fred DeFilippi and Adhemar Huughe of East Moline. He said that negotiations for the release of the Spring Valley man were conducted at a saloon at 21st and Washington Blvd. in Chicago. Frank Delbono and Mike Talarico finally agreed to a $3,000 ransom. DeFilippi also took the stand and admitted that during the last decade he had been engaged in an "illegal occupation" on occasion. While denying that he ever operated his own still, he did confess to selling corn sugar to others who were operating stills. He had arranged to meet with Talarico and Victor Ciesielski to sell them some sugar. Wesley Prichett and Carlo Delbono were two of the guards at the hideout. Frank Delbono dictated the ransom letters that were sent to the pastor of SS Peter and Paul Church in Spring Valley, P.M. Mahoney, the editor of the Spring Valley Gazette, and to his wife.

Three men, Joe Bruno, Mike Talarico, a leading liquor mobster regarded as Davenport's "Public Enemy No. 1," and Frank Delbono received 42-year prison sentences. Wesley Prichett was to serve 20 years. Victor Ciesielski, and Carlo Delbono were given 2-year sentences. Commenting on the kidnapping of the Spring Valley man, Judge Louis Fitzhenry said, "I think that a crime of this kind is second only to murder." George Johnson, the federal attorney who sent Al Capone to prison, added, " I've known that type. Their coming from the Lexington Hotel in Chicago is very significant. It is the capital of the Capone crowd. These men are very typical of the men seen around there." (2)

The successful conclusion of the DeFilippi case was not the only reason for many happy faces in the Valley. In the nation's capital, lawmakers had been arguing the merits of the Collier Beer Bill. After two days of heated debate, the proposal allowing the legalization of 3.2% beer was approved by the House of Representatives 230 to 165 in

December 1932. The bill was sent on to the Senate. The end of prohibition enforcement was voted on in late January 1933. Enforcement funds were dropped to $8.4 million, and there would be no wiretaps allowed to collect evidence against prohibition violators. Although the end was near, there were still a number of legislative steps that needed to be taken before enforcement units would be disbanded. In the meantime, federal task forces continued to carry out prohibition mandates.

In northwestern Bureau County, federal authorities continued their investigations of illegal distilleries. The discovery of yet another still concealed in a barn took place on March 14. Members of a liquor syndicate operating in western Illinois and eastern Iowa had made an arrangement with John DeCrane, a farmer in rural Tampico. He was alleged to have rented his barn in exchange for two barrels of whiskey and $50 a month. The syndicate men constructed six mash vats and were beginning to assemble the other equipment for the distillery. The federal agents did not become suspicious of the operation until the barn burned to the ground only two days after the first batch of mash had started to ferment in a 5,000-gallon vat. DeCrane not only lost his barn, two cows, and 50 hogs, but also his freedom. Federal agents took him into custody as he stood near the charred remains of the only remaining vat. He implicated Joe Schreiner of Erie, Illinois as the man who rented his barn. Schreiner, who was arrested two days later, was out on bond for another prohibition violation. (3)

National attention focused on inauguration day in March 1933. Would the new president carry out the Democrats' promise to end prohibition? After Roosevelt took the oath of office, he was confronted with numerous problems, but he did not forget his pledge to rid the country of the restraints of the Volstead Act. On March 13, he sent a message to Congress that many had long sought. In a short text, the new president said, "I recommend to the congress the passage of legislation for the immediate modification of the Volstead Act, in order to legalize the manufacture and sale of beer and other beverages of such alcoholic content as is permissible under the constitution." The response to the surprise request was thunderous as the House broke into wild applause. (4)

In the meantime, Springfield legislators were working on a bill of their own. One of the provisions of the pending beer regulatory bill specified that "no alcoholic beverages may be sold within four miles of a university, normal school or college." This would have a serious impact on the Illinois Valley with St. Bede College located between Peru and Spring Valley. There was also the question of the status of L-P-O junior college in LaSalle. Illinois Governor Henry Horner argued that the provision was "too drastic," and it would "halt the sale of liquor in almost every large city in the state." He promised that he would send the bill back for rewording. (8) The final law also provided that retailers would have to pay a $50 state license fee. Downstate governments could also charge up to $200. There was no limit set on Cook County fees. It also forbid the use of the word "saloon" in advertising and limited the sale of beer to places that also sold food.

Meanwhile in Washington on Mar. 21, the House of Representatives passed a bill to allow the sale of 3.2 beer and wine. The bill was sent to the Senate the following day for its approval. The end of beer prohibition was just a pen stroke away. President Roosevelt finally signed the legislation making beer and wine legal at the stroke of midnight, April 7, 1933. The bill had passed in only nine days since the president had proposed the legislation. Plans were drawn up to grant licenses to brewers, and revenue stamps had been printed. According to Lyle Kennedy of Streator, who still recalls the happy occasion over 70 years ago said, "The town went berserk. Factory and train whistles were blown and bells were tolled. There was an impromptu parade down Main Street with autos and trucks blowing horns as if it was New Year's Eve." The old word "saloon" was replaced by the word "tavern" which seemed to give the old establishments a touch of class.

Roosevelt also took up the problem of dealing with those in federal custody. He called upon the Attorney General to determine how many of those individuals would not have been found guilty under the new legislation. Most pending cases were simply dropped.

On Mar. 22, Henry Hoerner announced that he had filed an application for one of the federal permits to manufacture 3.2 beer at Star Union. However, he would wait until the permit arrived before authorizing the necessary modifications to the processing equipment. Estimates ranged from two to three months for the changeover. But Hoerner assured Star Union customers that beer would be brought in from other sources in the interim to be distributed by his company. George Zippel, the former brewmaster at Star Union, was being contacted to return to his role in the operation. In the meantime, Henry and his son, Martin Hoerner, had participated in a Chicago conference of regional brewers to discuss various options in terms of distribution.

The legalization of beer had a tremendous impact on the Valley. Immediately hundreds of job applications were filed at Star Union and Peru Products. It was estimated that approximately 200 men would be hired. Although the companies had continued to produce soda pop and a few other products, a much larger workforce would now be needed.

Legalization would also stimulate the local economy in other ways. Brewing equipment would need to be upgraded. Additional trucks would have to be purchased for distribution. Large quantities of kegs and bottles would also be necessary. The Rock Island and other railroads would also benefit from the increased traffic bringing in larger quantities of hops and barley. If the same numbers of bars opened as had existed before prohibition, licensing revenue amounting to an estimated $45,000 would flow into the LaSalle-Peru city coffers. Former speakeasies would have to pay the fees to operate, but the new law would probably encourage the opening of an estimated two dozen new taverns in the local area. (6)

Star Union Products in Peru was gearing up for the big day. Notice the caveat inserted in this ad – "as soon as it is legalized." It was still illegal on April 1, 1933 when this ad appeared in the LaSalle *Daily Post.*

The ads of the day reflected the changing attitudes in the Illinois Valley. There would be new jobs for brewery workers; speakeasies would no longer have to be described as "soft drink" parlors and could operate legally; and the cities, states, and nation could now collect needed revenues from taxes and licensing fees. It was a much-anticipated event.

The lack of legal beer was even reflected in the movies being shown in LaSalle. For 25 cents, Buster Keaton and Jimmy Durante would entertain moviegoers at the Majestic Theater in LaSalle. The film title was very appropriate when this ad was place in the LaSalle *Daily Post* on April 4, 1933. It would still be a few more days until beer would be legal and widely available once again.

In the flurry of activity surrounding the re-introduction of legal 3.2 beer, the Illinois General Assembly worked into the night on April 5 trying to arrive at a satisfactory bill to license and regulate the beer retailers. So there was a short period when the state would not be able to collect fees from those businesses. That being the case, it was up to individual counties to pass their own ordinances to regulate sales. Local taverns were awaiting

shipments from Wisconsin, but Sheriff Welter reminded tavern owners that sales would not be legal until 12:01 a.m. on April 7. (7)

Princeton never seemed to have the problems of liquor enforcement that characterized cities in eastern Bureau County and LaSalle County. "Benny" Benson, manager of the Princeton Bottling Works, welcomed the law allowing for the legalization of 3.2 beer. He was ready to distribute beers from the Atlas and Berghoff Brewing companies to 37 towns around Princeton. The licensed distributor said that he expected that the new beers would be "far superior" to the near beer that was available during prohibition. Anticipating large sales for the first day of legal beer, he told his customers that he would only accept cash for their orders. (8)

Princeton Mayor Brown was not the least concerned about the reaction of the local population. The local stores had a sufficient supply according to the *Bureau County Republican* although it was noted that 12oz. bottles were initialing selling for 20 cents, the price soon dropped to a more reasonable 15 cents. A case of beer sold in the first days of legalization for $2.75 in Princeton.

The Chicago breweries, many of which had been operating illegally, were barely able to keep up with the urban demand. The Peru breweries had adequate bottling facilities, but it took awhile for the Peru breweries to come up to full production. However, bottling plants seemed to spring up everywhere in the Illinois Valley.

Beer ads, which had been virtually non-existent during prohibition, now flooded the office of the LaSalle *Daily Post-Tribune*. The copy indicated how quickly the demand for beer was being met. Now there were bottling plants in Princeton, Mendota, Spring Valley, LaSalle, and Peru ready to deliver beer as soon as the ban was lifted at the stroke of midnight on April 7.

All ads pictured on this page and those following are reprinted from the LaSalle *Daily Post Tribune* during April 1933 unless otherwise indicated.

Some brands would be unfamiliar to 21st Century aficionados. In 1933, the Atlas, Edelweiss, Kingsbury, Budweiser, and Pabst labels were very familiar brands in the Illinois Valley. Ads at left and below are reprinted from the April 6, edition of LaSalle *Daily Post-Tribune*.

The celebrations in Chicago were tumultuous on April 7. At 12:01 a.m., 4,000 trucks and horse-drawn wagons besieged the shipping docks at the city's seven big breweries. Police escorts were needed to prevent hijacking. Everyone wanted a share of the 200,000 barrels of beer that were now available. At the city airport, eight planes were loaded. The first flight was headed to Washington, D.C. The special consignment included a 5' glass beer bottle that held 30 gallons for President Roosevelt. Revelers who could not squeeze into a downtown tavern lined the streets and cheered every time a beer truck passed by.

Local residents of the Illinois Valley had to wait a little longer for the first beer to arrive since the local breweries were still not in operation. Taverns

had shipments coming in by rail and by truck in anticipation of heavy sales. They were not disappointed. The Enterprise Bottling Works of LaSalle ordered a truckload of beer from Sheboygan, Wisconsin. In a short time, the entire shipment was depleted. Behind the taverns, there were large piles of empty beer cases and bottles.

Streator was not as fortunate. It wasn't until 10:45 a.m. that an Illinois Valley Ice Cream Co. truck arrived from Ottawa with 350 cases of Atlas beer. The Illinois Fruit and Produce Company was supposed to have an order of Schlitz coming from Milwaukee, but it never arrived for the celebrations. Local distributors of Anheuser-Busch, Blatz, and Prima Special were having the same problem.

The taverns were ready to go back to business as usual although prices would be somewhat higher. Before prohibition, a 12-oz. glass cost only a nickel, and a bottle went for a dime. Now the Streator taverns were going to charge a dime or more for a 10-oz. glass and 15 to 20 cents for a bottle. The specialty beers cost even more. There was also the new one-cent sales tax that was newly enacted by the General Assembly. The first beer came to Streator only in bottles. Later, barrels costing $18-$20 were brought to taverns. Real beer lovers could purchase a case for about $2.60 plus a $1 deposit for bottle return. According to Lyle Kennedy, who was an eyewitness to the events in Streator, there was another celebration similar to the one held in Streator when Roosevelt signed the act legalizing beer in March. He recalled how "people were lined up eight or ten deep in front of the bars, and they toasted the return of real beer more and more loudly far into the night."

Edelweiss beer could soon be purchased at 226 Joliet Street in LaSalle across the street from City Hall. This April 6, 1933 ad appeared in the LaSalle *Daily Post-Tribune*.

Happy Days Are Here Again

That Nationally Known Good Beer

Drink **Edelweiss** BEER

THE PERFECT MALT AND HOP BREW

At All Dealers or Phone 245

We Are Now Accepting Orders from Dealers as Well as Home Trade for Delivery in Order of Receipt

Telephone today, we will deliver a case to your home Friday. Out of town customers send post card and we deliver direct to your home.

Phone Your Order Now—Call 245

Edelweiss Distributing Co.

226 Joliet Street—La Salle   PHONE 245   Opposite City Hall

The Illinois Fruit and Produce Company, which had distribution outlets in several cites in the Illinois Valley besides their office at 1203 Fulton St. in Ottawa, invited prospective buyers to make inquiries before April 7th. They would be the exclusive distributors for Schlitz beer in LaSalle, Livingston, Grundy, Marshall, and Woodford Counties once real beer was legalized. This ad appeared in the Mar. 31 edition of the Ottawa *Daily Republican.*

Atlas beer was another popular brand in the Illinois Valley. The local Atlas sales office in Ottawa was located at 1037 Fulton Street. This April 3, 1933 ad in the *Daily Republican* represented the initial efforts in Ottawa to encourage bars to stock up. However, there was not the heavy emphasis on the availability of beer in clubs and restaurants as there was in LaSalle. Such ads became less frequent in Illinois Valley newspapers other than in LaSalle after April 7th.

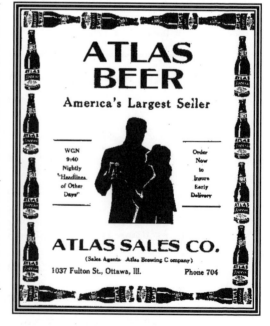

The LaSalle *Daily Post* enjoyed a tremendous increase in advertising revenues from the beer distributors and retail outlets. The ad at left appeared in the April 24, 1933 edition. Surprisingly neither the Streator *Free Press* nor the *Bureau County Republican* published any beer ads when beer became legal.

The opening of old and new taverns in the Valley caused a ripple effect. Other businesses would also benefit from the sale of beer. The Peru Sheet Metal ad appeared in the LaSalle *Daily Post-Tribune* on April 24, 1933.

Some ironic situations developed in the midst of all the celebrations. Although beer would now be legal, moonshine was not legal yet. On the eve of the legal sale of beer, federal agents raided a farm two miles northwest of Oglesby and found a distillery that had opened in December. The owner had essentially constructed a Hollywood-type façade. The barn on the property was easy to see from the road. The big barn doors and windows were wide open. There was no outward appearance of an operating distillery. However, the clever operators had constructed an addition behind the stables and out of sight of patrolling federal agents. The two-story structure held the vats and a still on the ground floor. The larger tanks were located on the second floor. Hundreds of empty one and five-gallon cans were found. Empty sugar sacks were strewn about. Six 2000-gallon mash vats, two 1000-gallon receiving tanks and one 1000-gallon tank were used to process the alcohol. The 75-year old farmer, who owned the barn, was not arrested. It was well known that most of the farmers of the area only benefited in terms of a small monthly rent payment from the syndicate that operated the distilleries. (9)

Dozens of beer-laden trucks were soon on the roads. These made tempting targets for the syndicate. As taverns tried to replace their depleted stocks, the Enterprise Bottling Works at 1117 Eighth Street, LaSalle sent for additional beer from Sheboygen. One shipment of 5,000 cases carried by 11 trucks was hijacked in the Rockford area. Of that, one truckload of 400 cases was supposed to reach LaSalle. In order to prevent a repeat hijacking, the next shipment went by way of Joliet adding 50 extra miles to the normal 215-mile trip. It took ten hours, but the beer was safely in LaSalle. (10)

Enterprise Bottling ad reprinted from LaSalle *Daily Post-Tribune* April 6, 1933.

One of the best-known distributors in LaSalle was Kelly & Cawley. Ad reprinted from LaSalle *Daily Post-Tribune* April 13, 1933

Not only were Kelly and Cawley in the distribution business, but they also established a club on 1st Street in LaSalle, that became one of the most popular places to spend some time from the 1930's into the 1950's. The Kefauver Crime Commission investigations during the Eisenhower administration marked the beginning of the end for this popular establishment.

These ads appeared in the LaSalle *Daily Post-Tribune* on April 14 (above) and April 27, (right) in 1933.

With the end of the ban on real beer and wine, many residents of the Valley were ready for good food, dancing and drinking at one of LaSalle's hot spots, Kelly & Cawley's. The ad at left was printed in the LaSalle *Daily Post* on May 11, 1933

First Street LaSalle in the 1930's became the destination for many seeking a good time on the weekends. Kelly and Cawley's was located on the left side of this 1930's photo.

Kelly & Cawley's as it appeared in the 1950's on 1st Street in LaSalle. Source- LaSalle Historical Society.

There was a seemingly endless list of places where one could legally obtain beer after April 7th. The Deer Head Tavern opened its doors at 228 Gooding in LaSalle. Reprinted from *LaSalle Daily Post,* April 6, 1933.

The Kaskaskia Hotel, located at 2nd and Marquette in LaSalle, was a favorite with businessmen. Ads from LaSalle *Daily Post-Tribune* April 6, 1933.

The Kaskaskia Hotel as it was pictured in the 1930's. LaSalle Historical Society

The village of Cedar Point shed its unenviable reputation as a major producer of illegal alcohol. Soon its beer gardens would be widely enjoyed by Valley residents. Ad from LaSalle *Daily Post-Tribune* April 13, 1933

Across the Illinois River in Oglesby some of the old Walnut Street speakeasies never reopened, but there was plenty of room for new taverns and restaurants. Ad from the LaSalle *Daily Post-Tribune* April 21, 1933.

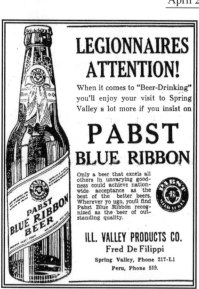

When the American Legion held their District Homecoming Convention in Spring Valley in July 1933, Fred DeFilippi was ready to distribute his Pabst Blue Ribbon beer. Ad reprinted from July 29, 1933 edition of LaSalle *Daily Post-Tribune.*

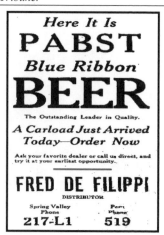

Fred DeFilippi had little trouble in recovering from his kidnapping ordeal and began selling legal beer through his distributorship in Spring Valley. Ad appearing in the April 10, 1933 edition of the LaSalle *Daily Post-Tribune.*

New companies sprang up overnight to distribute beer in the four-county region. Few people remember the Italian-American Importing Co. in LaSalle. Another major distributor in the four-county area was Cassiday Bros. with their facilities at 129 E. St. Paul in Spring Valley. Ads at left and below reprinted from LaSalle *Daily Post-Tribune* July 7, 1933.

The Big House in Spring Valley once was the residence of Sam Dalzell, manager of the Spring Valley Coal Co. Later, it was converted into a restaurant rumored to have been a dining establishment frequented by Al Capone.

The Big House also sought the business of the American Legion in the ad below printed in the LaSalle *Daily Post-Tribune* on July 28, 1933

Preparing for the first night of legalized beer, Ottawa's speakeasies took down the heavy drapes that barred the inquisitive eyes of the local constables. The familiar brass rails at the bars were polished, and several of the establishments remodeled their interiors.

There were some changes. One of these was the price of beer. No longer was beer sold for a nickel; the price was raised to ten cents a glass. There was also a conspicuous absence of large bowls of pretzels and the customary free lunch.

In Ottawa, there was a bit of a wait before beer arrived at the local taverns. Some proprietors traveled to nearby cities, which had a limited supply and came back to the county seat with a case or barrel, if they were lucky. Some truckloads finally arrived at 2 a.m. on the 7th after fighting their way to the brewery loading docks in Chicago. The competition was fierce. One truckload from Monroe, Wisconsin arrived at one distribution company in Ottawa at 6:30 a.m. The truck was quickly emptied of its cargo of 750 cases of beer and then headed back to Monroe, a distance of 125 miles, for another load.

Prima Sales was located at 501 W. Main in Ottawa. Ad reprinted from the April 5, 1933, Ottawa *Daily Republican.*

The Ottawa police were pleasantly surprised at the lack of unruly activity near the downtown bars. The Ottawa *Daily Republican* described the evening for patrolmen as "just a hum-drum night of beat walking." The police recalled how "the inebriated were clustered on the street corners and parading all parts of Ottawa, as they took advantage of the last fleeting minutes of the saloon days." (11)

Beer did not arrive in Morris, Illinois until 6 a.m. Two trucks were seen unloading at local distributors. Cases were being distributed to local taverns in small trucks for $2.50 - $2.75 per case. Customers had to pay an additional $1 deposit on the bottles.

Later in the morning, a Rock Island freight was on a siding while beer was unloaded. When the eastbound Golden State

Limited briefly stopped at the Morris station (above), those on the platform observed the amber drink on the tables in the dining car.

A semi owned by Mid-West Transportation overturned on Rt. 7. The truck was packed to the roof with cases of beer. The 365 cases were wedged in so tightly that only one bottle was broken. Farmers from the surrounding area rushed to the scene to help unload the truck since the load was too heavy to put the trailer back on its wheels. One farmer whose fence was damaged in the mishap said that he would not hold the trucking company liable if the trucker would only leave a case of beer. The driver offered a single bottle of brew to another man who offered him a lift to the nearest phone. By the time the truck was righted and reloaded, there were a number of empties strewn along the highway. Truckers no longer had to fear prohibition agents as they drove down from Wisconsin with cases of beer exposed for all to see.

The speakeasies in Morris were transformed over night. Partitions to back rooms were removed; the windows were washed and signs were changed. One of the managers of a local tavern said, "I am glad this sneaking and snooping feature of the liquor business is over. It will be a relief to know that everything from now on is in view of the public and a dealer will not have to live from day to day or night to night with the fear of arrest or something worse hanging over him." The barstools had been taken out of some of the twelve taverns that had secured a $200 license from the city council. Before prohibition, Morris had 22 bars in town - each paying a $500 fee.

Ad reprinted from *Morris Daily Herald* April 7, 1933.

The familiar tall barstools were also removed in some taverns. One enthusiastic patron commented, "I want my stomach right against the bar this morning and when I can no longer reach my beer I'm going home." The bartender said that he had not even had time to have a glass of beer himself since he was so busy serving everyone else.

Morris bars were again featuring free pretzels and sandwiches for a nickel with a beer purchase. Bar patrons recalled the good old days with 4% Gebhard beer.

The Morris City Council had endured serious financial losses during prohibition. Approximately $1200 had been taken in annually from licensing of beer, billiards, and pool in pre-prohibition years. Now, not only would the city benefit financially from the renewed source of income, but distributors stood to make $40 on every a barrel even after paying a $5 federal tax and their brewery bill of $15 a barrel. (12)

In spite of the availability of beer in almost every town in the Valley, there were still individuals producing moonshine. Federal agents along with Dave Cooper of Marseilles, who was working with them, discovered one rather large operation three miles southwest of Streator. When the agents arrived on April 13 at 8:30 p.m., they found Dominic Sabitino hard at work. As the agents were searching the barn, another man, Carl Ritto, came in at about 1:30 a.m. They were both taken to the LaSalle jail. The owner of the barn, Clarence Whalen, was ordered to appear in Ottawa for the hearing before the U.S. commissioner.

As a result of the raid, there was a large amount of distillery equipment to haul away. The 500-gallon St. Louis style still, a re-cooker, condenser, cooler, pre-heater, 15-hp boiler, and three steam pumps were all destroyed. Only one of three 3,000-gallon vats had any mash cooking, and it was only half full. Several hundred tin cans were found empty. Only five tins were found with alcohol. Apparently, certain individuals were still in business and were going to extremes to continue their illegal pursuits. (13)

This was not an isolated incident. On April 23, another large operation was found on the John Peterson farm located southwest of New Bedford in northwestern Bureau County about 15 miles from Princeton. Federal agents in Rockford had been suspicious of a large truck that had been driving around the city and finally making a delivery of alcohol. Rather than arrest the driver immediately, the agents followed the empty truck back to the New Bedford farm.

With the discovery of the Greenville Township distillery, the agents planned a Sunday morning raid. Two agents from the Rockford office, together with Chief of Police Ward Miller, Sheriff Neill from Dixon, and Princeton Deputy Gene Flaherty arrived at 4 a.m. Later, they explained to a reporter from the *Bureau County Republican* that they could smell a distinct odor of alcohol as they approached the farm. The bootleggers, who were found loading another shipment of alcohol, were taken completely by surprise. Two of the men, Howard Plumley and Joe Schreiner were from Erie, Illinois. The other man, Clement McKey, was from East Moline. Schreiner, was the same individual who was involved in the Tampico distillery investigation in March. He had a reputation as the "kingpin" of the local bootleggers in the region. Peterson, a tenant farmer, drove to his house, but after seeing "strangers on the premises," he left hurriedly.

Three large trucks were being used. Plumley was stopped only a half-mile west of the farm while driving a truck loaded with 240 gallons of alcohol. Another truck was loaded with 250 gallons and appeared to be ready for delivery. Subsequent investigations revealed that the New Bedford operation was supplying Sterling, Rock Falls, Rockford, and other cities in northern Illinois. (14)

The officers dismantled the huge still and loaded it into one of the bootleggers' trucks. The fermentation vats held 25,000 gallons of mash. The addition of kerosene to the mash by the officers completely destroyed any further use of the mix. In addition, the 5,600 pounds of sugar and 450 pounds of yeast were also confiscated. After everything was loaded, the prisoners and equipment were taken back to the county jail for processing. The $4,000 plant was effectively out of business. (15)

In addition to policing alcohol production, governmental bodies also had to contend with a number of legal loose ends. For one thing, LaSalle had passed one of the most stringent ordinances regarding the sale of beer. As the ordinance was initially proposed, a loophole in the new permit system was discovered. The city council did not want to see convicted bootleggers back in business. While the new regulation specifically outlawed their acquisition of a beer permit, it did not prohibit a friend or relative from obtaining one. So it could be "business as usual" by only changing the name of the permit holder. (16)

Another problem was the matter of enforcing the new permit regulations. Each tavern or restaurant that wanted to serve beer and wine had to file an application for a permit. At first, a number of the establishments simply refused to take the time to apply. Perhaps it was because former owners like Pete Daukezas and John Grosskreutz had been denied a permit. (17) By July, 55 proprietors complied with the new ordinance. Only two applicants were denied a permit. However, there was a continuing problem in the county where a number of rural taverns had not obtained a beer license. (18)

A lively debate also flared up in the Peru City Council meeting in July. Initially the council had voted to establish a midnight closing time for bars in the city. In one heated exchange an alderman exclaimed, "Some of our aldermen have wishbones where they ought to have backbones." Nonetheless, the restriction was lifted by a 6-5 vote. Bars in Peru could be open 24 hours a day. (19)

Even before the legalization of beer, the Ottawa city council had drawn up a series of revisions to its ordinances to deal with the regulation of beer distribution. Taverns would be classified as Type "A" establishments. Distributors would fall into the Type "B" classification.

Both would be required to pay a $200 annual fee. Other regulations forbid the granting of a beer license to convicted felons and barred all slot machines and other gambling equipment. Beer parlors had to close at midnight and could not reopen until 6 a.m. They also had to close every Sunday. In addition, the location of taverns could not be within 200' of hospitals, schools, churches, or veterans' homes. Mayor H.J. Hillard signed the emergency measure went into effect on April 15. (20)

LaSalle County officials had a different problem. What should be done about the dozens of individuals who had been charged with the sale of 3.2 beer but had not yet had their day in court? From time to time, the state's attorney simply removed such cases from the docket when the court calendar was overloaded with more serious offenses. With the passage of the new beer law in Congress, many hoped these old prohibition cases would be dropped and those serving time in county jails would be immediately released. In response to an inquiry from LaSalle, District Attorney Dwight Green in Chicago interpreted the March 22 law in such a way that those serving time for the manufacture of home brew would have to serve their entire sentence. The legalization of beer manufacturing would not serve as a mitigating factor in shortening anyone's sentence. (21)

While beer and wine may have been legalized, there was still the battle to repeal the 18th Amendment. The 21st Amendment, which would carry that out, had been proposed by the Congress, and the ratification process was making its way across the country. It would require the approval of 36 states to allow the sale of alcohol. In Illinois, the voters registered an emphatic 4-1 majority in favor of adopting the change. In Chicago, 90% of the voters were in favor of ending prohibition. Illinois was the 9th state to vote for ratification, and so far no state had voted to retain the 18th amendment. (22) One by one, the states voted to ratify the 21st Amendment. In August, Texas voted for repeal thus extending the unbroken line of states in favor of repealing the 18th Amendment to 22. On September 10, Maine raised the number to 26. This was a historic event since Maine had been dry for the last 75 years! But it would still take ten more states to make the 21st Amendment the new law of the land.

As the ratification process continued, local governments and the state legislators in Springfield wrestled with various plans to regulate legalized beer through licensing and taxation. Although beer was now legal, there were many retailers that did not want to be burdened with licensing fees. Oglesby Police Chief James Kneebone ran into this problem with Linto Lolli, a truck driver for Fred DeFilippi. In spite of numerous warnings, Lolli continued to bring loads of beer into Oglesby without paying the $50 annual fee to the Oglesby coffers. As of August, only three of the distributors operating in the city had secured a license so it was anticipated that more arrests would be made. (23)

News of raids on rural stills became non-existent so moral crusaders aimed at other vices that had always existed but were seldom controlled. B.H. Pyszka, one of LaSalle's city commissioners, proposed that the city rid itself of prostitution and gambling. Accordingly, Chief Walloch conducted a raid at the establishment at 101 First Street owned by John Ostrowski. It had been the target of several raids during prohibition days, but since beer was now legal, the police filed new charges – maintaining a "disorderly house." They arrested two young ladies and confiscated a number of slot machines. However, it was one of the few successful attempts to crackdown on vice. Mayor H.M. Orr noted in the September city council meeting someone had tipped off the gambling joints with the result that the slot machines in the city had disappeared overnight in advance of the raids. Commissioner and moral crusader Milera Mason commented, "Somebody certainly was not loyal and was not fair to the county." She had hoped that the discussions in the city council chambers would remain quiet while the police conducted their investigations. Because of such naiveté, gambling and other forms of vice would, in the decades that followed, brand LaSalle as "Little Las Vegas" well into the 1950's.

November 9, 1933 was set as the deadline for closing all bars in LaSalle that did not obtain the $100 semi-annual license to stay in business. Commissioner Milera Mason said that they would have to "pay up or shut up." The city council had allowed beer parlors to continue in business under the old "soft drink parlor" licensing designation until that expired. Some owners said that they decided to get out of the business rather than pay. In 1933, 68 retailers and wholesalers did secure permits to sell beer. Chief of Police Walloch was ordered to close down the four drinking establishments that were bucking the ordinance. (24)

The village of Tonica was conspicuous in the lack of any efforts to control the use of alcohol throughout the prohibition years and, indeed, for most of its history as an organized municipality. There was a unique explanation for this situation. A provision in the land grant that established the community, that had been almost religiously adhered to, specified that the ownership of any property that was used for the sale of intoxicating liquor would automatically revert to the heirs of the previous owners. That provision was maintained until April 1933, when 3.2 beer was legalized. Such beer was now designated as a non-intoxicating beverage. As the final ratification of the 21st Amendment loomed in December 1933, the village board had to deal with the historic land grant clause. Tonica Mayor Woodke said, "Hard liquor will be just naturally barred." The local Methodist minister, Rev. Schult, who had even fought and lost the battle over licensing of retail outlets, joined that sentiment. The 3.2 beer would be tolerated in the three local establishments that paid an annual $5 fee to the village, but any beverage with a higher alcohol content would be barred for sale in the village. (25)

Streator had a special interest in the repeal of the Volstead Act. Anticipating that prohibition would soon be eliminated and there would be a tremendous demand for bottles, the Owens-Illinois Glass Co. fired up one of its furnaces to begin the production of liquor bottles. The smoke rising from the stacks was a welcomed sign to the many unemployed workers.

On Dec. 5, 1933, Utah became the 36th state to ratify the 21st Amendment. The local and state governments had to devise new laws to regulate every aspect of liquor and beer production and sales. Most important was legislating the license fees and other tax revenues that were desperately needed. The General Assembly in Springfield struggled throughout 1933 in its attempt to adopt legislation to regulate the sale of beer. When a bill was finally passed, only Senator Noah Mason of Oglesby voted against it. One of several provisions in the law was especially bothersome to the local politician. Local brewers such as Star Union and Peru Products would be barred from owning any taverns and could not extend credit to retailers for more than the customary 90 days. In Mason's opinion, the only recourse for the companies would be to sell their numerous local taverns and all of the fixtures. (26)

By 1933, regulation had replaced prohibition. The "soft drink" parlors (speakeasies) of the 20's that survived the constant raids became licensed taverns. Cities could now collect substantial amounts of tax revenues from the sale of alcohol to fund the growing need for public works projects and relief programs as the depression deepened and soup kitchens fed a growing number of unemployed men. The front-page stories of federal raids had vanished. Bank robberies, milk strikes, and labor disputes now warranted banner headlines. Special prosecutors, such as Hanson and Dowd, either retired or found new challenges in law enforcement. Bootleggers were out of business. Al Capone faced many more years of confinement in the Atlanta penitentiary and faded from history, but others took his place, as new rackets became profitable.

The "Roaring 20's" had passed into history. The "Noble Experiment," as President Hoover described the enforcement of the 18th Amendment, turned out to be a unique struggle between moral crusaders and a restless generation that challenged the prevailing order. FDR's New Deal closed the chapter that defined heroes such as Charles Lindbergh and villains like "Scarface" Al Capone. Now, the new president had more important problems to confront as the Great Depression worsened.

Chapter 18
Legacy of a Bygone Era

More than eight decades have passed since the prohibition era began. Most elements of that unique period have faded from memory and from view. The few remains of the once-huge breweries - Star Union, Peru Products, Ottawa Brewing and Gebhard - give only a hint of the size and importance, that they had in the social and economic aspects of the river towns before and after the Volstead Act. With few exceptions, the illegal stills and mash vats were destroyed or recycled as scrap.

However, there are a few signs of the times that one can still find. No doubt a few area residents cling to a hidden family heirloom in the form of an old cooling coil or an old beer keg gathering dust in a basement, garage, or barn. The empty amber bottles of Star Union and Peru Products beer are still treasured collectors' items. A few of the old speakeasies made it through those turbulent years and were turned into perfectly legal drinking establishments. Many other buildings, especially the soft drink parlors along First Street in LaSalle and Walnut Street in Oglesby were abandoned or torn down. Old timers might still reminisce about raids by Hanson or Dowd or perpetuate rumors of Al Capone and his boys visiting the area when they wanted to take in a show or go duck hunting along the river. The following pages provide a glimpse of that time in American history called the "Roaring '20's" that can still be viewed today.

Many small, neighborhood bars trace their history back to a time when they were the local distributors for Star Union products. This one is

located at the corner of Hennepin and St. Paul Streets in Mark. Having gone through a number of owners and a variety of uses over the years, this former tavern was re-christened the Coal Miners Café in 2003.

Another Mark tavern, once owned by owned by Alfonse Mazzini in the 1930's, also traces its origin to Star Union sponsorship. Located on the southwest corner of Mark's famous four-corners, it was converted to apartments in recent years.

While most of the furnishings from prohibition-era bars disappeared over the years, these chairs, which are emblazoned with a Star Union logo (☆UBCO) on the backs, were once used in the Mazzini tavern in Mark. Art Piccioli collection.

The four-corner's intersection of Peoria and 4th Streets in Peru with the 1902 Hoerner building on the northwest corner is a reminder of the man who ran the Star Union Brewing Co. The site was unique in that it was the location of one of the very first bars in Peru, the Conrad Eickenfeldeis Saloon, dating back to around 1857. The holdings of the Star Union company included much more than its brewery on Water Street in Peru. During the prohibition years, the soda bottling facility was located at 5th and Peoria in Peru.

The cornice on this building at 1059 8th Street in LaSalle bears the year 1901. The lower level was once a Star Union tavern. The distinctive turn-of-the-century architecture is found on many of the buildings in LaSalle and Peru.

Dresbach Distributing now operates out of this old Star Union building near the waterfront. Pabst Blue Ribbon Beer is still available through the distributor.

Little remains of the Star Union Brewery - only the old bottling section of the plant. The brewery building, the Cellars cooling house and the other structures have all fallen victim to the wrecking ball. Bricks and large limestone blocks litter the neighboring lot to the east along the old Rock Island tracks. William Dresbach, a former Star Union employee, stayed with the operation long after Star Union was bought out by Canadian Ace Brewing. When Pabst purchased the property from Canadian Ace, they offered Dresbach a distributorship, which he accepted in the 60's. Although retired from active participation in the day to day operation, he still stops by on occasion.

Only that portion of the building on the right side is original. The section at left was added in more recent years

On the north bluff, overlooking the Illinois River, James Hebel is restoring the main office building of the Peru Beer Co.

In the above photo, the building at left was the automotive department where beer trucks were maintained. Left photo-bottling department. The old Peru Beer Co. buildings are located are located along the Rock Island tracks.

Once the scene of vibrant economic activity, the bottling plant of the Peru Beer Co. still bears the "Bottling Department" name.

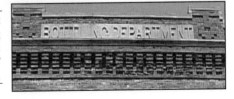

Perhaps one of the most popular gathering places in LaSalle that dates back to prohibition days is located at 959 Ninth Street. The two-story, red brick building was built in 1883 as a social center and gathering place mainly for the Polish immigrants of LaSalle.

The year at the top of the building is 1883, but Benedict Doll did not use it as a bar until 1885. The second floor was converted to an apartment for the Waszkowiak family in 1938.

The 24' long "Del Monte" back bar at today's *Machelle's Backstreet* was manufactured by the Brunswick Corp. in 1903. The company ceased making such bars in the 1920's. The ornately carved woodwork was made from mahogany and cherrywood. Three mirrors are bordered with additional wooden carvings.

Even before prohibition, the building went through many owners and operators, Benedict Doll, Tom Miles, Theo Jagodzinski, B.J. Gatza, and Brony Pyszka. It continued to function as a soft drink parlor during prohibition under the operation of Joe Manicki, Marion Sment, Paul Waszkowiak and Martin Waszkowiak. Like many neighborhood establishments, it was raided from time to time, and small quantities of illicit liquor were found. The tavern business survived and continued through the depression and WWII. It is still a thriving business today under the ownership of Machelle Urban, who takes great pride in preserving its rich history.

Another LaSalle bar built before prohibition days is located at 1026 First Street.

Built in 1904, it opened under the ownership of Mathias and Vincenzia Komp. It was sold to Valentine Cigolle in 1920 who ran it as a soft drink parlor. Although it was vacant from 1930-1933, Joseph Cigolle reopened it as Cigolle's Liquors when prohibition ended. From 1945 until 1962, it was known as Club LaSalle. In recent years, it was renovated by the current owner, Dennis Kaszynski.

The art deco back bar dates from the 1930's when prohibition ended. The new owner has attempted to preserve the theme of the 20's and 30's with extensive renovation. The collection of Star Union memorabilia makes this a unique establishment in LaSalle.

Anyone who visits Utica can not help but notice the so-called "Flatiron Building," better known as Duffy's, located on Mill Street. Built in 1892, there was a saloon at the south end and a bank at the north end of the two-story structure. A dentist and a medical doctor occupied the upper floors in the early 1900's. Harrington's Drug Store occupied the building at one end, and a store replaced the bank after 1929. It became a restaurant and in the 1960's was purchased by Mr. Duffy who converted it back to a tavern, which it remains today under the under the ownership of Tom McConnell. At the far right of the photo at 123 Mill St. was another saloon, which began before prohibition. All taverns became soft drink parlors during prohibition in order to stay open. It remained a tavern until the 1940's and was vacated after the 1950's.

At right is the ice house used by the Ottawa Brewing Association.

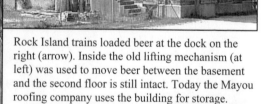

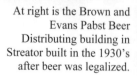

Rock Island trains loaded beer at the dock on the right (arrow). Inside the old lifting mechanism (at left) was used to move beer between the basement and the second floor is still intact. Today the Mayou roofing company uses the building for storage.

At right is the Brown and Evans Pabst Beer Distributing building in Streator built in the 1930's after beer was legalized.

In Morris, the Gebhard brewery sits in silent testimony to an age when immigrants with strong backs could find work with little trouble and, at the end of a hard day, enjoyed a pint of their favorite beer. Only the shell of the building remains today. It only takes a little imagination to picture the plant in full production with barges loaded with barley that would tie up next to the plant along the Illinois-Michigan Canal.

The brewery has been long abandoned and ravaged by the elements.

One can easily speculate that Louis Gebhard purchased coal for his boilers from the Alexander Tefler Coal Mine near the Rock Island tracks in Morris. Later, he may have found fuel at the Morris Coal Company that opened in 1907.

When prohibition began, William Gebhard sold his business. In February 1920, a 22-year old Chinese entrepreneur, Mr. Hu, who represented a syndicate of businessmen, negotiated the purchase of the brewing equipment. The boilers, fermentation tanks and other equipment was dismantled and transported to New York where it was loaded onto a ship bound for the Panama Canal. Once through the locks, the ship sailed across the Pacific to Shanghai, China. This was part of a concerted effort by the Chinese who acquired another brewery in St. Louis and two on the Pacific Coast.

Local businessmen decided to use the old buildings. They pooled their resources to invest in the Morris Milling Company managed by Dan Brown. For a time, carloads of wheat were being ground into flour, but the company went bankrupt during the depression. The Puritan Milling Co. of Chicago leased the property, valued at $60,000, in December 1932. Since prohibition was still in effect, a clause in the lease specified that no intoxicating liquor or malt could be manufactured at the Morris plant, now renamed the Century of

Progress Milling Co. The flour milling business continued and was renamed the Brown Milling Co.

In 1946, Lindsay Light and Chemical took over. Sunflame Appliance (SF) bought the plant in 1953 and they sold it again to

American Wick. Each company was involved with the manufacture of thorium-coated gas mantles. It was estimated that the plant turned out about 45,000 of the rayon sacks every week to supply the needs of campers and decorative lighting outlets. A British firm, Valor International Ltd., of London bought the business in 1986. Because of the radioactive nature of thorium, special permission for manufacturing had to be granted by the Illinois Department of Nuclear Safety. Growing concerns about the presence of the radioactive material together with the widespread applications of asbestos lead to condemnation proceedings. The Morris city council tried to have the buildings torn down since the 1990's, but only some of the steel beams were removed. An effort was made to preserve the remaining buildings as a historic site since the buildings are still structurally sound.

While beer brewing continued in the Illinois Valley at Star Union and Peru Products after prohibition ended, the larger operations eventually took over most of the market. Although there are a number of American brands available, three major companies, Budwieser, Miller, and Coors dominate the market today.

In the summer of 1994, a microbrewery began operations in Hennepin using the familiar name of the Star Union Brewing Co. The president, John Redshaw, along with 18 investors hoped to take advantage of the slump in mass marketed beers to produce a variety of specialty beers. Among the local employees were John Holmbeck, operations manager, Theresa Judd, sales and marketing manager, and Dave Urnikis, brewmaster.

The Hennepin plant was the first commercial brewery to open in central Illinois since the closure of the Pabst facility in Peoria Heights in the 1980's. The new Star Union brewery was located on 4.6 acres of land acquired from LTV Steel. Below are the labels used for three varieties of beer produced at Star Union in Hennepin. John Redshaw collection.

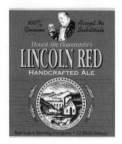
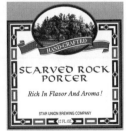

Locally the Star Union products, such as Starved Rock Amber Ale and Star Model, were distributed by Mautino's distributing in Spring Valley. The Hennepin brewery started with a 5,000 barrel per year capacity but had sufficient space to produce as much as 15,000 barrels annually. One of the main differences between the old Star Union of Henry Hoerner's day was that the new Star Model would be a wheat-based brew using Briess malt and Cascade and Tettnanger hops. After nine days of fermentation and another month of cold storage, the beer was ready for distribution. The company's "Taste the History" slogan was an attempt to remind beer drinkers of the Peru brewery's Star Model 120-year reputation for quality products.

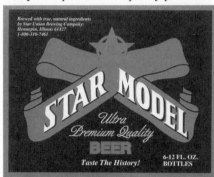

Unfortunately, the Star Union Brewing Company in Hennepin was not a financial success. Intense competition and the unfamiliar wheat-based brew contributed to the company's problems. The plant ceased operations in 1996. Artifacts bearing the famous Star Model logo again became only historic collectibles.

Ironically, it is in Morris, only a few blocks from the old Gebhard buildings, that one finds the only operating brewery in the Valley. Begun in 2000, the Firehouse Restaurant and Brewing Co. offers its patrons a choice of five

different varieties, Fire House Light, Prairie Fire Wheat, Spotted Dog Pale Ale, Fire Engine Red and Night Watch Dark. Although the names are not as familiar as Star Model, they offer a nostalgic reminder of a bygone era.

The new restaurant in Morris is not really a firehouse in spite of the firehouse-like doors.
It's really a restaurant and microbrewery that produces five different varieties of beer.

Brewmaster Matt Van Wyk takes charge of polished copper tanks and metal beer kegs holding five varieties of beer. It is currently the only location one can find in the Illinois Valley for a close-up view of how beer was once made.

The era of speakeasies, gangsters, secret stills, moonshine, and home brewed beer has long since passed into history. For some, it was a lawless decade, while others look back on the illegal activities with a nostalgic smile. What was once a crime is today a thriving business employing thousands of workers nationwide and providing a relaxing respite from the tedious workday- not unlike the satisfaction enjoyed by the weary coal miners and factory workers of the Illinois Valley eighty years ago.

Published Sources

Abbreviations used – LSDPT (LaSalle Daily Post Tribune) MDH (Morris Daily Herald), BCR (Bureau County Republican) PCR (Putnam County Record) SFP (Streator Free Press), ODR (Ottawa Daily Republican).

All stories are found on page one unless otherwise indicated.

Chapter 3

1. "Senate Rejects Veto by Wilson by 65 To 20 Vote," LSDPT, Oct. 28, 1919.
2. "Chicago's Plan for 'Big Night' Are Postponed," LSDPT, Nov. 15, 1919.
3. "Supreme Court Opens Hearing on Prohibition," LSDPT, Nov. 20, 1919.
4. "Big Beer Stock Held From Sale by U.S. Dry Law," LSDPT, Nov. 27, 1919.
5. "Supreme Court Overrules All Wet Arguments," LSDPT, Dec. 15. 1919.
6. "Fight is Begun by New Jersey in Upper Court," LSDPT, Dec. 16, 1919.

Chapter 4

1. "Wine and Women Seized in Raid on Valley Home," LSDPT, Jan. 8, 1920.
2. "Moonshiners Will be Taken Into US Court," LSDPT, Jan. 10, 1920.
3. "Didn't Know it Until Too Late," MDH, Jan.12, 1920.
4. "Booze Stills Unearthed By Gum Shoe Men," MDH, Feb. 13, 1920.
5. "Seek to Legalize Beer and Wine," LSDPT, Jan. 22, 1920.
6. "Nab Still and Booze in Ottawa," LSDPT, Feb. 26, 1920.
7. "Allow N. Jersey To File Attack on Prohibition," LSDPT, Mar. 15, 1920.
8. "Convict Owner of Ottawa Still," LSDPT, May 20, 1920.
9. "Revenue Man is Accused by Two Liquor Sellers," LSDPT, 1920.
10. "One Drink Cost Ciganovich $75," LSDPT, Oct. 18, 1920.
11. "Sheriff Nabs 18 Barrels of 3.10 Pct. Beer," LSDPT, Oct. 22, 1920.
12. "Violators of Dry Law Fined at County Seat," LSDPT, Oct. 22, 1920.
13. "Oglesby Plans a Curb on Soft Drink Parlors," LSDPT, Nov. 18, 1920.
14. "Oglesby Man is Placed in Jail as Moonshiner," LSDPT, Dec. 9, 1920.
15. "Brundage Wars on 'Wet'Saloons of LaSalle Co.," LSDPT, Dec. 15, 1920.
16. "Mayor Sends Ultimatum to Saloon," LSDPT, Dec. 17, 1920.
17. "Summon Saloon Men to Appear Before Landis," LSDPT, Dec. 18, 1920.
18. "Failed to Heed, Tip, Saloon Man Put Under Bond," LSDPT, Dec. 20, 1920.

Chapter 5

1. "Ottawa Saloon Man Acquitted by Landis Jury," LSDPT, Jan. 5. 1921.
2. "Landis Cites 3 Saloon Men For Contempt," LSDPT, Mar. 3, 1921.
3. "Landis Issues Writs Against Twin City Bars," LSDPT, Mar. 15, 1921.
4. "Sheriff Ayers and Aides Raid 2 Saloons Here," LSDPT, Mar. 21, 1921.
5. "Local Saloon Man Pays $300 Fine in Court," LSDPT, Mar. 24, 1921.
6. "Third Oglesby Man Draws Fine," LSDPT, April 1, 1921.
7. "Druggists Can Buy Booze on April 1st," LSDPT, Mar. 17, 1921.
8. "2 Local Saloon Men Draw Fines," LSDPT, April 8, 1921.
9. "Raid A Saloon at Seatonville; Owner on Trial," LSDPT, April 22. 1921.
10. "Doffs Uniform, Nabs Salesman as Bootlegger," LSDPT, April 23, 1921.
11. "4 More Saloons in Oglesby and Peru Visited," LSDPT, April 25, 1921.
12. "Shack Reveals Itself As Home of Moonshiner," LSDPT, April 26, 1921.
13. "Moonshiners Admit Guilt; Sent to Jail," LSDPT, May 12, 1921.
14. "Oglesby Mayor Serves Notice on Law Evaders," LSDPT, May 10, 1921.
15. "Warrants Served on Oglesby Saloon Men," LSDPT, May 12, 1921, p. 2.
16. "Finds Booze in Pool of Water Under A House," LSDPT, May 17, 1921.
17. "Officers Raid Still Hidden in Timber on Farm," LSDPT, May 20, 1921.
18. "Uses Moonshine Still to Raise Farm Mortgage," LSDPT, July 16, 1921.
19. "Beer Isn't Safe Even in Village Jail," LSDPT, July 1, 1921.
20. "Sheriff Raids Wine Cache on Bank of River," LSDPT, July 25, 1921,
21. "Nephew Looted Mischke's Wine Cellar Report." LSDPT, Aug. 9, 1921.
22. "Still Found in Vacant House in Seatonville," LSDPT, July 28, 1921.

23. "Two Are Nabbed as Moonshiners," LSDPT, Aug. 4, 1921.
24. "Wholesale Raid on Moonshine 'Joints' at Depue Monday," LSDPT, Aug. 4, 1921.
25. "New Arrest is Made Today As Result of Raid." LSDPT, Aug. 6, 1921.
26. "Spring Valley Saloon Man is Found Guilty," LSDPT, Sept. 8, 1921.
27. "Seeks 2.75 Beer With Heavy Tax," LSDPT, Sept. 8, 1921.
28. "Ottawa Police Officer Nabbed As Booze Seller," LSDPT, Sept. 19, 1921, p. 2.
29. "Ottawa Police Officer Freed by Court of Bootlegging," LSDPT, Sept. 26, 1921.
30. "Ottawa Police Officer Nabbed As Booze Seller," LSDPT, Sept. 19, 1921.
31. "Mendota Homes Raided; Take 2 As Bootleggers," LSDPT, Sept. 22, 1921.
32. "Wallop on Head Saves Evidence in 'Booze' Raid," LSDPT, Sept. 23, 1921, pp.1-2.
33. "60 Days in Jail for Booze Sales." LSDPT, Sept. 29, 1921.
34. "Police Raid 3 Saloons in West Ottawa," ODR, Oct. 6, 1921.
35. "LaSalle Booze is Poured into Ottawa Gutter," LSDPT, Oct. 19, 1921.
36. "Found Guilty on 2 Counts," ODR, Nov. 18, 1921.
37. "Senate Bans Medical Beer," ODR, Nov. 18, 1921.
38. "Leland's Mayor Catches Man As He Sells Booze," ODR, Dec. 1, 1921.
39. "Booze Joint Raid Maid by Police Chief," ODR. Dec. 9, 1921.
40. "Ottawa Brewery Accused of Making and Selling Real Beer," LSDPT, Dec. 17, 1921.
41. "Brewery is Under Guard of Federal Agents," ODR, Dec. 21, 1921.
42. "Police and Deputies Raid Saloons Here," LSDPT, Dec. 19, 1921.
43. "Seizes 4 Stills and Bottles of Moonshine, Etc." LSDPT, Dec. 27, 1921.
44. "2 Nabbed at Earlville as Moonshiners." ODR, Dec. 29, 1921.
45. "Name Kline As Operator of Whisky Still," ODR, Dec. 31, 1921.
Chapter 6
1. "Ayers Nabs 3 in First Booze Raids of Year." ODR, Jan. 9, 1922
2. "Streator Boys Tell of Buying Illicit Liquor," LSDPT, Mar. 8, 1922.
3. "Jury convicts Man for Sale of Booze," LSDPT, Mar. 9, 1922.
4. "Moonshine Jug and Moonshine Jag End in Cell," LSDPT, May 10, 1922.
5. "Nab Leland Man as Bootlegger," LSDPT, May 22, 1922.
6. "Still Found in Peru By Ayers," LSDPT, July 12, 1922.
7. " Sheriff Finds Booze in Auto; Driver is Held," LSDPT, July 29, 1922.
8. "Spring Valley Widow is Fined For Booze Sale," LSDPT, Aug. 3, 1922.
9. "Sheriff finds Moon in Hiding –2 Are Arrested," LSDPT, Oct. 16, 1922.
10. "Sheriff Finds Booze in Peru," LSDPT, Dec. 18, 1922.
Chapter 7
1. "Welter in Raids in Oglesby Bars," LSDPT, Jan. 8, 1923.
2. "Oglesby Men To Get Trial Today," LSDPT, Jan 10,1923.
3. "Sheriff Raids Four Barrooms in LaSalle County," LSDPT, Jan. 15, 1923.
4. "Warrants for 5 in Beer Seizure," LSDPT, Feb. 25, 1923.
5. "30 barrels of Beer Seized in Morning Raids," LSDPT, Feb. 19, 1923.
6. "Brewery Raids Now Hit Ottawa; 19 BBLS. Seized." LSDPT, April 24, 1923.
7. "Star Union Case Opens in Court," LSDPT, May 24, 1923.
8. "Say Beer Was 4 Per Cent." LSDPT, May 25, 1923.
9. "Jury is Out in Peru Beer Case," LSDPT, May 29, 1923.
10. "Court to close Peru Products," LSDPT, July 14, 1923.
11. "20 Gallons of Moonshine is Found in Home," LSDPT, Feb. 26, 1923.
12. "Booze Seizures Reach Big Total," LSDPT, April 4, 1923.
13. "2 Saloons Yield Stock of Booze," LSDPT, July 20,1923.
14. "City Starts to Enforce A Law It Just Passed," LSDPT, July 20, 1923.
15. "Bellrose Sits All Night Over Beer He Seized," LSDPT, Oct. 4, 1923.
16. "Putnam County Moonshiner is Placed In Jail," LSDPT, Nov. 1, 1923.
17. "Sheriff Seizes 75 BBLS of Beers in LaSalle Raid," LSDPT, Nov. 12, 1923.
18. "Booze Flood Wets Chicago; Get All Kinds," LSDPT, Dec. 19, 1923.
19. "Launch Move to Close Saloons in Marseilles," LSDPT, Dec. 27, 1923.

Chapter 8
1. "Elgin's Beer in River Stream," LSDPT, Mar. 5, 1924.
2. "Dozen Federal Agents 'Mop Up' Along First St.," LSDPT, April 11,1924.
3. "Sheriff Seizes Still, 'Moon,' and Mash in Oglesby." LSDPT, April 16, 1924.
4. "Get Evidence in Four Places; Six Found O.K.," LSDPT, May 1, 1924.
5. "Three Get Jail In Booze Cases," LSDPT, May 8, 1924.
6. "Booze Raiders Active Today in Twin Cities," LSDPT, June 4, 1924.
7. "18 Ordered To Appear Before Commissioner," LSDPT, July 29, 1924.
8. "Find Still in Home of Man 80 Years Old," LSDPT, June 16, 1924.
9. "Welter Gets Men and Booze in Four Raids," LSDPT, June 6, 1924.
10. "Confiscates Two Stills and Moonshine," LSDPT, July 31. 1924.
11. "Beer Runner is Given $500 Fine," LSDPT, Oct. 2, 1924.
12. "Hanson Opens His Drive Against Liquor Sales," LSDPT, Dec. 3, 1924.
13. "Utica Saloon Cases Come Up on Dec. 12," LSDPT, Dec. 4, 1924.
14. "Sheriff Raids Many Streator Bars and Homes," LSDPT, Dec. 4, 1924, p. 2.
15. "Hanson Meets Set-Back in Fight on Saloons," LSDPT, Dec. 15, 1924.
16. "It's Expensive," LSDPT, Dec. 15, 1924,
17. "State's Attorney Asks Closing of 20 Saloons," LSDPT, Dec. 16, 1924.
Chapter 9
1. "Court Closes 3 Streator Buildings," LSDPT, Jan. 3, 1925.
2. "Hanson Closes Two Places By Court's Orders," LSDPT, Jan 14, 1925.
3. "Proprietor Admits that He Broke Law," LSDPT, Jan. 13. 1925.
4. "Hanson Seeks to Close Business House," LSDPT, Jan. 21, 1925.
5. "Kozlowski Is Fined $500 on Booze Charges, " LSDPT, Feb. 4, 1925.
6. "Owner of Bar is Bound to Grand Jury," LSDPT, Mar. 3, 1925.
7. "Three Places Are Called on Over Week-end," LSDPT, Mar. 9, 1925.
8. "Home of Smith Bombed," SFP, Mar. 11, 1925.
9. "Smith Cottage in Streator is Blast's Target," LSDPT, Mar. 11, 1925.
10. "Spring Valley, DePue, Seaton, Ladd Visited," LSDPT, Mar. 13, 1925.
11. "Liquor Found Hidden Under Foundation," LSDPT, Mar. 20, 1925.
12. "Deputies Raid Bar in Rutland," LSDPT, Mar. 21, 1925.
13. "Places Raided After Autoist Makes Charge, LSDPT, Mar. 23, 1925.
14. "Buy Home Brew, Then Read Warrant," LSDPT, Mar. 24, 1925.
15. "Nertney's Bar is Visited by Mop Up Squad," LSDPT, Mar. 26, 1925.
16. "Hanson's Crew Uses Shovel to Unearth Booze," LSDPT, Mar. 31, 1925.
17. "Bottles Were Brushed Into Hole in Floor," LSDPT, April 11, 1925.
18. "Hanson Files Information in Circuit Court," LSDPT, April 25, 1925.
19. "LaSalle Bar is Closed By Write of US Court," LSDPT, April 10,1925.
20. "Seven are Fined in Booze Cases in Court Today," LSDPT, April 20, 1925.
21. "Bootlegger is Given 6 Months in County Jail," LSDPT, April 23, 1925.
22. "First St. Man Helps Officers Locate Booze," LSDPT, April 24, 1925.
23. "Truckload of Liquor Seized at 12 Places," LSDPT, April 27, 1925.
24. "Find 4 Barrels of Wine and a Bottle of Moon," LSDPT, Apr. 28, 1925.
25. "Derby Tickets and Ball Pools Taken By Them," LSDPT, May 1, 1925.
26. "Gambling Raids Spread to LaSalle," LSDPT, May 9, 1925.
27. "Bonded Booze is Seized By 3 Constables," LSDPT, July 14, 1925.
28. "Hanson's Men Have Busy Day at Local Bars," LSDPT, July 31, 1925.
29. "3000 Bottle of Home Brew in His Cellar," LSDPT, Aug. 3, 1925.
30. "40 Gallons of Booze Is Also Located There," LSPDT, Aug. 5, 1925
31. "Dumping Board Helps them Get Evidence," LSDPT, Aug. 6, 1925.
32. "Booze Raiders Catch Eight in Week-End Work," LSDPT, Aug.10, 1925.
33. "Manager Korb is Ordered to Appear Today," LSDPT, Aug. 12, 1925.
34. "Valley Police Nab Trio Who Fired on Them," LSDPT, Aug. 13, 1925.
35. "Beer Runners Who Shot at Officers Given $250 Fine," BCR, Oct. 8, 1925.

36. "Hanson and Aides Mop Up West End," LSDPT, Aug. 22, 1925.
37. "Order Issued for Destruction of Seized Liquor," LSDPT, Aug. 24, 1925.
38. "Star Union Brewery Swept by Fire," LSDPT, Aug. 28, 1925.
39. "Owners Planning To Rebuild Star Union," LSDPT, Aug. 29, 1925.
40. "Gets Wine and Moon on Visit To Oglesby Bar," LSDPT. Aug. 31, 1925.
41. "Continue Raids in Twin Cities," LSDPT, Sept. 14, 1925.
42. "Find Still in One Place With a Small Model," LSDPT, Sept. 5, 1925.
43. "Latino Car Shows But One Bullet," SFP, May 27, 1925.
44. "Hanson's Deputy Shot in Gun Clash," LSDPT, May 25, 1925.
45. "Constable Smith's Home Dynamited," SFP, Sept. 14, 1925.
46. "Dry Agent and His Family in Narrow Escape," LSDPT, Sept. 14, 1925.
47. "Hanson to Ask Fund to Assist in Such Cases," LSDPT, Sept. 14, 1925.
48. "Sheriff's Men Outwit Saloon Keeper Here," LSDPT, Oct. 1, 1925.
49. "5 More LaSalleans Caught," LSDPT, Oct. 2, 1925.
50. "Quinto Ossola Facing Second Liquor Charge," LSDPT, Oct. 3, 1925.
51. "Sixty Days in Jail given to the Offender," LSDPT, Oct. 5, 1925.
52. "Smith, Liquor Raider Quits As Hanson Aide," LSDPT, Oct. 7, 1925.
53. "Cherry Man Goes Back to Jail in New Booze Case," LSDPT, Sept. 9, 1925.
54. "Federal Agents Seize Brewing Plant in Ladd," BCR, Sept. 17, 1925.
55. "Chicken Farm At Ladd Revealed," ODT, Sept. 14, 1925.
56. "LaSalle Bootlegger Forces Way Into Jail," BCR, Oct. 22, 1925.
57. "Booze to Be Destroyed By Court Order," LSDPT, Oct. 31, 1925.
58. "County Ward Pays His Fine in Booze Case," LSDPT, Nov. 3, 1925.
59. "Court Injunctions Close 21 Buildings in County," LSDPT, Nov. 5, 1925.
60. "Sheriff Raids Two Homes in LaSalle Last Night," LSDPT, Nov. 17, 1925.
61. "Oglesby Bar is Raided Friday," LSDPT, Nov. 21, 1925.
62. "Hanson Helps Place Bars on Ransom Saloon," LSDPT, Dec. 2, 1945.
Chapter 10
1. "Hanson's Men Raid 4 More," LSDPT, Jan. 8, 1926.
2. "Hanson's Men Raid 4 More," LSDPT. Jan 8, 1926.
3. "Hanson's Men At Work Early This Morning," LSDPT, Jan.9, 1926.
4. "Claim to Have Evidence From Both Saloons," LSDPT, Jan. 7, 1926.
5. "Hanson's Men Get Evidence in Two Local Raids," LSDPT, Jan. 14, 1926.
6. "Two Truckloads Secured From 4 Homes There," LSDPT, Jan. 27, 1926.
7. "Find Liquor in Raid on Saloon," LSDPT, Feb. 12, 1926.
8. "Tonic Beer Holds Little cheer For Beer Drinkers," LSDPT, Mar. 31. 1926.
9. "Hanson Aides Seize Auto of 3 Bootleggers." LSDPT, April 29, 1926.
10. "Admits He Was Brewing Beer, Lands in Jail," LSDPT, June 5, 1926.
11. "Secure Liquor in Raid Close to County Seat," LSDPT July 2, 1926.
12. "Wine, Gin, Moonshine, Seized in Oglesby Raids," LSDPT, July 13, 1926.
13. "Nine Oglesby Men Jailed in Liquor Raids," LSDPT, Aug. 21, 1926.
14. "Record Haul in Liquor Raids," LSDPT, Aug. 13, 1926,
15. "Hanson's Men in Search for Few Who Fled," LSDPT, Aug. 14, 1926.
16. "Record Haul in Liquor Raids," LSDPT, Aug. 13, 1926, p. 2.
17. "Record Haul in Liquor Raids," LSDPT, Aug. 13, 1926, p. 2.
18. "Hanson's Men in Search for Few Who Fled," LSDPT, Aug. 14, 1926.
19. "Nine Oglesby Men Jailed in Liquor Raids," LSDPT, Aug. 21, 1926.
20. "Sewers Get Much Booze," LSDPT, Nov. 13, 1926.
21. "Home Brew Is Given Andrew's Permission," LSDPT, Dec. 29, 1929.
Chapter 11
1. "Booze Taken In Home Raid," LSDPT, Dec. 30, 1926
2. "Liquor Raids Are Staged By Sheriff Clark," LSDPT, Jan. 6, 1927.
3. "Clark Raids Home of Candidate in Ottawa Election," LSDPT, Feb. 26, 1927.
4. "Spring Valley Saloons Under Federal Raid," LSDPT, Jan. 21, 1927.

5. "Forty Liquor Warrants Are Being Served," LSDPT, Feb. 24, 1927
6. "Liquor Raid Victims Are Arraigned," LSDPT, Feb. 25, 1927.
7. "Wildcat Brewery Seized at Arlington," LSDPT, Mar. 24, 1927.
8. "Women Taken in Two Raids in Oglesby," LSDPT, Mar. 10, 1927.
9. "Much Liquor Taken By Raiding Party," LSDPT, Apr. 22,1927.
10. "Sledge Used in Raid on Ottawa Joint," LSDPT, May 2, 1927.
11. "Sheriff Gets Booze Supply," LSDPT, June 30, 1927.
12. "Sheriff Arrests Two After Raid; Intoxicants Taken," LSDPT, Aug. 18, 1927.
13. "Sheriff Gets Beer in Raid in Streator," LSDPT, July 9, 1927.
14. "Beer, Moon, Mash in Raid Loot," LSDPT, July 14, 1927.
15. "Raiders Visit Seven Places; Booze Found," LSDPT, Aug. 25, 1927.
16. "Sheriff Mops Up in Bureau," LSDPT, Aug. 28, 1927.
17. "Sheriff Raids Utica Saloons," LSDPT, Aug. 29, 1927.
18. "Ottawa Drug Store Raided; Booze Taken," LSDPT, Sept. 3, 1927.
19. "Big Brewery Located At Spring Valley," LSDPT, Sept. 21, 1927.
20. "Police Find Peach Brandy Still on Chartres St.," LSDPT, Sept. 28, 1927.
21. "Cherry Raid Yields Big Liquor Loot," LSDPT, Oct. 21, 1927.
22. "Three Raids Are Made by Sheriff Clark," LSDPT, Oct. 24, 1927.
23. "Liquor is Taken in LaSalle Booze Raids," LSDPT, Oct. 29, 1927.
24. "Saloon of Politician Under Raid," LSDPT, Oct. 31, 1927. p.13.
25. "Hetherington Former Motor Cop Arrested," LSDPT, Nov. 8, 1927.
26. "Booze Found By Raid Squad," LSDPT, Nov. 14, 1927.
27. "Prohibition Head Denies Large Number," LSDPT, Nov. 16, 1927.
28. "Sheriff Gets Liquor Haul," LSPDT, Dec. 17, 1927.
29. "Hundreds of Gallons Are Clark's Loot," LSDPT, Dec. 19, 1927.
30. "Attempted to Bribe Deputy Charge Made," LSDPT, Dec. 20, 1927.
31. "Hundreds of Gallons Are Clark's Loot," LSDPT, Dec. 19, 1927.
32. "Cedar Point Still Taken," LSDPT, May 4, 1927.
33. "Hundreds of Gallons Are Clark's Loot," LSDPT, Dec. 19, 1927.
Chapter 12
1. "Sheriff finds Giant Still," LSDPT, Jan. 5, 1928
2. "Booze Taken in Raid in Arlington," LSDPT, Jan. 20, 1928.
3. "Big Liquor Haul Made in Cedar Point," LSDPT. Feb. 13, 1928.
4. "Sheriff Gets Much Booze in Oglesby Raid," LSDPT. Mar. 19, 1928.
5. "Alcohol Car Burns; Laden With Liquor," LSDPT, April 27, 1928.
6. "Five Arrested in Depue Raid," LSDPT, May 11, 1928.
7. "Sheriff Raids Ransom Hotel," LSDPT, June 6, 1928.
8. "Clark Raid Ottawa Saloon," LSDPT, July 31, 1928.
9. "Morris Wrung Dry in Raids," LSDPT, July 23, 1928.
10. "Sheriff and Aides Using Their Sponge," LSDPT, Aug. 6, 1928.
11. "Real Liquor With Bay Rum," LSDPT, Aug. 31, 1928.
12. "Thirty-Seven Are Taken in Raid in Dana." LSDPT, Sept. 5, 1928.
13. "Liquor Taken in Raids on Three Homes," LSDPT, Nov. 23, 1928.
14. "Liquor Flows Freely As New Year Appears," LSDPT, Jan. 2, 1929.
Chapter 13
1. "700 Gallons of Alcohol Are Seized," ODR, Jan. 10, 1929.
2. "Defendants Released on $4000 Bonds," LSDPT, Jan. 12, 1929.
3. "Defendants Released on $4000 Bonds," LSDPT, Jan. 12, 1929.
4. "Police Chief Says Officers Knew Nothing," LSDPT, Jan. 31, 1929.
5. "Peru Police Force Before Federal Grand Jury in Chicago," LSDPT, Jan. 23, 1929.
6. "Vinegar Odor is Alibi of Peru Police," LSDPT, Jan. 24, 1929.
7. "Probe Reveals $286,000 Paid in Graft By Liquor Syndicate," LSDPT, Jan. 24, 1929.
8. "Second Graft Collector is Being Watched," LSDPT, Jan. 25, 1929.
9. "LaRue Seeks Connection of Capone With Liquor Mob," LSDPT, Jan. 24, 1929.

10. "Federal Jury Concludes Its Investigation," LSDPT, Feb. 1, 1929.
11. "Federal Men Raid Village in Putnam Co." LSDPT, Mar. 27, 1929.
12. "Federal Men Confiscate Booze Plant," LSDPT, Mar. 28, 1929.
13. "Federals Raid Mark 2400 Pints Taken," PCR, Mar. 28, 1929.
14. "Death As Well As Liquor Is Distilled in Wildcat Plants," LSDPT, Mar. 29, 1929.
15. "Federal Men Confiscate Booze Plant," LSDPT, Mar. 28, 1929.
16. "Federal Sponge Squad Dries Up Mark Distillery," PCR, Apr. 4, 1929.
17. "Ferroni, Piccoli, Green Plead Guilty," LSDPT, Apr. 22, 1929.
18. "Dowd Tells of Tracing Fraud From Ferroni," LSDPT, Apr. 24, 1929
19. "Judge Orders Acquittal of Accused Two," LSDPT, Apr. 25, 1929.
20. "Urbanowski is Guilty Says Jury," LSDPT, April 27, 1929.
21. "Uranowski Gets Prison," LSDPT, May, 3, 1929.
22. "Urbanowski Returns Home to Peru," LSDPT, Mar. 24, 1930.
23. "Eighty-Five Gallons Taken by Patrolman," LSPT, Jan. 25, 1929.
24. "Police Hold Saloon Owner in Booze Case," LSDPT, Jan 26, 1929.
25. "Sheriff Raids Booze Still in Streator," LSDPT, Feb. 8, 1929.
26. "Morris Liquor Supply Stopped by Federal Raid," LSDPT, Feb. 8, 1929.
27. "Peru Saloon Yields Wine," LSDPT, Feb. 13, 1929.
28. "Clark Raids Peru Stills," LSDPT, Feb. 22, 1929.
29. "Clark Raids Three Places," LSDPT, Feb. 26, 1929.
30. "Kewanee Man Stands Trial," LSDPT, Feb. 26, 1929.
31. "Hundreds of Gallons of Booze Taken," LSDPT, Feb. 28, 1929.
32. "Bureau Co. Booze Squad Stages Raid," LSDPT, Mar. 4, 1929.
33. "Bootleggers Must Go Says Bureau Judge," LSDPT, Mar. 5, 1929.
34. "Three Raids in Streator," LSDPT, Mar. 6, 1929
35. "Clark Makes Raid; Undercover Results," LSDPT, Mar. 8, 1929.
36. "Thirteen Taken in County Seat Saturday Night," LSDPT, Mar. 11, 1929.
37. "Ferguson's Bartender Rearrested," LSDPT, Mar. 12, 1929.
38. "Bootleggers' Association Active, Declares LaRue," LSDPT, Mar. 11, 1929.
39. "Twenty-Eight Taken in Federal Custody," LSDPT, Mar. 15, 1929.
40. "Dry Agents to Remain," LSDPT, Mar. 26, 1929.
41. "Found Liquor in Tea Room Near Cedar Point," LSDPT, Mar. 26, 1929.
42. "Two Peru, One LaSalle Man Waive Hearing," LSDPT, April 19, 1929.
43. "Prohibition Agents Make Booze 'Buy'," LSDPT, April 6, 1929.
44. "Spring Valley Saloons Under Sheriff Raid," LSDPT, April 30, 1929.
45. "Peru Saloons Raided," LSDPT, May 14, 1929.
46. "Federal Charges Prepared Against Hybki by Agents," LSDPT, May 17, 1929.
47. "Twardowski Ran Still to Pay Off Mortgage On Property," LSDPT, May 18, 1929.
48. "Former Chief of Police is Sentenced," LSDPT, May 21, 1929.
49. "Peru Politician is Taken by Raiders," LSDPT, May 18, 1929.
50. "Federal Dry Men, Police Apply Sponge," LSDPT, June 20, 1929.
51. "Council Seeks Answer to What is Soft Drink Parlor," LSDPT, July 23, 1929.
52. "Four Towns Visited In Mop Up," LSDPT, July 29, 1929.
53. "Basement is Cache of Big Booze Supply," LSDPT, Aug. 19, 1929.
54. "Arrest Three, Secure 30 Cases Liquor," LSDPT, Nov. 20, 1929.
55. "Earlville Bootlegger is In Jail," LSDPT, Dec. 16, 1929.
56. "George Crank Arrested by Sheriff Force," LSDPT, Dec. 18, 1929.
57. "150 Quarts of Liquor Seized After Crash," LSDPT, Dec. 18, 1929.
Chapter 14
1. "Prohibition's Tenth Anniversary Today," LSDPT, Jan. 16, 1930.
2. "Mike Mura Sought As Still Owner," LSDPT, Jan. 29, 1930.
3. "Mike Mauro Surrenders," LSDPT, Feb. 7, 1930.
4. "Mark Plant Destroyed," PCR, Jan. 30, 1930.
5. "Federal Squad Discovers Big Still in Mark," LSDPT, Jan. 31, 1930.

6.   "Seatonville Still Taken," LSDPT, Feb. 3, 1930.
7.   "US Endeavors to Confiscate Local Moonshine Farm," PCR, May 8, 1930.
8.   "Most Modern Booze Plant Ever Taken," LSDPT, April 30, 1930.
9.   "Latest Still Is larger, More Modern Than Usual," LSDPT, April 30, 1930.
10.   "Dry Raiders Seize Ladd Still," LSDPT, May 2, 1930.
11.   "Invoke Old Revenue Code For Forfeiture of Farms," LSDPT, May 3, 1930.
12.   "Sheriff Clark Raids Big Wenona Still," LSDPT, May 7, 1930.
13.   "Sheriff Clark Raids Another Big Distillery," LSDPT, May 10, 1930.
14.   "Applen Raids Seven Bureau County Places," LSDPT, May 19, 1930.
15.   "Eight Soft Drink Oases Are Raided," LSDPT, May 28, 1930.
16.   "Seize brewery and Still in 3 Raids Today," LSDPT, May 28, 1930.
17.   "Streator Cops Get Abandoned Still in Raid," LSDPT, June 16, 1930.
18.   "Double Plant and Product Seized," LSDPT, June 26, 1930.
19.   "Streator Raid Yields Big Moon Still," LSDPT, June. 21, 1930.
20.   "Seize Three Streator Stills," LSDPT, June 25, 1930.
21.   "Double Plant and Product Seized," LSDPT, June 26, 1930, p. 2.
22.   "Double Plant and Product Seized," LSDPT, June 26, 1930.
23.   "Oglesby Home Nets 2 Stills," LSDPT, July 11, 1930.
24.   "Four Are Fined After Raids at Mark," LSDPT, July 25, 1930.
25.   "Still From Ladd Home is Located," LSDPT, Aug. 25, 1930.
26.   "Booze Running Aviator Drops Warning Letter," LSDPT, Aug. 23, 1930.
27.   "Capone Booze Plant Seized at Mark," LSDPT, Sept. 19,1930.
28.   "Deny That Capone is Near Lacon," LSDPT, Sept. 19, 1930.
29.   "Distillers Are Linked in Big Booze Ring," LSDPT, Dec. 4, 1930.
30.   "Mark Liquor Defendants Plead Guilty," LSDPT, May 12, 1931.
31.   "Belief Grows That Dry Law Change Will Be Made," LSDPT, Nov. 12, 1930.
Chapter 15
1.   "Distillery is Seized at Cedar Point," LSDPT, Jan. 8, 1931.
2.   "Distillery is Raided in LaSalle City," LSDPT, Jan. 16, 1931.
3.   "Sheriff Seizes LaSalle Wine Supply," LSDPT, Jan. 24, 1931.
4.   "Baima Held in Liquor Raid," LSDPT, Feb. 2, 1931.
5.   "LaSalle Hit By Wickersham Report," LSDPT, Mar. 4, 1931.
6.   "Four Facing Rum Charges," LSDPT, Mar. 7, 1931.
7.   "Raiders Find Liquor in Streator Establishments," LSDPT, April 8, 1931.
8.   "Alcohol Is Seized At Cedar Point," LSDPT, May 21, 1931.
9.   "Huge Liquor Plant Found By US Men." LSDPT, May 21, 1931.
10.   "Dry Agents Raid Still at Seneca, Operator Seized," MDH, May 22, 1931.
11.   "Find Plants Near Seneca and LaSalle," LSDPT, May 22, 1931.
12.   "Wm. Block is Facing Charge in US Court," LSDPT, June 4, 1931.
13.   "Local Stills in Huge Ring," LSDPT, June 5, 1931.
14.   "Two and Half Years, $10,000 Fine in Sight," LSDPT, June 16, 1931.
15.   "Hunt Capone Fugitives in LaSalle," LSDPT, June 19, 1931.
16.   "Sand Bar is Holding Rum Fleet Today," LSDPT, July 18,1931.
17.   "Refuel Here; Craft to Make Grafton Today," LSDPT, July 20, 1931.
18.   "Toluca Scene of Escape of Rum Prisoners," LSDPT, July 25, 1931.
19.   "Army of Federal Agents Swarm Into City," LSDPT, July 30, 1931.
20.   "Slot Machines Also Taken in County Visits," LSDPT, Sept. 28, 1931.
21.   "Former LaSalle Cop Charged," LSDPT, Sept. 23, 1931.
22.   "Two Stills, Man Seized," LSDPT, Oct. 9, 1931.
23.   "Federal Men Raid House in LaSalle," LSDPT, Oct. 13, 1931.
24.   "Facing Third Rum Charge," LSDPT, Nov. 4, 1931.
25.   "Arrest Six in Valley Raids," LSDPT, Dec. 5, 1931.
26.   "Dixon Sheriff Jails Oglesby Rum Runner," LSDPT, Dec. 29, 1931.

Chapter 16
1. "Still Found Operating in Ladd House," LSDPT, Jan. 23, 1932.
2. "Equipment is Seized, Taken Into Peoria," LSDPT, Feb. 13, 1932.
3. "Sheriff Raids Oglesby Homes," LSDPT, Mar. 2, 1932.
4. "Four Held in Liquor Raids," LSDPT, Mar. 16, 1932.
5. "Peoria Raiders Mop Up in County," LSDPT, May 12, 1932.
6. "Liquor Laden Cars Taken At Peru, Mendota," LSDPT, May 31, 1932.
7. "Sheriff Wrecks Big Distillery," PCR, June 9, 1932.
8. "Putnam County Sheriff Raids Huge Alky Still," LSDPT, June 6, 1932.
9. "Leggers Attempting to Seize Plant Equipment," LSDPT, July 7, 1932.
10. "Still Seized in Cedar Point," LSDPT, July 9, 1932.
11. "Raid Still Turn Guns on Equipment," LSDPT, Sept. 12, 1932.
12. "US Arrests 54 in Six Cities," LSDPT, Oct. 15, 1932.
13. "Dry Agents Visit Valley," LSDPT, Oct. 18, 1932.
14. "Welfare Body Sends Warning Message to Merchants," LSDPT, Dec. 13, 1932.
14. "Illinois Dry Law Stands in Way of Beer," LSDPT, Nov. 9, 1932.
15. "DeFilippi Safe At Home," BCR, Dec. 29, 1932.
16. "Welter Sees Showdown in Kidnapping," LSDPT Dec. 14, 1932.
Chapter 17
1. "Bruno Released From Rockford Police," LSDPT, Feb. 14, 1933.
2. "Three Given 42 Years Pen." LSDPT, May 11, 1933.
3. "Tampico Farmer Held on Federal Liquor Charge," LSDPT, April 6, 1933.
4. "Roosevelt Asks For Booze At Once," LSDPT, Mar. 13, 1933.
5. "Joker Endangers Liquor Sale Here," LSDPT, Mar. 17, 1933.
6. "Peru Brewery Seeks Permit," LSDPT, Mar. 22, 1933.
7. "Rural Beer Places Will Be Watched," LSDPT, April 6, 1933.
8. "Benson Ready for Legal Beer," BCR, April 6, 1933.
9. "Operators of Still Flee," LSDPT, April 7, 1933.
10. "Say Hijackers Rob Eleven of Huge Trucks," LSDPT, April 10, 1933.
11. "Restrictions Lacking As Legal Beer Returns," LSDPT, April 7, 1933.
12. "Beer Flows Freely in Morris Today, Welcome Quiet," MDH, April 7, 1933.
13. "Three Face Rum Charge," LSDPT, April 13, 1933.
14. "Agents Knock Off Still Near New Bedford," BCR, April 27, 1933.
15. "Liquor Plant Confiscated," LSDPT, April 24, 1933.
16. "See Loophole in Beer Plan," LSDPT, April 28, 1933.
17. "Launch Beer License Drive Here," LSDPT, June 21, 1933,
18. "Beer Licenses Sold 53 Here," LSDPT, July 3, 1933.
19. "Peru Beer Closing Hours Lifted," LSDPT, July 8, 1933.
20. "Ottawa Beer Plan Given," LSDPT, April 5, 1933.
21. "Old Liquor Cases Still On Docket," LSDPT, May 11, 1933.
22. "Illinois Puts Repeal Over Quarter Way," LSDPT, June 6, 1933.
23. "Beer License Law Enforced," LSDPT, Aug. 9, 1933.
24. "Four Beer Parlors in LaSalle Are Closed," LSDPT, Nov. 9, 1933.
25. "More Kick to Put Tonica on Spot," LSDPT, Nov. 16, 1933.
26. "Sell Buildings Only Recourse, Mason's View," LSDPT, Feb. 3, 1933.

About the Author

R.G. Bluemer has a distinguished career as an educator in the Illinois Valley having taught in the Putnam County schools since 1967 and at Illinois Valley Community College in Oglesby since 1999. His academic training in social science (BA-ISU '67) and history (MS-ISU '72) prepared him for his educational pursuits and his writing career. In addition to his literary works, Bluemer is also a freelance reporter for the LaSalle Daily News-Tribune. He is also a much sought after public speaker and has made presentations to Rotarians, church groups, literary societies, and civic organizations.

Speakeasy, is Mr. Bluemer's fourth published book, and is the third in a series on the history of the Illinois Valley. The other books in the series included **Black Diamond Mines** (2001), which described the coal mining operations in the Valley and **Rails Across the Heartland** (2002), which documented the role of numerous railroads in the development of the area. In his current work, the author described the era of the 1920's with regard to prohibition enforcement and the ties to organized crime.

The author is a native of the south side of Chicago, who moved to the Illinois Valley with his wife, Peggy, in 1967. He has lived in Granville for the last 36 years.